Fraud, Corruption and Sport

Fraud, Corruption and Sport

Graham Brooks
Senior Lecturer in Fraud and Corruption, University of Portsmouth, UK

Azeem Aleem
Principal Lecturer in Risk and Security, University of Portsmouth, UK

and

Mark Button
Reader, Institute of Criminal Justice Studies, University of Portsmouth, UK

palgrave
macmillan

First published 2013 by
PALGRAVE MACMILLAN

Palgrave Macmillan in the UK is an imprint of Macmillan Publishers Limited, registered in England, company number 785998, of Houndmills, Basingstoke, Hampshire RG21 6XS.

Palgrave Macmillan in the US is a division of St Martin's Press LLC, 175 Fifth Avenue, New York, NY 10010.

Palgrave Macmillan is the global academic imprint of the above companies and has companies and representatives throughout the world.

Palgrave® and Macmillan® are registered trademarks in the United States, the United Kingdom, Europe and other countries.

ISBN 978–0–230–29978–8

This book is printed on paper suitable for recycling and made from fully managed and sustained forest sources. Logging, pulping and manufacturing processes are expected to conform to the environmental regulations of the country of origin.

A catalogue record for this book is available from the British Library.

A catalog record for this book is available from the Library of Congress.

Contents

Table

1
Introduction: Fraud, Corruption and Sport

There is a wealth of literature on the sociology of sport (Newman, 1968, Taylor, 1971; Newman, 1972; Dunning and Sheard, 1979; Chinn, 1991; Philips and Tomlinson, 1992; Giulianotti, 1999; Dunning, 1999; Horne et al., 1999; Hoberman, 2001; Gutmann, 2004; Dimeo, 2007; Giulianotti and Robertson, 2009; Millward, 2011; Spaaij, 2012; McGuire, 2012; Horne et al., 2012; Dennis and Grix, 2012). This covers a range of specific sociological, political and cultural issues in sport, such as racism, gambling, images of sport, globalisation and club ownership. The focus of this book, however, is the reach and depth of individual and organisational fraud and corruption in sport; as such, we see it as a pioneering study of the subject and hope that it provides a contribution to the wealth of ongoing sociological debates and the world of sport.

There are a few historical rather than sociological accounts of specific fraud and corruption in sport, such as Issac (1984, American college basketball), Sack (1991, American college football), Figone (1989, 'vested gambling interests' in college basketball), Thelin (1994, corruption in intercollegiate athletics), Ginsburg (1995, corruption in amateur and 'modern' baseball) and Jennings (2007, organisational corruption in international sporting bodies).

Sport is therefore more than an athletic endeavour and reaches beyond 'pitch and track' into the worlds of politics, business, fashion, entertainment, film and 'crime'; it is often used as a 'tool' to promote a nation's credentials on an international stage (Allison, 2005; Cronin and Mayall, 1998; Riordan and Kruger, 1999; Wilson, 2009). This 'national promotion' is only one part of the usefulness of sport;

it has provided legitimacy to military regimes, increased international prestige and national pride and stimulated economic and commercial success (Gems, 2006; Ok, 2006). These important roles that sport has played are not in order of importance and are open to manipulation. Instead of trying to put them in some sort of order, it is better to see sport as playing a collective social, political and cultural role, of which the associated elements of commercial interests are a recent development.

One of these commercial interests, gambling and its associated negative elements, however, has a reputation for damaging the integrity of sport (Brooks 2012b). In the past few years there have been numerous cases of fraud and corruption. These are diverse and include match-fixing in football (Foot, 2007; Jennings, 2007; Hill, 2008, 2010; O'Connor, 2010; Blitz, 2011; Pfanner, 2011; Lee, 2011) spot-fixing in cricket (Atherton, 2011; ICC Report, 2011; Mahmood, 2011; Radford, 2011), use of illegal substances in baseball (Mitchell Report, 2007), vote-rigging in sporting institutions (Crowther, 2002; Jennings, 2007), money-laundering (Brooks, 2012, Christian Aid, 2010; Foot, 2006) and ticket fraud for major sporting events such as the European Football Cup Final in Istanbul and Moscow to name a few. These frauds and acts of corruption encompass athletes, officials, judges/referees and sporting institutions.

While fraud and corruption in sport are nothing new, the context in which some frauds and acts of corruption occur, however, is now different. The changes – the codification of sport from amateur to professional status (Horne et al., 1999; Malcolm, 2011, 2012), the manipulation of sport as a form of national propaganda (Wilson, 2009) and the increased commercialisation of sport – have all contributed to acts of fraud and corruption. However, rather than dwell on the fear that professional codification would lead to increased corruption, which has been dealt with elsewhere (Tranter, 1998; Horne et al., 1999; Roberts, 2011) and the abuses of athletes by nations in search of glory and justification of political systems (Ungerleider, 2001; Dennis and Grix, 2012) we primarily focus on the cultural and commercial development of sport. Fletcher and Herrmann (2012) recently suggested that there is the 'internationalisation of corruption'. However, sport, if anything, unless there is a gambling scandal or corrupt sporting institution, is often downplayed as an aberration in need of self-regulation by its relevant self-governing body.

Furthermore, the international commercial sponsorship of sport has changed the way in which we watch, pay for and experience it (Gorse and Chadwick, 2012). Sport is a global business that now seeks muscular competition in the boardroom as much as athleticism on the pitch and track. The sponsoring of major sporting events and the competitive nature of winning contracts can, however, lead to fraud and corruption, particularly if the sporting institution tasked with 'running the sport' is considered corrupt (Simson and Jennings, 1992; Jennings and Sambrook, 2000; Crowther, 2002; Jennings, 2007; Leahy and Fontanella, 2010; Blitz, 2011).

Prevention of and responses to fraud and corruption in sport are dependent on the sport and type of corruption they are associated with. There is, however, little coordination in countering fraud and corruption within some sports, and it is therefore hardly surprising, even when encountering the same type of fraud (such as match-fixing), that sporting institutions offer little advice and/or assistance to one another. Instead, self-regulation and the promotion of personal and organisational interests rather than regulatory oversight are how sport is controlled. If the sporting institution has integrity its self-regulation is seen as a positive development; however, if it is seen as corrupt it damages the reputation of the sport more than a wayward athlete.

The occurrence of fraud and corruption in sport, as with other sectors, suffers from the same problem. Due to the internationalisation of sport and international tournaments it is difficult to define what we mean by fraud and corruption. For example, the British Olympic Committee (BOA) had a system in place, until 2012, which prohibited all athletes found guilty of employing illegal substances to increase personal performance from representing them in the Olympics; this was different to other nations that used the talents of an athlete once the prohibition period expired (Kidd and Broadbent, 2012).

Indeed, this is compounded when trying to review the social, cultural and legal 'attitudes' towards fraud and corruption. Attempting to define fraud and corruption, particularly across jurisdictions, is therefore a problem. Even with a clear definition, which would be difficult, if not impossible, to implement, the measurement of fraud and corruption is also problematic (Brooks et al., 2011), and due to the secretive nature of fraud and corruption, it is difficult to police (Sandholtz and Gray, 2003). The complex nature of these acts, and differences in social, cultural and political developments, only 'muddies the waters' of what fraud and corruption *is*, and who has jurisdictional control once an act has been discovered.

There are common elements of corruption such as the misuse of power, violation of trust and position, and personal or organisational financial benefit (Bowman and Gilligan, 2007). These elements are not exhaustive, as typologies of corruption have developed in an attempt to classify what is 'corrupt'; to make this matter increasingly difficult, corruption, of which fraud is a part (see Chapter 2), is part of a continuum ranging from legal but unethical acts to illegal and criminal acts. In saying this, we still attempt to classify the types of fraud and corruption in sport below as a 'guide' to the extensive list of fraud and corrupt acts in international sport.

Fraud and corruption in sport

There are wide-ranging types of fraud and corruption to be found in sport. The table below is not an exhaustive list; rather, it is intended to show that sport as a business is not immune to fraud and corruption; in fact, it is an area in need of specialist attention and research. A recurring theme in this book is that fraud and corruption, though part of sport, are often ignored or downplayed and defended as different from that occurring in other businesses. This is incorrect. Sport is a business and as such it will countenance the same types of fraud and corruption as businesses everywhere, such as payroll fraud, procurement fraud, vote-rigging, tax evasion, as well as the more sensational and specific problems of match- and spot-fixing (Brooks et al., 2012).

While there are many different types of fraud and corruption in sport, which are found elsewhere, below is a table with a brief description of how they might be defined, along with a description of what the acts might consist of. While the table is a 'guide' to the range of corruption in sport rather than a comprehensive account of all corruption, it offers a flavour of the range of fraud and corruption that is found in sport. Many of the acts below will also have common characteristics and blur the boundaries as to what category they should fall under. For example, there is the category of *bribery* and *gifts and hospitality*; in the category of *bribery* an 'inducement' could be offered

Table 1.1 Fraud and corruption in sport

Category	Definition/description	Sporting example
Bribery	The offering, promising, giving, accepting or soliciting an advantage as an inducement for an action that is illegal, unethical or breach of trust. Inducements can be gifts, loans, private school fees and/or other rewards	Bribing sports players and/or sports officials to fix the outcome of a match/competition. *Or* Securing a vote in an election or sporting competition
Collusion	A secret arrangement between individuals, 'groups' of people and/or organisations in the public or private sector aimed at securing illicit financial/competitive advantage	Two teams playing in a qualifying round of a tournament play for a draw so both progress to next stage of tournament and/or financial benefit of going further in a tournament and/or eliminating a 'dangerous' team
Conflict of interest	A person or organisation for which a person works is confronted with choosing between demands and duties of the position of employment and their own private interests	A sports official purchasing a service, for example, security from a company she has a financial interest in rather than the best and most suitable bid and services for their club
Embezzlement	Theft of resources and misappropriation of funds	Taking money from the transfer of player(s) between clubs/teams without authorisation
Extortion	Money or resources extracted by coercion, such as through threats of violence or use of force	Kidnapping players from teams and/or family members to ensure the 'right result' in match
Cronyism/ nepotism	Favouritism based on acquaintances and relationships whereby a person exploits his/her official position to provide a job or position to a family member or friend who is not qualified for or deserving of the position	A manager of a team awarding a player a position in a side based on a personal relationship or a chairman promoting his son/daughter onto a sporting body's board even though he/she is unqualified and unsuitable for the post

Table 1.1 (Continued)

Category	Definition/description	Sporting example
Fraud	The act of intentionally deceiving someone in order to gain an unfair financial advantage in the present or future	Players and/or officials fixing the outcome of a specific match or selection of matches or part of a match; for example, the number of red cards in football, and spread of points in basketball
Gifts and hospitality	A gift or hospitality could affect or be perceived to affect the outcome of business transactions and are not reasonable and bona fide	Providing sporting bodies' officials with gifts and free hotel accommodation in an attempt to persuade them to vote for a particular company/nation in a commercially sought after contract; for example, running the Football World Cup. Such gifts/hospitality might also be solicited from the sporting body and/or its members
Lobbying	Any activity carried out to influence an institution's policies and decisions in favour of a specific cause or outcome. Even if allowed by law, these acts can become corrupt if disproportionate levels of influence are apparent from individuals or organisations.	An individual paying for high-level access to a club to arrange an international tour and/or an organisation making special requests such as waiving visa rules for international delegates
Money-laundering	The process of concealing the origin, ownership or destination of illegally or dishonestly obtained funds by hiding them within legitimate economic environments, such as offshore banks or trusts	The buying and selling of players at inflated prices between two clubs and siphoning off some of the money and placing it in an offshore bank account

Revolving door	An individual who moves back and forth between public office and the private sector, exploiting his/her connections in both sectors	A minister of sport moving into a position in a private sector pressure group, national sporting body or international sporting body (and back again)
Abuse of authority	An elected representative using his/her influence to achieve a desired end, which they will either personally benefit from immediately or at a later date	A minister influencing planning permission for a new stadium for a club that s/he supports or has a financial interest in
Trading in influence	Influencing a key decision by promising to return a favour due to the position of power the individual holds	Trading votes in a competition, such as by voting for one country in a contest that has agreed to vote for your athletes/country in a competition
Illegal disclosure of information	Passing on information and disclosing sensitive information that should be kept secret	Inside knowledge of injury to an individual athlete or animal (horse racing) still playing/running in a competition
Vote-rigging	Either controlling the number of candidates that enter a contest or controlling the number of votes that are counted in an election	A sporting body electing a president who has ensured election by dispensing or promising inappropriate favours, or manipulating numbers of votes, such as by illegal counting

if the 'correct' service or outcome is provided, but in the category of *gifts and hospitality* a 'free' ticket to an event is dispensed in appreciation and recognition of 'services' completed. Furthermore, it is useful to keep in mind that corruption is part of a continuum and as such corrupt acts range from unethical and legal to illegal and criminal.

As can be seen from the above table the opportunity to commit fraud and corruption in sport is substantial. Furthermore, the complex nature and blurring of boundaries as to what is acceptable is a recurring theme in the rest of this book. Some examples will be obvious acts of fraud and/or corruption, but others will be on the cusp of illegality and can be seen as morally questionable while still legally acceptable.

Organisation of the book

This book has been written by three authors, and while we mostly agree as to what we think fraud and corruption in sport comprise, and how they should and can be defined, there are elements based on our personal, cultural attitudes that reflect the differences, documented in this book, as to what fraud and corruption *is* and how it can be countered and dealt with. In this sense, we simply reflect the present and ongoing problem of trying to classify acts of fraud and corruption in a national and international context.

The book is split into two main sections. Part I, *Fraud, Corruption and Sport in Context,* consists of four chapters: Chapter 2 focuses on the definition of fraud and corruption in sport and the development of a typology to help explain the diverse types of frauds and corrupt acts that are found in international sport. We highlight the problem of distinguishing between 'cheating' to gain an advantage in a match/sport, breaking a set of codified rules, the culture of corruption in sport, and gambling and its influence on people and the integrity of sport.

Chapter 3 addresses the problem of measuring fraud and corruption in sport. While this problem has been documented elsewhere (Gee et al., 2009, 2010; Button and Brooks, 2012) there are similar issues that arise here, as with other types of businesses, although there is a dearth of contemporary academic analysis, with the exception of Gorse and Chadwick (2012). There is therefore little research available that attempts to analyse and examine a variety of different sports and how they counter and deal with fraud and corruption above and beyond recourse to a criminal justice system.

To assess the level of fraud and corruption in sport and the reach of the problem beyond sensational media coverage, a measure of fraud and corruption is needed. Measuring fraud has, however, been referred to as a chimera (Levi, 2008); we suggest that measuring fraud and corruption is difficult rather than impossible and akin to looking for a mythical beast. It is difficult, as is measuring crime in general (Maguire, 2007), and made increasingly difficult because of the deceptive nature of fraud and corruption (Doig and Levi, 2009; Doig and Macaulay, 2008; Gannon and Doig, 2010) and the legality and illegality of these acts; it is, however, a worthwhile if flawed task.

In Chapter 4 we focus on why people involved in sport, such as athletes, officials and referees, commit fraud and acts of corruption. Drawing on existing theoretical approaches, we apply Sykes and Matza's (1957) techniques of neutralisation and Dittenhofer's (1995) classification of syndromes. These, as far as we are aware, have not been used to explain why those involved in sport, in particular sport 'stars', commit acts of fraud and corruption. We also examine the organisational context of acts of fraud and corruption in sport and the social and cultural explanations offered so far which are useful in helping our understanding of them.

In Chapter 5 we consider the impact that the Internet has had on sport. The main focus of this chapter is how the Internet is used as a medium to commit fraud via gambling websites. Furthermore, while it is seen as a feature of 'vested gambling interests' to use such a medium, we dispel this myth by highlighting how online gambling sites are the focus of organised criminal elements and therefore are a bulwark against (Brooks, 2012) rather than a conduit of fraud and corruption, depending on the jurisdiction, and help inform sporting institutions of 'suspicious' gambling of which they would otherwise be blissfully unaware.

In Part II, *Fraud and Corruption in Sport: Key Bodies: Enforcement and Governance,* each chapter is a case study of a particular sport. There is a brief review of the extent of the main types of fraud and corruption that are primarily associated with the sport, attempts to counter and prevent fraud and corruption and/or how the structure and management of the sport is a contributory factor in the fraud and corruption it encounters. Some suggestions are then made, if possible, on how to increase detection and prevent acts of fraud and corruption in the future.

The sports reviewed are football/soccer (Chapter 6; we prefer to use the term football as the majority of the world refers to it as such and it is, as mentioned above, our cultural interpretation of this sport). The number of leagues around the world is phenomenal; so is the potential for fraud and corruption. We review the most damning aspect of corruption in football – match-fixing. This is, however, only one type of fraud committed and thus ticket sales, money-laundering, paying of agent fees, and questionable player transfers comprise the subject of this chapter as well.

This is followed, in Chapter 7, by a review of corruption in cricket. Played primarily by members of the British Commonwealth it is nonetheless an international sport and is so popular in India and Pakistan that it is seen as a national sport. Often exposed for its association with 'gambling interests', international cricket has been beset by fraud and corruption (Atherton, 2011). Exposing such fraud and corruption is, however, difficult as this chapter explains how 'witnesses' to such acts are often also involved in them. Finding a credible witness is a problem that all national and international law enforcement bodies encounter and evidence is often tainted.

Chapter 8 is concerned with horse racing. Referred to as the 'Sport of Kings', it has often succumbed to fraud and corruption. This is perhaps because its survival is linked to gambling (Forrest and Simmons, 2010). This dependence is a double-edged sword, as gambling is a source of funding for the sport as well as being the cause of many acts of fraud. We, however, move beyond 'putting in the fix' to secure a gambling coup and highlight the ease with which fraud and corruption occurs at thoroughbred auctions.

The sport of basketball is dominated by the USA as we focus in Chapter 9 on fraud and corruption in the National College Athletic Association (NCAA) and the professional National Basketball Association (NBA). In particular we focus on the impact of gambling on the sport and the issues of point shaving (Bernhardt and Heston, 2009) (playing to win a match while failing to cover the spread of points set) and tanking (losing matches mostly at end of the season to secure high-ranked players the following year). The NCAA and NBA are aware of the problem of preventing these 'acts' and have attempted to deal with them. However, they have failed to dissuade college basketball players from 'putting in the fix', and working with vested gambling interests, as this chapter will show.

Chapter 10 is a review of pugilism (boxing) that is portrayed more than any other sport as corrupt, with links to organised crime, particularly in the USA (Sammons, 1990). The focus of our attention here, however, is on more than 'fixed 'fights'; it is also concerned with the treatment, organisation and structure of the sport which leads to the abuse that boxers encounter in a brief and brutal career from the managers, promoters and sanctioning bodies that determine the contestants and location(s) of fights.

Chapter 11 is concerned with baseball. If the USA has a national sport, this is it. However, it has successfully transported it to Cuba and also to Japan, Korea and Taiwan, where it is a very popular spectator sport. Drawing on examples of fraud and corruption regarding match-fixing in the USA and Taiwan (Junwei, 2007), we also provide examples of how fraud and corruption in sport reaches beyond adults to children. The Little League Baseball tournament held in the USA was subjected to manipulation by the Taiwanese state in search of national glory and political prestige. We also consider the willingness of players to consume illegal substances and Major League Baseball's (MLB) progress towards 'making the sport clean' and protecting players and MLB's own personal vested interests (Mitchell Report, 2007).

In Chapter 12 we reflect on the key themes raised and suggest that this is the start of preventing fraud and corruption in sport. By drawing on other 'business' sectors, both private and public, throughout the book we hope we have highlighted the need for sporting institutions and sport to 'raise the bar' in the attempt to prevent acts of fraud and corruption. While they may be impossible to stop, vested interests, which sometimes include the governing body, need to take the matter of fraud and corruption seriously to secure the integrity of their sport. Sport tainted with fraud and corruption might lose the all-important commercial contracts and sponsorship (Gorse and Chadwick, 2012) on which some are so dependent; however, we also note that this increased commercialisation and revenue might also be the catalyst for such fraud and corruption, and as such, unless attempts are made now to counter fraud and corruption in sport, recent scandals will recur.

Part I

Fraud, Corruption and Sport in Context

2 Defining Fraud and Corruption in Sport

Introduction

In this chapter we explore what is meant by fraud and corruption. These 'terms' are contentious regardless of the country and legal system in which they are defined. In some cases, depending on the legal system, codifying fraud and corruption are recent. For example, until the Fraud Act 2006 in England and Wales there was no specific codified offence of fraud, relying instead a succession of 'theft acts' (Goldspink and Cole 2002; Ormerod and Williams, 2005; Doig, 2006). Passing laws might codify an offence, but in a common law system such as that in England and Wales there is room for contestation and interpretation of 'laws'.

Therefore, we start this chapter by examining the difficulties in defining both fraud and corruption (Arlidge and Parry, 1985; Doig, 2006; Iyer and Samociuk, 2006; Gilligan and Bowman, 2007; Fletcher and Herrmann, 2012). While we are aware that it is difficult to clearly define fraud, and in particular corruption, as fraud is part of corruption but corruption will not necessarily entail fraud, we set the scene by highlighting the contested and problematic attempts to define such complex acts and crime(s).

In the final section of this chapter we build on the work of Maennig (2005), Transparency International (2011) and Gorse and Chadwick (2010, 2012) and attempt to place acts of fraud and corruption into a typology. While difficult due to the nature of fraud and corruption, this framework, we hope, is a useful contribution to explaining the complex range of fraud and corrupt acts in sport.

Defining fraud

There are now a few national and international definitions as to what an act of fraud *is* and *how* it can be defined (see Wells, 1997; Arlidge et al., 1996; Doig, 2006; Smith et al., 2010). While there are some differences as to what constitutes fraud across and within jurisdictions, a common theme of fraud is that it is based on deception in an attempt to secure some type of financial benefit. Even if the financial benefit is not immediate it can be secured in time, for example through the use of false documentation to employ football players to secure promotion, without whom it would be difficult (Foot, 2007) (see Chapter 6 and the discussion of false passports in Italian football).

However, before we proceed, a 'working definition' of fraud is needed. To be able reduce the level of fraud in an organisation we must know what we are dealing with and thus some definition of the problem is a prerequisite for appreciating the complex nature of fraud. This appreciation will be limited, but without a working definition of the key elements of fraud, no matter how contested, is needed if we are to progress.

There is no legal definition of fraud under French law; instead there is a wide range of 'crimes' defined as 'fraud', such as breach of trust, violation of a data system and counterfeiting; in Ireland, there is also no legal definition, but fraud is seen to contain acts that are deceptive; the German Criminal Code views fraud as provoking or affirming a mistake and distorting or suppressing facts; and in the USA fraud is defined in law as a false representation of a matter of fact – whether by words or by conduct, by false or misleading allegations, or by concealment of what should have been disclosed (Fletcher and Herrmann, 2012).

In the England and Wales it was hoped that the passing of the Fraud Act 2006 would clarify 'what is fraud' and thus increase the chances of the successful prosecution of a complex and deceptive crime (Summers, 2008). To achieve this aim the Fraud Act 2006 in England and Wales abolished the numerous offences of deception that were part of previous complex and overlapping legislation (see Doig, 2006; Smith et al., 2010) and made fraud an offence if it involved false representation (section 2 of the Act), failure to disclose information (section 3 of the Act) and abuse of position (section 4 of the Act).

However, while Summers (2008) has suggested that the passing of the act would help with investigating and prosecuting fraud, Ormerod (2007) described the Fraud Act as too broad, with its focus on the intention to commit fraud rather than the act of committing fraud. This legal shift has thus moved away from proving a person committed the crime of fraud to one of intent. As Ormerod (2007: 2) has said, this has 'criminalized lying'. However, lying is part of a deception, and deception is the basis of fraud, regardless of the jurisdiction; and rather than dwell on the discussion on the legal advantages or disadvantages of the Fraud Act 2006 here, which has been dealt with elsewhere (see Smith et al., 2010: 15–18) we turn our attention to the international nature of corruption found in sport that is committed by individuals alone or with others and sporting bodies expected to protect the integrity of the sport. Regardless of the reason(s) behind frauds, deception is an integral part of the crime.

These legal and non-legal definitions of fraud are wide-ranging, as is the act of fraud, and the world of sport is not immune to different types of fraud. In fact, sport lends itself to the frauds that all businesses suffer, such as counterfeit products, tax evasion and money-laundering, but also from frauds that are specific to sport, such as match-fixing (Foot, 2007; Hill, 2008) (see Chapters 6, 7, 9 and 10, on football, cricket, basketball and baseball, respectively). Most frauds are dealt with under civil rather than criminal law and sport is again no different. The problem for sport is often compounded by the fact that those tasked with maintaining the integrity of a sport lack the expertise and knowledge of fraud to deal with it and rely on 'policing bodies', whose own professional knowledge base has been criticised as limited (Button et al., 2008), apart from a few specialised bodies is some jurisdictions, such as the Serious Fraud Office in the UK.

Furthermore, due to the internationalisation of sport, it also encounters the problem of jurisdictional control regarding fraud. For example, if a match is fixed in a Football World Cup in Germany with players on one team, such as Poland, with an official (referee) from Costa Rica by people living England and working in India, who is responsible?

Fraud then, regardless of the sector, has a few common elements; it is based on deception with the intention of securing some advantage – immediate or in the future – and depriving a third party such as individual(s), a small group of people or an organisation of honest services or benefits at the expense of other individuals and organisations. We are aware that this is not an airtight definition of fraud, this in itself is perhaps impossible; instead it offers a framework and key elements of what an act of fraud might contain, if discovered.

Defining corruption

The conceptualisation of the term 'corruption' is intertwined with ideological, moral, cultural and political perspectives. There is no clear international accepted definition of corruption (Iyer and Samociuk, 2006; Gilligan and Bowman, 2007; Transparency International, 2011). However, there is growing body of literature which has attempted to define corruption (McMullan, 1961; Leff, 1970; Nye, 1970; Scott, 1972; Gibbons and Rowat, 1976; Rose-Ackerman, 1978; Gillespie and Okruhlik, 1991; AAPPG, 2006). This literature tends to associate the term 'corruption' with the misuse of public office for private gain (McMullan, 1961; Nye, 1967; Klitgaard, 1998; Rose-Ackerman, 1999). The literature therefore addresses narrow and specific examples of corruption, such as influence-peddling or misuse of office for personal gain. Furthermore, although international anti-corruption organisations seek to produce a uniform definition of corruption, it often falls into a description of an exchange between an 'official' receiving a 'benefit' provided by a party with an interest in the outcome of a decision (Henning, 2001). The benefit is financial or a gift and the party is an individual or group/organisation which will gain an advantage in present and/or future transactions and/or decision(s).

This, however, is a limited and narrow view of corruption, with a tendency to focus on the act of bribery and excluding other types of corruption. Akindele (2005) has suggested that corruption is not just an economic exchange with a financial incentive, nor an exclusively political act motivated by the desire to attain or retain political power. The justification for the above definition(s) is that much corruption occurs at the interface between the private and public sectors, as it can with sporting institutions and state institutions; for example, the London Olympics of 2012 were delivered by the Olympic Delivery Authority (ODA), which is the public body responsible for developing new venues and infrastructure for the Olympics and use of stadia for the public after 2012, and the London Organising Committee of the Olympic and Paralympic Games (LOCOG), which is a private company responsible for preparing and staging the London 2012 Olympic Games. Funding and sponsorship, however, are perhaps a double-edged sword where the image of the sport is tainted (Gorse and Chadwick, 2012) if sponsored by a corrupt company that uses sport as a vehicle for a company to 'clean' its image on a world stage.

Regardless of the complexity of trying to understand corruption, it is still possible to grasp some understanding of the many and varied acts; it is better to view corruption as a range of acts, some of which are legal but seen as corrupt and others that are both corrupt and illegal. Corruption is therefore very broadly defined or broken down into its constituent elements and can contain illegal or legal acts but unacceptable practices (Johnston, 2005). As the literature suggests, there have been numerous attempts to classify corruption and provide a systematic method for approaching this complex phenomenon. These are:

- Political corruption
- Bureaucratic corruption
- Electoral corruption

Hodees (2004: 11) described political corruption as involving:

> a wide range of crimes and illicit acts committed by political leaders before, during and after leaving office. It is distinct from petty or bureaucratic corruption in so far as it is perpetrated by political leaders or elected officials who have been vested with public authority and who bear the responsibility of representing the public interest.

Bureaucratic corruption is the use of a public office for a pecuniary gain. It can involve the practice of purchasing monopoly positions in some sectors and, as Mbaku (1996: 101–2) put it:

> provides civil servants with the opportunity to raise their compensation above what the law prescribes... the practice of corruption, private entrepreneurs are able to capture and maintain monopoly

> positions in the economy...obtain the resources they need to purchase security and continue to monopolize the supply of legislation.

Bureaucratic corruption therefore allows inefficient organisations – public (Mbaku, 1996; Johnston, 2005) and private – to remain in business for the benefit of a few to enrich themselves from those seeking profitable commercial contracts from state institutions and private institutions. Bureaucratic and political corruption, however, is possible in the world of sport (Jennings, 1996; 2007). Electoral corruption is another form of corruption and is often a prominent feature of politics and of elections in 'old' and 'new' established democratic states (Gyimah-Boadi, 2004; Rose-Ackerman, 2006; Kunicová, 2006) and also sporting institutions (Blitz, 2011). The concept of electoral corruption embraces a range of practices intended to 'control' and influence the outcome of elections – such as buying votes and electoral fraud (Lodge, 1999; Kurer, 2001; Kunicová, 2006). The present body of literature on corruption has primarily placed corrupt acts into the three types above, which seem to define corruption as a public sector problem (Rose-Ackerman, 1996). However, corruption involves a wide spectrum of practices of varying form and significance that are a major feature of the interface between the public and private sector; it is here where international sporting institutions work and, as we suggest, more research on these nationless bodies is needed as they claim to represent peace and humanitarian ideals when representing vested interests (Guthrie-Shimizu, 2009). As with other sectors sport encounters acts of fraud and corruption; however, rather than rely on a classification of political, bureaucratic and electoral corruption it is better to have a typology specifically of fraud and corruption in sport to classify the reach and types of corruption that are part of the world of sport.

Developing a typology of fraud and corruption in sport

This section will focus on developing a typology of sport. While some sports lend themselves to fraud and corruption more than others, and some make headline news, such as the cricket scandal and sentencing of three Pakistani professional cricket players to prison in 2011 in the UK (Wilde, 2011), all the cases cited below damage the integrity and profitability of sport (Gorse and Chadwick, 2012). Many of the cases also have common characteristics and blur the boundaries as to what part of the typology they should fall under.

Furthermore, it is the complex nature and blurring of boundaries as to what is acceptable that is a recurring theme in the rest of this book. Some of the examples will be obvious acts of fraud and/or corruption, but others will be on the cusp of illegality and be seen as morally questionable but still legally acceptable. Perhaps the best way to clarify these boundaries is to have a working framework on which we can place acts of fraud and corruption in sport.

All of the examples of fraud and corruption in Table 1.1 in Chapter 1 can be placed into a typology of fraud and corruption. We have encountered, as has other research (Maennig, 2005; Remote Gambling Association, 2010, Transparency International, 2011), that providing a framework on which to examine corruption and fraud in sport is problematic. For example, fraud and corruption in sport is classified in three ways:

- *competition fraud and corruption* (use of illegal substances)
- *a systemic problem* (part of the structure and culture of the organisation; for example, vote rigging)
- *influence of gambling* on sport (for example, match-fixing) (Transparency International, 2010).

A system of classification from Maennig (2005) is that sport is divided into:

- *Competition corruption* (athletes and/or officials involved in the outcome of result/s)
- *Management corruption* (sporting officials and/or governing institutions not part of competition).

Furthermore, Gorse and Chadwick (2012) are developing a database with a focus on the affects of corruption and sport sponsorship. The classification system they have employed utilises the:

- Year
- Country
- Athletes involved

- Sport
- Type of corruption
- Impact.

All of these are useful and make a contribution to the ongoing problem of trying to classify corruption in sport. None of them, however, refer to cheating as part of corruption. Cheating – violating the rules of sporting conduct but staying within the law – is, we argue, part of the continuum of corruption; after all, as we stated in Chapter 1, corruption is sometimes legal and well as illegal and as such needs to be recorded even if no case is brought, as some of the cases we use exhibit.

To compound this matter a typology of corruption is determined by 'culture' and thus shifts in attitude to rules of the competition and expected conduct of athletes and sporting officials change, and as such acts that were once seen as corrupt are now seen as acceptable. For example, in the first Tour de France in 1903 there were clear rules prescribing that the race was a contest between individuals. While a team can now race a leg of the Tour on behalf of their leader, this was considered illegal in 1903. In the 1903 race, two riders, Lucien Pothier and César Garin, ceded victory to teammate Maurice Garin. All three riders were later disqualified from the Tour by the French Cycling Federation and Henri Corner was declared the winner, as 'riding for the team' was consider unacceptable practice (Wheatcroft, 2003).

A more modern version of this 'attitude' is in Formula 1. In 2002 Team Ferrari 'ordered' one of its members, Rubens Barrichello, to move aside at the Australian Grand Prix and allow his teammate Michael Schumacher to pass him before the finishing line (Maennig, 2005). Therefore, while there are, and always will be, difficulties in producing a typology, as these examples have shown, we offer our current and contemporary working framework of fraud and corruption in sport, drawing on a combination of the above approaches.

The art of bending and breaking the rules: a continuum of corruption

To 'cheat' in a sporting event is nothing new, but to define what cheating is is not as straightforward as it seems. There are those incidents in a match that we might consider cheating, such as 'diving' in a penalty area in a football match when tackled to win a penalty kick, blocking a player in basketball, intimidating player(s) in a cricket match with verbal abuse (also known as hazing and sledging), and getting a 'extra' payment to physically injure a player in what has become know as the 'bounty scandal' in American Football. These could be defined as cheating; however these are attempts by athletes to bend the rules, or codes of sporting conduct, rather than break them. There is, however, a fine line between bending rules and breaking them. For example, polishing a cricket ball by hand to affect the surface and flight of the ball is considered part of the sport, as is bowling the cricket ball hard into a playing surface, which can slowly produce an uneven surface on the ball and affect its bounce, making it hard for batsmen to judge the movement of the ball and score runs; but applying some substance to affect the surface and flight of the ball is seen as cheating, as is gouging the ball with a sharp object to roughen the surface of the ball to affect its flight, bounce and trajectory (Radford, 2010). There is, however, a continuum of 'cheating'; this is not to suggest that players who bend rules will then break them, but these are not distinct and separate acts.

Therefore, we have decided to include cheating as part of our typology, but make the distinction between bending rules and breaking them. Players bending the rules might receive a penalty on the field of play; for example, an ice hockey or rugby player can be sent off for a period of time to the 'sin-bin'. Some of these actions are often in the 'heat of the moment' and players sometimes behave in an unacceptable way, but nevertheless choices were made to gain an unfair advantage rather than play by a strict code of conduct (the 'rules' or 'laws' of the game). However, breaking the rules can also be a calculated, planned act that can involve one or more people on a team and, we argue, should be considered an attempt to 'gain an unfair advantage'. We are not suggesting that the above examples are frauds, but we emphasise that cheating and corruption are a continuum, and they can sometimes defraud fans and opposition players of a genuine sporting contest. Then there is cheating to 'gain an advantage', which is often accepted as part of a sport; this is cheating by knowingly breaking sporting codes, which is calculated, planned and a clear act of deception. For example, in a quarter-final Heineken Rugby Football Union (RFU) Cup match in 2009 (now known as bloodgate), a Harlequin player, Tom Williams, was substituted because of a facial injury. It was later discovered that this injury was 'manufactured' by inserting a blood capsule in his mouth. The reason for this was to replace a player on the pitch, which could not have been done without the 'manufactured' injury. This was not an isolated incident as the investigation discovered that Harlequins had used this 'tactic' in at least four previous matches. Williams was originally banned for 12 months, but this was reduced to four months after an appeal; the then Director of rugby at Harlequins, Dean Richards, was banned for three years; the club physiotherapist Steph Brennen was originally subject to a two-year ban, but this was overturned in January 2011, with the club fined £260,000 and the Harlequins doctor, Wendy Chapman, was temporarily suspended by the General Medical Council (GMC) for cutting Tom Williams' lip (European Rugby Cup Decision Disciplinary Committee, 2009; Transparency International, 2011). However, Chapman has since been told by the GMC that she is free to practise again, even though the GMC found her guilty of serious misconduct (Jenkins, 2010).

The RFU established a 'taskforce' to examine and counter the various types of corruption. The taskforce produced a number of recommendations in a report named *The Image of the Game*, with changes to the rules to bolster the integrity of the RFU (Transparency Iinternational, 2011). These recommendations were however, 'after the event', as this type of cheating had occurred more than once. For some, however, the above example might still be a 'grey area' and come under 'bending the rules' rather than outright corruption. This, we suggest, is misleading as the event was planned and executed by a team of professionals in an attempt to secure an unfair advantage. It should therefore be seen as a form of corruption.

A clear example of corruption, however, is using illegal, banned substances to increase performance throughout a season, competition or single event for a human or equine athlete. The rewards and risks for this type of cheating are substantial; winning key matches and/or events and medals can attract personal sponsorship, fame, international recognition and wealth, particularly if an Olympian; see the case of Marion Jones (Connor and Mazanov, 2009; Jones, 2010).

Jones is only one of many athletes who have been caught using illegal, banned substances. In 2008 there were 621 cases of 'substance use' by athletes in international sports (Remote Gambling

Association, 2010). Of these 621, 382 were found guilty by their representative boards and subject to a variety of different sanctions, with 160 suspended from competition, or given a lifetime ban, in 2010. This type of cheating is nothing new; there is a 'modern' history of athletes breaking the rules to secure an advantage in a sports competition. Some sports such a cycling, particularly the Tour de France, have regularly had to contend with cyclists caught injecting, digesting and masking substances that increase performance (Walsh, 2006) and organisations such as the International Olympic Committee (IOC) banning athletes at successive Olympics (Hard, 2010).

The problem in developing any typology of fraud and corruption in sport is that different sports react in a completely different way to acts of fraud and corruption. Furthermore, the same sport can react differently to the same or similar act in a different way. For example, the British sprinter Dwain Chambers was banned for life from representing Team GB in the Olympics by the British Athletics Board until 2012. However, LaShawn Merritt, an American 400-metre Olympic champion banned by the IOC for a failed test in 2010 and suspended for 21 months, was cleared to run in the same competition by the Court of Arbitration of Sport (CAS) (Kidd and Broadbent, 2012). The US Olympic Committee challenged the rule that any athlete banned for more than six months and serving his ban should not be prevented from competing. The British Athletics Board, however, has a very different opinion to that of its US counterpart; if banned for ingesting or injecting illegal substances the athlete is not welcome as part of the Olympic Team (see Chapter 4 for a discussion of the British Olympic Association and Dwain Chambers appeal).

Self-regulation is normal in sport and there is therefore limited accountability and transparency on judgments of corrupt acts. Athletes, however, do not have a monopoly on cheating, fraud and corruption in sport; many of those tasked with preventing fraud and corruption and maintaining the integrity of the sport are also corrupt, and it is this systemic problem to which we now turn.

A culture of corruption: a systemic problem or protecting vested interests?

While athletes might ingest banned, illegal substances to increase personal performance and win major events, which in turn attracts commercial sponsorship and recognition, those administrators entrusted with 'running' the sport and protecting its integrity are all too often also found to be corrupt (Jennings, 2006; Hill, 2008).

However, as discussed above, not all corruption is illegal, and national sporting institutions and individuals manipulate, or bend, the rules. For example, voting to hold the Olympics (Jennings and Sambrook, 2000; Barney et al., 2002). The 1996 Atlanta Olympics, however, represented a qualitative change in the involvement of commercial interests in the Olympics, with an unprecedented degree of corporate involvement, which was thought to have increased the potential for corruption (Crowther, 2002: Guttmann, 2004). Following this, the IOC changed its method of voting in an attempt to counteract corruption.

Winning the bid to organise a high-profile sporting contest is not always as straightforward as it seems. In 2010 Amos Adamu was banned by Fifa for three years for soliciting bribes in exchange for his vote to hold the Football World Cup in 2014 and 2018. In 2011, Lord Triesman, then Chair of the England World Cup bid, gave evidence to a UK Government Select Committee for the Department of Culture, Media and Sport where he alleged that six members of Fifa's executive committee had engaged in 'unethical conduct' relating to the Football World Cup bid. This allegation, while vigorously denied at the time, has some merit as Fifa banned Mohammed Bin Hammam, the Fifa representative from Qatar (Transparency International, 2011).

However, it is Fifa, rather than an external organisation, that primarily investigates these matters; things reached a stage where Fifa expanded its own investigation to include another 10 of its members in 2011, with Sepp Blatter, the Fifa President, promising reform at Fifa.

Furthermore, Jennings (2006) claims, drawing on official Fifa documents, that demands are made on the potential host country that wishes to hold a World Cup for tax breaks and free hotel rooms, as well as that visa restrictions be lifted for some of its members. This last issue is in contravention of both United Kingdom and European Union laws and yet the England World Cup bid agreed to these and all other Fifa demands (Transparency International, 2011). The desire to hold a Football World Cup then appears to be a systemic problem, as both Fifa and *some* of its members, but also those wanting to host such an event, engage in breaking the rules relating to holding a major sporting event.

So far we have shown that athletes ingesting and injecting illegal, banned substances is nothing new in the world of sport and neither is the corruption of some of those invested with the power to protect the integrity of sport; there is, however, a third threat to the credibility of sport; this is the influence of gambling. This 'threat' completes a potential triptych of dangers that sport must contend with as the temptation to 'put in the fix' as an athlete, sport star, official or referee overshadows the allure of honest competition.

Gambling: a cause of fraud and corruption in sport?

Due to the international media coverage and the commercialisation of sports, the behaviour of sports stars on a field of play is well documented. These can range from the spectacle of histrionics on the pitch to the leaking of details of 'personal relationships'. In addition, when a major story of corruption breaks and an international organisation is involved it too is widely covered. However, one constant complaint is the effect gambling has on sport (Figone, 1989; Ginsburg, 1996; Brooks, 2012) along with its links to organised crime and the potential for addiction, with a focus primarily on the athletes rather than officials or administrators (Donaghy, 2009).

It is often thought that players are the only ones involved in match-fixing; this is incorrect. Players are required to fix a match, but not always. Referees (Hill, 2010; Pfanner, 2011), club officials, owners and players have all been involved (Foot, 2007; Hill, 2008) in some capacity in sports such as baseball, football and horse-racing. There are many international examples of the corruption of football referees working with criminal elements to defraud bookmaker(s), and club owners offering money, gifts, holidays and sexual services to 'persuade' officials to 'act in the right way' (Foot, 2007; Hill, 2008). Such corruption is an international problem (Maennig, 2005) rather than the province of one country.

We offer as an example the recent match-fixing scandal in the Korean League (K-League), which amply shows the effects of gambling interests on sport.

The K-League Cup is an 'auxiliary' competition held on weekdays (similar to the League Cup in England and Wales). This competition attracts little interest, and teams field weakened sides playing reserve players. Players from Daejon Citizen attempted to fix the outcome of this match when playing Pohang Steelers in April 2011; Daejeon Citizen lost the match 3–0. It was later discovered in an investigation that players accepted money from betting organisations to fix specific results in selected matches, rather than one match. In this case a total 46 footballers and 11 others, including 'gambling brokers', have been indicted and permanently expelled from the K-League for match-fixing (*Korean Herald*, 2011; Brooks et al., 2012).

There is some evidence that football matches around the world have been fixed at all levels of the sport (Foot, 2007; Hill, 2010; Pfanner, 2011). As with other frauds elsewhere (Levi, 1999; Gill 2005; Doig, 2006) the reason(s) put forward for match-fixing are that professional athletes have a brief sporting career and will sometimes succumb to match-fixing to 'earn' extra money. Players in all sports justify these acts as 'bending the rules' rather than corruption; they often explain that the match in question was insignificant and that everybody is involved and that such fraud and corruption is 'common practice' (see Chapter 4 for a discussion on athletes' justifications for acts of corruption).

However, rather than blame gambling as the sole reason for fraud and corruption in sport a more balanced view is needed. With the development of Internet gambling, people can gamble on an event online and listen or watch in real time anywhere around the world. While the Internet has increased the reach of gambling it alone is not a cause of corruption; it is a new medium used for an old crime.

Gambling corruption existed before the development of the Internet (see the Black Sox scandals in baseball; Ginsburg [1995]). Rather than always viewing online gambling as negative, some organisations such as Betfair, a betting exchange in the UK, have memorandums of understanding with sporting bodies to keep them informed of any suspicious gambling on a sporting event. Information is passed to these bodies to determine what action should follow. In this way, technology is used as a system of surveillance. This system, however, is only of use for legal gambling; in the case of illegal gambling, such as in India, bookmakers' association with organised crime often fills this void. It is better to have some system of regulation and thus an element of control, otherwise gambling becomes, as history has shown (Figone, 1989), a business opportunity for organised crime.

Conclusion

This chapter has primarily illustrated that it is difficult to clearly define fraud, and especially corruption. This is due to the complex nature of fraud and corruption; there is a range of acts that are potentially, but not always, illegal. In providing examples and descriptions of sporting fraud and corruption and a working typology for analysing and categorising fraud and corruption in sport, we have contributed to the ongoing debate about how to determine what is 'bending the rules' and what is cheating, and means of developing acceptable ways of working to define outright fraud and corruption.

We have provided many examples of fraud and corruption committed by both individuals and sporting institutions. All participants are capable of committing acts that ruin the integrity of the sport they are involved in and diminish the enjoyment that sport can offer to athletes, spectators or organisations.

In the next chapter we move beyond trying to define fraud and corruption and focus on *how much* fraud and corruption is committed in sport. This is difficult, as little research has been undertaken into the *extent* of fraud and corruption in sport. There are, however, a few useful examples of surveys and investigations that highlight the problem of measuring and preventing fraud and corruption in sport.

3
The Extent of Fraud and Corruption in Sport

Introduction

In this chapter we examine the extent of fraud and corruption in sport. As Chapter 2 illustrated, fraud and corruption are difficult to define and, as such, this will affect the extent to which fraud and corruption in sport can be measured. We do not hold the view, however, that it is impossible to measure fraud to some extent (Levi, 2008); it is more the case of how it is measured that is a problem (see Gee et al., 2009, 2010, 2011; Méndez and Sepúlveda, 2009). Fraud, like all crime, and especially corruption, are nonetheless difficult to measure, and this is further compounded by the lack of interest and limitations that sporting bodies have in recognising and then dealing with this problem, as the cases throughout the book will show. The majority of sporting bodies often fail to accept that sport is a victim of fraud or corruption, play down the potential for fraud and corruption or claim that fraud and corruption is under control. This, as we will demonstrate, is far from the truth. Even if these sporting bodies accept the threat fraud and corruption have on the integrity and commercial revenue of sport (Gorse and Chadwick, 2012), the starting point is to record and measure the cases of fraud and corruption and put measures in place that reduce and counteract such a threat.

This chapter therefore starts with a discussion of the challenges of measuring fraud and corruption. The categorising of some frauds and acts of corruption are open to contestation and acts in the world of sport are no different. We then review the limited studies that have attempted to measure the level and depth of fraud and corruption in sport. We also draw on official reports on corruption in international cricket (Condon, 2001; Qayyum Commission, 2000; King Commission, 2000) and the problem of steroid use in baseball (Mitchell Report, 2007) as they highlight, even though it was not the task of these investigations, the reach of corruption in sport. This is followed by an examination of the limitations of these methods and the problem of surveying a 'hard to reach' population of corrupt individuals and sporting bodies protecting the vested interests of the sport they are charged with keeping clean.

The influence of gambling on sport is then assessed; this, though, is not as straightforward as it might appear. Legal gambling is often blamed for fraud and corruption in sport (Brooks, 2012); however, gambling was part of sport even before official 'bookmakers' became legal (Chinn, 1991). It is not so much the act of gambling that is the problem; rather it is the development of difficult-to-control technology and opportunity that has possibly 'caused' an increase in fraud and corruption in sport. We suggest that the gambling sector is one of the best placed to monitor sporting transgressions, particularly match-fixing, and as such is useful in recording known, but also suspicious, gambling as an estimate of potential fraud.

The problem in measuring fraud and corruption in sport

In Chapter 2 we highlighted how difficult it is to define fraud and in particular corruption. This, obviously, impacts on the measurement of them (Seligson, 2006). Although we discuss some of the ways in which fraud and corruption are measured, these processes are, like the definitions, still contentious. *The Fraud Act 2006* (Home Office, 2006), *The Bribery Act 2010* (Home Office, 2011), the *Improper Payments Information Act of 2002* (IPIA), now followed by the more recent *Improper Payments Elimination and Recovery Act of 2010*, the Financial Action Task Force *Strategic Surveillance Survey* (2009) and *Laundering the Proceeds of Corruption* (2011) and the *Foreign Corrupt Practices Act 1977*, watered down in 1988 and now updated again in 2010, to name a few, have gone some way to providing a working framework to clarify acts of fraud and corruption, particularly in legal circles, and also for those of us unfamiliar with the language of jurisprudence.

However, while legislation is passed in the hope of deterring crime we might not even be aware as individuals and organisations that we have been defrauded. Furthermore, it can become complicated as to who the victims are.

The clearest example of fraud and corruption in sport is where individuals or a collection of players in a sport fix the outcome of a match for personal or vested gambling interests. 'Losing to win' is fraud, and paying spectators, people watching a televised match at home, owners of the team, players not involved in the fix, officials, commercial sponsors and all employees of the club are defrauded and denied an honest sporting contest.

However, unless the case is discovered we are unaware of the fraud and that corruption has occurred. In many instances we could be unaware that the outcome of the sporting event we are watching has already been decided. This is even more difficult if a small part of a match, such as the spot-fixing scandal in cricket at the Lord's Test Match between England and Pakistan in 2010, is 'predetermined' (Mahmood, 2011, 2012). Unlike fraud and corruption in other sectors where an individual could be a victim (Button et al., 2011), in sport there are always multiple victims, as sport is played before the public and is influenced by commercial sponsorship and illegal gambling interests. This increases the problem of measuring the extent of fraud and particularly victimisation; should, therefore, the act of fixing the result of one football, boxing or baseball match be recorded as one act with a single victim or many?

The problem is how this victimisation is measured. If we have paid to watch a sporting event only to discover later on that is was fixed, we have been defrauded of a fair, open sporting contest; this is not in doubt. However, have we also been denied the services for which we have paid? This is clear when purchasing a service and/or product in other sectors; for example, if we buy a ticket to a sporting or music event online that is not delivered because the website we have accessed is an illegal site, or if a ticket is delivered but is a forgery, we are a victim of fraud.

In addition to this, even when knowingly victimised, individuals and organisations fail to report the act. An individual may feel embarrassed and fail to report the crime; an organisation might investigate the fraud in-house and decide that it would be best to resolve the matter internally, even though a crime has been committed, to protect its public reputation rather than open a 'Pandora's box' (Levi, 1987: 132) and expose the level and depth of fraud and corruption in their company and/or sporting body (Russell, 1998; Smith et al., 2010).

There are many measures of fraud and corruption that are limited. There is always a margin of error. We should not, however, dismiss those surveys that often measure the level of fraud and corruption (Méndez and Sepúlveda, 2009). We must be aware that different methodological approaches, both theoretical and empirical, are used and some are less rigorous than others; corruption is thus open to theoretical interpretation as Cadot (1987), Shleifer and Vishny (1993) and Guriev (2004) suggested some years ago on *how much* fraud and corruption is 'out there' (Svensson, 2003; Clark and Xu, 2004).

Furthermore, the role of the police is critical, as we often rely on official statistics for information. However, the police in England and Wales are often seen as incapable or uninterested in dealing with fraud (Brooks et al., 2009). This lack of police interest has been confirmed by a number of studies (Doig, 2006; Button et al., 2009) along with the Fraud Review Team (2006) that uncovered this lack of interest, with the view that the investigation of fraud is extremely expensive in terms of hours spent obtaining statements and preparing a prosecution case, which may be unsuccessful.

This lack of interest has led many organisations to develop or increase their own fraud investigative resources or to turn to the private sector (Gill and Hart, 1997; Doig et al., 2001; Doig, 2006). Sporting bodies, however, still rely on the police as they have little power to punish offenders beyond imposing bans for a breach of sporting code and prohibiting them from participating in the sport for a period of time or holding any role that is relevant to the sport, such as a coach.

The attitude of the police in England and Wales regarding fraud, however, is not surprising when one considers that there is only one police force with a performance indicator related to fraud – the City of London Police, and the police infrastructure for combating fraud is limited to the Serious Fraud Office, with a total of 307 employees (Serious Fraud Office, 2010), with an estimated 524 police officers in fraud squads (Fraud Review Team, 2006a, 2006b) and the Serious and Organised Crime Agency (SOCA) whose remit is still somewhat vague regarding frauds, with an emphasis for the police to focus on core policing issues and key indicators.

This lack of interest is perhaps reflected in the low numbers of fraud cases that reached court from the SFO in 2009–10. A total of 24 defendants in 13 trials were tried, with 22 convictions and one civil recovery order. Of these 91.7 per cent were convicted, with an average sentence of 31.8 months (Serious Fraud Office, 2010: 23). While this was a high conviction rate, only 13 cases reached the trial stage; this could have been for a variety of reasons; lack of evidence, funds or available investigators, and the complex nature of fraud. This attitude, however, varies depending on jurisdiction as the example of the *Guardia de Finanza* (Financial Guard) in Italy shows; this is part of the Ministry of Economy and Finance and has approximately 68,000 employees (*Guardia de Finanza*, 2010).

Furthermore, there are also many surveys estimating the level of fraud in the public and private sector (KPMG, 2004, 2008, 2009; National Fraud Authority, 2010) but few academic or official public bodies or private sector organisations have focused on sport. It is, however, to the 'sporting surveys' and official reports that we now turn.

Surveys and estimates of fraud and corruption in sport

There are only a few surveys that directly focus on fraud and corruption in sport that we are presently aware of; these are Sack's (1991) survey of college basketball and football in the USA, Transparency International's (TI) (2010) perception survey on fraud in sport and corruption in sport, the PKF (2011) survey on British football clubs' resilience to fraud and Gorse and Chadwick's (2010, 2012) focus on sponsorship and corruption.

In Sack's survey (1991) a third of those playing college basketball claimed they had accepted illegal payments to fix matches, with many of the athletes seeing nothing wrong with such conduct; the PKF survey revealed that many football clubs are unaware of the seriousness of fraud, and therefore fail to put in place counter-fraud strategies to protect the club's income from fraud and services provided to paying customers. The TI survey is more wide-ranging and focuses on the perception of corruption rather than fraud, which was no doubt influenced by the numerous scandals that had occurred regarding national and international sporting stars and bodies in

2009–10, while Gorse and Chadwick (2010, 2012) are developing a database of known acts of fraud and corruption.

These surveys/methods are open to criticism, as are all surveys and research that attempts to record criminal acts. The difficulties associated with criminal justice research are well documented; there is a lack of objective data regarding reported and recorded criminal offences (Box, 1983; Bulmer, 1984; Jupp, 1989; Maguire, 1997); self-report and victimisation surveys are problematic (Coleman and Moynihan, 1996); and acts of fraud and corruption are difficult to detect (Slapper and Tombs, 1999; Button and Brooks, 2009; Brooks et al., 2009). Detection and the necessary evidence is part of successfully prosecuting fraud, but due to the complex nature of the crime few cases reach court regardless of the jurisdiction. While this a problem for all criminal cases, in the case of fraud the level of evidence needed for a criminal prosecution is sometimes difficult to obtain.

In an anonymous survey of 648 basketball and football college athletes Sack (1991) discovered that 0.5 per cent admitted 'earning' money by gambling on college matches they were playing in or were part of the team in some capacity, for example as a substitute. While this is a low percentage figure, not all athletes, even if a survey is anonymous, will admit to using inside knowledge, and thus the real numbers involved in this illegal gambling might be substantially higher.

In other surveys of American sport, Sack (1991) discovered that 27 per cent of retired college football players admitting accepting illegal payments to 'influence' matches. This percentage is high; even taking into account that some of the responses may be incorrect, this percentage is hard to ignore. Furthermore, some of these players could have gone on to have a career in professional sport, as a coach for example, with the attitude that accepting illegal payments as a college athlete is 'part of the game' and an acceptable way to 'earn' extra income to supplement low income for who are professional athletes in all but name (see Chapter 9 on basketball in particular for this problem).

In 2010 TI commissioned Gallup, an independent polling organisation, to undertake a national opinion survey on the perception of corruption in England, Wales and Scotland. While it covered various aspects of corruption our concern is with its reporting of perception of corruption in sport. Of 16 sectors identified in the research from

2,012 respondents in England, Wales and Scotland, professional sport was seen as the second most corrupt sector after political organisations. Furthermore, respondents were asked 'who did they trust to fight corruption', which revealed that 34.1 per cent thought nobody capable, with 19 per cent not sure who was best placed to fight corruption. However, it was noticeable that the media was the highest ranked sector thought to fight corruption with 15.5 per cent (TI, 2010: 8) rather than the police and sporting institutions.

Building on this TI carried out a survey of each specific area in the perception survey. A combination of methods was used; drawing on academic texts, official reports, media and policy literature and interviewing key people in respective organisations with expertise on corruption and direct experience of combating corruption. Sport, however, is a complex field where there is a broad range of different types of corruption; these can range from serious matters such as match-fixing, use of illegal and/or banned substances to low-level cheating.

The findings from the research are useful and informative, but we are still in the early stages of exposing the level and depth of fraud and corruption in sport and thus preventing it. These findings have exposed a mixture of old and new issues; match-fixing is an old problem, but technology has changed the landscape in which people can anonymously place bets around the world, even if registered with an online account. Supported with qualitative interviews the TI (2010) research offers a nuanced analysis (Flick, 2010) providing a snapshot picture of the way fraud and corruption are defined, viewed and considered in different sectors of the sporting world.

The TI (2010) report, however, omits those it interviewed, but notes that responses to corruption were mixed dependent on the sport and the type of corruption. It did make clear that those interviewed were selected based on seniority within their own organisation, expertise and experience of combatting corruption. Furthermore, self-regulation, if there is any regulation, is the usual mechanism for dealing with fraud and corruption in sport. The problem with self-regulation, as has been seen in other sectors such as policing (Goldsmith, 1991; Punch, 2000; Chan, 2003) is that without independent oversight there is a lack of transparency and corruption is able to continue and/or accepted as part of the culture of the organisation (Handy, 1993; de Graaf, 2007).

PKF has produced the Annual Survey of Football Clubs Finance Directors Report for 10 years, and, for 2011, it was decided to extend the survey to assess the sector's understanding of fraud and the level of awareness and resilience it has in protecting itself from both fraud committed by internal employees and contracted external employees. In the economic climate of recent years, with the first Premiership Club, Portsmouth FC, going into administration, and the development of the UEFA Fair Play Financial Rules for the 2012 season assessed in 2013/14 (UEFA, 2011), football clubs now, more than ever, need to balance the books, particularly if wanting to play in the most prestigious European tournaments, which offer the greatest financial rewards. The PKF report illustrated how vulnerable football clubs in the UK are to fraud and corruption beyond match-fixing. They illustrate that substantial work is needed to counter fraud in football, and in particular, the English Premier League (EPL), the most commercially successful league in the world, which attracts £9 billion per annum in commercial 'rights' (Millward, 2011). While no individual clubs were identified in the report the analysis helped provide a map of the condition of the clubs surveyed and the resilience to fraud in professional football.

The key findings of the survey showed that: 24 per cent of all football clubs of those surveyed in England, Wales and Scotland have an internal audit function, 5 per cent have an agreed counter-fraud strategy, 5 per cent have an anti-fraud statement and 7 per cent have a fraud response plan. This, we suggest, is of some concern since, regardless of their league, some kind of internal audit function is a necessary element of any business. Such an omission leaves the club vulnerable to internal and external fraud, which, the most extensive research shows, can cost between 3 and 9 per cent of expenditure (Gee et al., 2009, 2012). Furthermore, a report by Christian Aid (2010) *'Blowing the Whistle': Financing the Beautiful Game*, highlighted that there is a lack of clarity of football club ownership in the Premier League, and that this lack of clarity allows unscrupulous people a veneer of public respectability.

Such surveys are rare in the world of sport; there are, however, other 'reports' which are of some interest. On 26 June 2000 Sir Paul Condon was appointed Director of the Anti Corruption Unit (ACU) of the International Cricket Council (ICC) after scandals of corruption in the sport. While the then ACU (now the Anti Corruption and

Security Unit – ACSU) interviewed people involved in the sport of cricket from around the world they discovered what amounted to a conspiracy of silence (ICC, 2001). This was also encountered to some extent by the Qayyum Commission (2000) in Pakistan and the King Commission (2000) in South Africa. It soon became apparent that players were reluctant to talk about corruption, as were some officials, as many did not want to be seen as informants and thus ostracised by fellow players and colleagues. Furthermore, there was no credible person or body to whom to report matters of fraud and corruption at this time; there was a justified fear that 'whistleblowers' would be penalised rather than supported (Radford, 2011), and that international careers would come to an abrupt end as a result of exposing the corruption in cricket, with some simply claiming that corruption would always be part of international cricket. This last view appears to have proved disappointingly correct (see Chapter 7 for other investigations and reports on corruption in cricket). All of these 'reports', however, did dispel the myth that cricket was free from corruption, with a few rogue players, but failed to produce any estimate or indication of the breadth and depth of international corruption.

A similar report on Major League Baseball (MLB), the Mitchell Report (2007), is a useful document that helped expose some, not all, of the extent of steroid, Human Growth Hormone (HGH) and other illegal substance abuse by players in MLB. This report was prompted more by a succession of scandals and concern from within baseball that substance abuse was ruining the integrity of the sport.

Finally, many American scholars have produced numerous empirical papers on point-shaving in basketball (Bernhardt and Heston, 2010; Gibbs, 2007; Wolfers, 2006); this is where players fail to cover the spread of points set by bookmakers in a match (for example, Team A is expected to win a match over Team B by at least twelve points; however, due to 'putting the fix', Team A wins the match by eight points and fails to cover the spread, but still wins the match, along with some money/gifts for failing to cover the spread).

Yet again, these studies are not surveys, but their authors have provided some empirical data to suggest that some basketball players or teams win basketball matches but by less than the spread of points that is set by bookmakers. They therefore win the basketball match while at the same time securing profits for those involved in the fix who have bet on this outcome.

We suggest that while these surveys, reports and academic papers are a useful way of exposing the level of fraud and corruption in a sport, they are a primarily a reaction to scandals rather than a strategic assessment of the state of the sport and its exposure to fraud and corruption and resilience to it. Constant measurement, even though limited, is part of a counter-fraud and corruption strategy, and for progress to be made in reducing the incidents of fraud and corruption in sport such surveys are invaluable in setting basic standards that could apply across all sports.

The limitation of surveys of fraud and corruption data

As a social practice involving individuals and organisations, corruption is inherently difficult to measure (Seligson, 2006; Urra, 2007). However, in recent years several organisations have developed a Corruption Perception Index (CPI) for the purpose of qualitatively assessing the pervasiveness of corruption around the world. At one level these CPIs are acknowledged as an important development in raising public awareness of corruption and promoting reform, particularly by Transparency International. However, these approaches are also criticised for a lack of methodological rigour in showing just one side of the corruption equation, for example, those that receive a payment or gift while ignoring those offering the bribe, often from the private sector (Otusanya, 2011). These CPI surveys, however, are also limited in their selection process; for example, which country is included in a CPI survey often reinforces stereotypical perceptions of corrupt regions of the world, and as such reflects the confusion and inadequacy and current corruption discourse (Christensen, 2006). A CPI then is not a reflection of a 'real' geography of corruption, and therefore their measurements are problematic.

A review of the literature on corruption reveals that a variety of theoretical frameworks have been used to analyse the incidence of, and recorded growth in, corrupt practices in recent years. Some approaches which have dominated corruption studies in the socio-political and economic literature are; capital accumulation as a theoretical lens (Szeftel, 2000; Khan, 2002) state and class (Dobel, 1978), a policy choice (Nas et al., 1986) and public choice approach (Mbatu, 1991). Furthermore, some have relied on modernisation theory and political development approaches (Huntingdon 1968, 1989;

Andvig, 2006), a cultural perspective (Anderson and Tverdova, 2003), the concept of globalisation (Glynn et al., 1997; Bakre, 2006) and a governmentality framework (Everett et al., 2007). However, perhaps a common theme in these different approaches is that without the involvement of intermediaries and professionals such as bankers, accountants and lawyers the flow of corrupt funds is impossible (Otusanya, 2011).

The methodological approaches used in surveys on fraud and corruption in sport also encounter similar issues, with many limitations of the methodological approaches mentioned in this section, and the use of professionals to obfuscate a process and exposure of corruption. For example, the TI Gallup poll (2010) survey was based on perception rather than fact. With a number of cases of fraud and corruption highlighted in the media – match-fixing in snooker, football, spot-fixing in cricket, illegal payments in football in 2009–2010 – it is perhaps hardly surprising that sport was seen as so corrupt. This perception then could be based on the period in which it was conducted rather than a 'real' perception of corruption in sports. However, TI (2011: 9) is aware of the limitations of this approach and recognises that 'due to its nature, the scale of corruption is impossible to quantify with precision'. While we agree that this is the case for corruption, which can be both illegal and legal, but morally reprehensible, fraud is often a criminal act and sometimes a civil offence; a conviction is one measurement we can use only in a limited way, because breaking the law will not necessarily end in a conviction, and corruption does not always defy the law.

The TI research also involved interviewing key personnel in relevant sporting bodies, but noted that access and information were limited. For example, TI (2010) made it clear that some sporting organisations were far more forthcoming with information than others. This could have been to protect the sport from further media interest and/or cover up that the organisation had failed to deal with fraud and corruption in its sport.

Furthermore, we have no indication of the number of people interviewed, nor how representative of the sport they are, and whether they had an 'agenda' to put forward instead of providing information about the level of fraud and corruption in sport. The same criticism could be aimed at the PKF (2011) research as well as it surveyed just 41 out of 102 potential clubs in England, Wales and Scotland.

These issues, however, are part of the survey method in general rather than specific to this research; all surveys can, if not designed properly, fail to ask the most important questions. Certain questions, however, can also be part of the survey, particularly if the survey is developed and designed in-house and if a compliant company is commissioned to provide the results 'expected'. Language in surveys is also another problem, as it may be misinterpreted, and make the task of defining corruption even more complex. This can affect the reliability of future studies as what is corrupt in one country is seen as common and accepted practice in another. However, we should not simply dismiss this method completely; it is still a useful way to deliver some objective, measured data on which to plan a strategy and assess the decrease or increase in fraud and corruption in sport.

The organisation of a sport, however, can differ substantially, with no set common basic standards on how a sport should be run. This is perhaps because many sports developed in local areas, with rules of the sport codified by well-meaning amateur individuals who feared that the professionalisation of sport would lead to fraud and corruption (Vamplew, 2004; Norridge, 2008). While there is some validity to this view, it is the expansion of sport rather than the nature of sport that has potentially increased the incidence of fraud and corruption.

Furthermore, it is perhaps the rapid and increased commercialisation of some sports, particularly in the UK, USA, Japan, South Korea, Australia and Canada, and the reluctance of governing bodies to recognise the associated potential for fraud and corruption that has led to the numerous cases exposed in the international media.

Even though we have been critical of the research in this section, we see this as the start rather than completion of the attempt to measure fraud and corruption in sport. In the following section we highlight why there is a need for more research and awareness of the potential for fraud and corruption in sport and of the influence that gambling has had on the development of sport.

Gambling and sport: measuring 'attempted' fraud and corruption?

A common theme throughout this book is that gambling and sport have a long historical association. For example, some sports such as horse racing rely on gambling to exist (Forrest and Simmons, 2010), while other sports have experienced substantial fraud and corruption due to the influence of gambling on the outcome of events and the involvement of organised crime (for example, for boxing, see La Motta, 1997; Newfield, 2003). However, gambling and its association with sport, particularly the Premier League, is now often an open commercial relationship with several gambling companies sponsoring teams.

One common recurring theme throughout the development of sport is that of fixing an event. Referred to as match-fixing it often involves the paying of bribes in gifts, cash or hospitality to secure a predetermined outcome, threats to the participants and/or family members, and/or paying for inside information on team selection and injury news ahead of the match. Other types of fraud and corruption have developed along with the expansion and financial success of sport, but it is this type of fraud that has attracted most attention, as it is newsworthy and sensational. It is however, only one type of fraud, as the previous chapter illustrated.

Rather than simply condemn gambling as a bad influence, however, we need to view this association in its social context. For example, gambling helped horse racing establish itself as a major sport around the world, providing formal structures for its development (Forrest and Simmons, 2012); however, the existence of gambling at its core also exposed the sport to the danger of fraud and corruption. Gambling can thus be seen as a doubled-edged sword, as both a way to fund the sport, but at the same time to discredit it. Not all sports needed gambling to develop, as they were commercially viable even without the interests of bookmakers and gamblers; these include football, baseball and basketball. Gambling on these sports is, however, now a major business, in both its legal and illegal forms.

Primarily played by amateurs until the 20th century, organised sport was seen as a form of exercise that was useful for a healthy body, mind and spirit (Vamplew, 2004; Macaloon, 2007), with gambling being seen as perverting an 'innocent pastime' and as 'public dissipation' (Munting 1997: 17). These views, however, failed to recognise or accept the extent of gambling on, for instance, amateur baseball in the USA and the reach and influence of gambling on other sports in their early development. Gambling on sporting contests, whether played by amateurs or professionals, is therefore nothing new (Leitzel, 2008). Now, with the expansion of sport the reach of gambling has also increased, and is seen as a potential threat to the integrity of many sports, such as football, baseball, basketball, cricket and boxing. Whether gambling is legal or illegal in a particular jurisdiction, it is still a threat to the integrity of a sport if it is abused. Simply making gambling illegal, however, has been shown to be difficult to police (see Chapter 9 on basketball); it is of far more use to put in place some system of regulation.

To counteract the effect of gambling on sport in the UK there is the UK Sports Betting Integrity Unit (SBIU) as recommended by the Parry Report (2010). The SBIU is part of the Gambling Commission in the UK, which under the Gambling Act 2005 is invested with the power to prosecute cases of sporting corruption, if they fall under its remit. However, the majority of investigations are referred to the relevant sporting governing body, with a small number passed on to the Crown Prosecution Service. Of these cases, 74 cases have been closed, 40 of which were passed to the relevant sporting governing body with one-third of the cases (24) involving British football (Transparency International, 2011).

Regulating gambling on sport is a complex matter involving legal, cultural and international issues (Hornle and Zammit, 2010). Most sports prevent competitors, officials and administrators from gambling on the sport that they are involved in; these rules, however, are often part of a code of conduct, and players involved in gambling are dealt with under these codes. It is, however, when those involved in a sporting contest can affect the outcome of a match, which few vested interests know in advance, that the integrity of the sport is threatened. This type of gambling on sport is perhaps akin to insider dealing, which is illegal in other business sectors. The temptation to place a bet on a sporting event and use this inside knowledge is difficult to resist; while many sports stars are multi-millionaires, many are only just surviving (see Chapter 11 on boxing, in particular) and thus can be 'persuaded' by individuals or organised criminal elements (Hill, 2010) to commit a fraud. It is therefore difficult to claim that legal gambling is a cause of fraud and corruption in sport; it is illegal gambling that is far more of a problem. If legal gambling affects 'modern' sport in any way at all, it is its sponsorship of sporting events that increases its profile and normalises gambling as a harmless activity to which some become addicted (Griffiths, 1995, 1999; Orford, 2001; Wardle et al., 2007). The legal gambling sector, more than the sporting bodies entrusted with protecting the integrity of the sport, is attempting to counteract the problem of match- and spot-fixing by monitoring and warning sporting bodies of any suspicious betting patterns (Brooks, 2012).

This 'real time' assessment of gambling transactions, if used correctly, helps expose potential fraud. Rather than be seen as a threat to the integrity of sports, legal gambling, with its ability to monitor transactions in detail, can provide a possible way to measure known, suspected and attempted frauds.

Conclusion

This chapter has primarily illustrated that there is lack of research into the level of fraud and corruption in sport. This, as we highlighted, is due to the complex nature of fraud and corruption, but also because sporting bodies do not all seem to consider seriously enough the magnitude of the problem they have encountered in a technological new age. This is in spite of the many highly publicised examples of fraud and corruption committed by players, owners, sporting institutions, amateur and professional athletes, coaches and managers.

We have also attempted to clarify the role of gambling in sport and the influence it can have, but also moved beyond gambling and match-fixing to show that fraud and corruption can manifest itself in a variety of ways that can damage the image and financial integrity of sport. In the next chapter we move beyond what and how fraud and corruption is committed in sport to explain *why* people commit acts of fraud and corruption.

4
Why Do Those in Sport Commit Fraud and Corruption?

Introduction

The first documented case of corruption in international sport is attributed to the athlete Eupolos of Thessalia (Maennig, 2005). There are also records of corruption of 'sports management' and administration in the ancient Olympics (Decker, 1995). Then, as now, however, there is no 'specific class' of people (Dittenhofer, 1995) that commits acts of fraud and corruption. As we have already illustrated, fraud and corruption is committed by athletes, sports administrators, professional coaches and managers working *in* or as individuals *for* sporting bodies; some of the examples in this book examine fraud and corruption in specific sports in more depth, but for now our attention is on why people involved in the world of sport commit acts of fraud and corruption.

The majority of frauds and acts of corruption are committed by those working in an occupation (Levi, 1988) and those involved in sport are no different. While presented something other than a business sometimes, sport is nevertheless the way many people earn an income and thus provides an occupation; for athletes their career might last a few years rather than a full working life, unless they go on to work in sport in some different capacity, such as from being an athlete to working in the media, but for a period of time they are a professional athlete, coach or manager, which is a full-time occupation.

In this chapter we focus on understanding why individuals commit acts of fraud and corruption and examine the theoretical approaches already put forward elsewhere that have been used to explain the underlying motivations and characteristics of such acts. We do this by drawing on literature that focuses on fraud in particular and the work of Dittenhofer (1995) and Gill (2005), as well as the sociological work of Sykes and Matza (1957) and Matza (1964) and their techniques of neutralisation, which, as far as we are aware, have not been applied to explain sports corruption.

We then follow this with a review of organisational acts of fraud and corruption, and the culture and environment and social and cultural understandings which affect individuals' work and propensity for illegal acts, drawing in particular on the work of Mars (1984).

In the conclusion we suggest that many of those in the 'sporting world' are no different to those in other businesses, and that previous work on fraud in general has some currency and value in explaining fraud and corruption in sport.

Individual athletes and acts of fraud and corruption

The explanations for the causes and occurrence of corruption can be found in the interaction of individual and social structures. The causes of corruption have been examined from a variety of perspectives, including the public choice model in which the individual is portrayed as a rational, calculating person who chooses corruption when the advantages of such an act outweigh its expected disadvantages (Rose-Ackerman, 1978; Klitgaard, 1988; de Graaf, 2007) and the idea of the 'bad apple' where the cause of corruption lies within a 'defective' individual (Punch, 2000; de Graaf, 2003). In much of the fraud and corruption literature, then, individualist explanations seek to reveal the underlying characteristics and motivations of the offenders (Smith et al., 2010). However, an alternative approach is to stress how similar rather than different are people who commit fraud and corruption (Coleman, 1999). Rather than review all literature here, however, we focus on key theoretical explanations as to why people commit fraud and corruption and use these to explain fraud and corruption in sport.

We start with the work of Cressey (1973) and his fraud triangle of 'pressure', 'opportunity' and 'rationalisation'. It is suggested that due to 'unshareable' stress – perceived or actual – personal failure, collapse or downturn of business, mounting debts and lack of recognition within an organisation and in relationships with employers, individuals have the potential to commit fraud. This is a wide-ranging and perhaps all-encompassing catalogue of factors. Personal pressure can manifest itself in many ways – financial, psychological and social – and as a result of pressure, opportunity and rationalisation combined with personal autonomy at work and environment and/or matters of personal life (Gill, 2005), it is suggested that people will commit fraud and corruption.

Albrecht et al. (1984) built on this fraud triangle of pressure, opportunity and rationalisation and included factors such as living beyond personal income, a desire for personal progression, high personal debt, excessive gambling (Orford, 2003), pressure from family and friends, lack of recognition and reward from employment, 'fluid moral values' and a desire to challenge and/or abuse the 'system'. These factors are also wide-ranging and broad and can be criticised for being all-encompassing, particularly if pressure is perceived rather than real and therefore all of us, at some point in time, could use some of these explanatory factors to explain motivations for fraud. Furthermore, some of these are instrumental factors while others are expressive and emotional. It is difficult to know what factors are responsible for acts of fraud and corruption, as they are as multi-layered and complex as fraud and corruption themselves. Instead, these factors, as with all attempts at profiling, are full of suggestive ambiguity and constitute a useful checklist of factors rather than a scientific method of prediction (Smith et al., 2010).

However, apart from interviewing those who commit fraud and corruption (Gill, 2005) it is still useful to have a system of classification to break down and explain the mixture of motivations of those prepared to commit fraud and corruption. Therefore, we draw on the work of Sykes and Matza (1957) (techniques of neutralisation) and Dittenhofer (1995) (classification of syndromes). While we are aware of the limitations of these approaches, they are still useful in explaining fraud and corruption. We have adapted them for our purposes here to highlight the usefulness of these theoretical approaches in explaining fraud and corruption, which draw on a criminological approach to a specific focus on fraud and integrity, or lack of it, in sport. While presented here as individual explanations many of the factors are combined and should be read in conjunction with one another rather than in isolation.

It is suggested that people commit acts of fraud and corruption due to financial need – perceived or real – and a personal appetite for wealth (Dittenhofer, 1995). This can arise from addiction, that can be illustrated by football players' excessive gambling (Orford, 2003) and alcohol addiction, and American football players and baseball players' (see Chapter 10 on baseball) recourse to illegal substances for both recreational and professional purposes. The temptation then could arise to pay for an uncontrollable habit or desire to succeed in competition at all costs. Athletes and coaches, however, might also be responding to short-term pressure; they may use illegal substances to increase personal performance in a competition to qualify for the Olympic team. However, in time, this brief dalliance with illegal substances can, and often does, turn into regular use, which is then rationalised as 'normal'. It is thus presented as common practice and justified. These rationalisations can be referred to as *techniques of neutralisation*, as defined by Sykes and Matza (1957) and can be used to explain both individual and organisational fraud and corruption. Many conventional criminological theoretical approaches at this time suggested that 'criminals' have a different and fixed moral code from that of 'normal' people who adhere to the law. Challenged by Matza (1964) it was instead suggested that offenders drift in and out of crime and acts of delinquency. Matza and Sykes (1957) felt that people are aware of the need to abide by the law, and possess the same internal code for avoiding illegal acts as the law-abiding, but when and if they succumb to temptation they employ a particular technique to silence misgivings or neutralise such behaviour and provide justification for their acts.

For many offenders, regardless of the crime committed, this often takes the form of a *denial of responsibility*. This is where offenders claim, in an attempt to neutralise the 'immoral' act, that they were victims of circumstance and/or were forced into a situation beyond their control. A further technique of neutralisation is where there is a *denial of injury*. This is where offenders insist their actions did not cause any harm or damage and that nobody was put in physical danger; an example would be that of a professional cyclist in the Tour de France who insists that substances ingested and/or injected to increase performance were legal and/or illegal but nevertheless safe. This technique is often a part of the *denial of responsibility* mentioned above. Professional cycling, however, has a recent history of corruption, with those involved being highly organised (Soule and Lestrelin, 2011).

Leading on from this example we have an *appeal to a higher loyalty*. Offenders suggest that the offence was 'for the team', for the protection of friends and/or the success of colleagues. Such an example is the systematic doping of the US Postal Service team in the Tour de France. Team mates of Lance Armstrong have admitted to using illegal substances such as EPO, a blood booster, and other endurance-enhancing substances, when racing. Several of the US Postal Service team have claimed that doping was part of the 'culture of the sport'. Perhaps the most telling justification was where team members said that 'we were going to do everything possible to help Lance win' (Walsh, 2011: 11 and 18).

While many of the US Postal Service team have now admitted illegal use of banned substances, at the time it appears that team loyalty and working as a team to achieve a set outcome was expected behaviour. The claim that 'I did it for the team' can, however, be employed in a completely different way; instead of appealing to those involved in the sport there is a 'passing of blame' or *disbursement of blame* where a team, co-accused or sporting body is caught committing an illegal act – be it breaking the rules of the sport or breaking the law of international competition. The disbursement of blame builds on some of the other 'denials' above and often appears in court cases where athletes have been charged with taking illegal substances. For example, the British sprinter Dwain Chambers, banned from the Olympics for testing positive for illegal substances, named several US athletes in his autobiography, claiming that he was aware of and familiar with other athletes injecting or ingesting such illegal substances (Chambers, 2009).

This disbursement of blame leads on to the technique of *misrepresenting the consequences*. Here offenders tend to psychologically minimise the injurious consequences of their actions and focus only on the rewards. The case of Chambers is useful to cite again here; he admitted that 'he hated having to cheat to win' in the competitive world of international athletics. A brief conversation with Victor Conte from BALCO recounted in Chambers' book, *Race against Me*

(2009), is enlightening. In conversation with Conte, Chambers asked about the then new synthetic substance THG:

> Chambers: 'Illegal?'
>
> Conte: 'It's undetectable'
>
> Chambers: 'Is it banned?'
>
> Conte: 'It is not on the prohibited list and neither will cause a positive test'
>
> Chambers: 'Isn't that cheating'?
>
> Conte: 'They're cheating you, Dwain. You're a talented athlete and you're not competing on a level playing field. Most of the top sprinters are on steroids. Every time you race you're at a disadvantage'

Chambers, however, was eligible to compete for Great Britain at the London Olympics of 2012 after his lifetime Olympic ban for doping offences was found to be unlawful by the Court of Arbitration for Sport (CAS). Furthermore, the CAS panel decided that the British Olympic Association's bylaw now violates the World Anti-Doping Agency (WADA) code. Great Britain is still the only country to enforce lifetime bans for athletes caught using illegal substances, and it will fight to keep the sanction as part of its Olympic regulations (Kidd and Broadbent, 2012).

An individual, organisation and nation can use all of these techniques as well. For example, an individual might deny responsibility, and an organisation can appeal to a higher loyalty.

Supporting this account of techniques of neutralisation is the work of Dittenhofer (1995) and Zeiltin (2001), in particular the syndrome of *injustice and dissatisfaction*. Behaviour in this category is defined as a sense of injustice felt towards an employer, particularly in a highly regulated work environment (Zeiltin, 2001). This does, however, raise a question that if employed in a highly regulated, rule-bound environment, how are fraud and acts of corruption possible? Furthermore, frauds are often committed in response to a sense of dissatisfaction and injustice brought on by missing a promotion or being marginalised by an employer, and then excluded from personal progression (Tucker, 1989) which leads to dissatisfaction and potential fraud. Such exclusion is determined by a person's organisational status and conditions of employment. If organisations are structured to differentiate employees by salary and rewards, this could lead to increased competition between employees, rather than building a sense of team spirit. However, such competition might be encouraged but also allow management to be selectively myopic and avoid personal responsibility for improving working conditions and wages. Even if handsomely paid, some athletes will use illegal substances with the aim of increasing personal sponsorship and commercial revenue. Examples of this are athletes ingesting a course of illegal substances to produce a 'best' performance to qualify for or win a race; this could be in the Olympics, Commonwealth Games or the Tour de France. Furthermore, it appears that steroids and Human Growth Hormone (HGH) have been injected by some baseball players to break batting 'home run' records, and that this practice is downplayed by some owners and managers of teams because such run chases increases crowd attendance (see Chapter 10).

Part of this sense of injustice also derives from the 'due me' attitude where employees, particularly those who have spent years at the same company, feel that their personal contribution to the company has not been fully recognised. Mars (1982, 1984) and Hollinger and Clark (1983) have pointed out that the 'due me' frauds are usually small and primarily used to correct a perceived lack of financial reward. In sport there is also ample opportunity to carry out frauds such as selling tickets privately for major events that should be sold to the public by an employee of the club and/or organisation promoting the event.

Building on this argument Mars (1984) has suggested there is a role for *Ego* in all this. Desire for financial reward is mixed with the need for recognition. In sport this could be from personal relationships and family, but also from public acclaim for sporting success and achievements. This syndrome is perhaps far more pronounced with athletes as esteem and recognition as a champion is a powerful motivation.

All of these explanations are of course limited; however, they do offer us a working framework for understanding why people in sport commit acts of fraud and corruption. These varying theoretical approaches complement one another as individuals' acts of fraud and corruption are not committed in a social vacuum, and as such we need to take account of the social context in which the individual athlete and sporting body function. It is to the organisational context that we now turn.

Sporting institutions and acts of fraud and corruption

Much of the literature on fraud and corruption notes that individuals do not commit acts of fraud and corruption in isolation (Smith et al., 2010). Individuals might work alone, but they are often part of an organisation, which can, and does, influence behaviour (Gobert and Punch, 2007). The culture of an organisation is seen as an important factor in explaining why people commit fraud and corruption and Mars (1982, 1984) has illustrated that the culture of organisations can differ, and that opportunity, interaction and workplace dynamics affect the propensity to commit fraud and acts of corruption. The extent to which a culture determines actions of individual employees is therefore dependent on a number of factors. These are: the degree to which employees' occupations are determined by set rules and regulations; the degree to which roles within an organisation are differentiated by distinction and/or status; and the degree to which people are physically isolated from one another. This shapes the culture of the organisation and the perceptions that employees hold of one another and the extent to which they are dependent on or in competition with one another.

While the culture of an organisation is important, sections of a company might also play a role in controlling or encouraging illegal behaviour. For example, working in an environment producing valuable products might lead to fraud, but if the culture of that section, which could be determined by a key individual, is one of personal and professional integrity, the desire to commit fraud and corruption is diminished. Therefore, we cannot simply refer to an organisation as corrupt, because some people working in such an environment will resist the temptation to commit illegal acts; it is better therefore to view key individuals and sections and structures of groupings in an organisation that might have a propensity to commit fraud and corruption. It is therefore impossible for us to state with confidence that all those employed by a sporting body are corrupt. It appears, however, that some members in positions of power have abused this to increase their own personal wealth and prestige; this does not mean that all those employed by a sporting body are corrupt. The problem here, though, is that constant scandals damage the integrity of those honest employees, while those that are exposed escape punishment, except for perhaps being excluded from holding a position in the sport (Jennings and Sambrook, 2000).

In order to understand organisational fraud and corruption and how it occurs, a distinction needs to be drawn between crime committed in the course of an occupation, as above, and collective, systemic rule-breaking of an organisation (Braithwaite, 1985). However, as Smith et al. (2010) have suggested, fraud committed by an organisation cannot, by definition, exist, as an organisation is unable to think and act as a conscious body aware of its own acts. Coleman (1999) dismisses this view and claims that though organisations are run by a collection of individuals, it is this collection of roles and functions that individuals occupy, and this shapes the conduct of employees' behaviour. As such, individuals' morality is of less importance than the structure in which s/he works (Boisjoly, 1995). It is not the moral standards and virtues of the individuals that determine the conduct of the organisation, it is the structure and culture of the organisation that directs human action and interaction in the context of a structured working environment.

This view, however, is nothing new. Edwin Sutherland (1949) sought to understand why 'successful' people committed acts of white-collar crime (which term he invented). Employing the theoretical approach of differential association, for Sutherland crime was explained as a preponderance of criminal attitudes instead of non-criminal attitudes; an individual learnt to be socialised into such attitudes by coming into contact with other individuals who held such thoughts. This, however, fails to explain how and why other employees did not adopt such attitudes towards white-collar crime. In fact, Braithwaite (1985) denounced differential association as a platitudinous attempt to explain organisational crime. This theoretical approach, however, did at least attempt to explain 'crimes of the powerful' and increased interest in sub-cultures of crime. An example of 'the structure and culture of the organisation that 'directs' human action and interaction' is Sykes and Matza (1957) and the technique of *denial of the victim*. This is where offenders believe the victim deserved to be victimised, and refuse to recognise 'inappropriate' behaviour and the consequences of physical, psychological acts and the impact on people personally or on the reputation of a sporting body running a sport.

Furthermore, if caught 'cheating' and/or committing a crime another technique is to *condemn those critical of them*. Offenders would maintain that those who condemn them do so out of spite, or are attempting to shift responsibility.

For Braithwaite (1995) whether an organisation is or will be criminal is dependent on the degree to which its aims can be achieved legitimately. If it is unable to progress legitimately an organisation might resort to illegal methods to achieve its desired aims of success (Levi, 2008). Most organisations, however, are structured in such a way that they can be manipulated to behave in a legal or illegal manner. The structure is only part of the problem. It is the role and attitude of senior management that can turn a legitimate organisation into one that is inherently 'criminogenic'. As Slapper and Tombs (1999) have indicated, due to demands for profits, organisations will and do commit fraud in response to economic, financial and legal pressures. Consequently, Box (1983) has illustrated that fraud increases in organisations – regardless of size – in a recession (Cook and Zarkin, 1985; Dow, 1998; Knoop, 2004). Some of this increase, however, can be attributed to the de-regulation of capital and business markets in 1980s and 1990s (Pomeranz, 1995) and this suggestion perhaps has some validity in explaining the corruption in some sporting bodies. This is further supported by Taylor (1999) who suggested that the intensification of international competition and a struggle for survival in worldwide markets has potentially increased the ethic of individual irresponsibility, as individuals are socialised into placing organisational objectives before personal achievement. In this increased competition for profits, sport has become a major beneficiary as advertising and sponsorship (Gorse and Chadwick, 2012) have raised the profile of most sports beyond recognition.

This enhanced profile of sport, however, has increased interest in academic studies and in particular in integrity management as a strategic reaction to the 'moral deficit' in sport and sporting institutions (Maesschalck and Vanden Auweele, 2010). It is debatable, however, whether the numerous high-profile sporting scandals mentioned in this book reflect a decline in moral integrity in sport or a decreased tolerance of sporting 'violations' and their exposure in the media. Regardless of the reason(s) behind this increased exposure there are those such as Forster and Pope (2004), Jennings (1996) and Morgan (2006) who contend that sport has not been renowned for its self-criticism and that important changes to sport tend to be enforced by external moral condemnation and, most of all, financial pressure rather than any notion of moral integrity.

However, we need to clarify what we mean by integrity and 'integrity management'. For the purposes of this chapter we view integrity as an application of accepted values and codes of conduct in common practice in sporting institutions. Integrity management, then, is the process and actions undertaken by senior management to stimulate and secure integrity and prevent violations within a particular organisation. There are, however, two types of approaches to integrity management; these are the rules-based external approach, which is a system of formal, detailed procedures used to enhance integrity and prevent corruption; and the other approach is based on values and focuses on guidance and internal control, that is, control is exercised by organisational members and is about supporting rather than controlling individual members. Rather than an either/or approach, it is best to use a combination of both; the rules-based approach provides an elementary legal framework and if the values are 'correct' within the organisation, individual members will 'police' one another (Maesschalck and Vanden Auweele, 2010).

There are, however, barriers to the success of such organisational conduct. These often derive from senior management and a culture of denial that anything is amiss. It is possible that there are no integrity issues in an organisation, but it is impossible to make such a claim unless an appropriate detection system, as part of an integrity management framework, is used to monitor behaviour and gather knowledge of the prevalence of violations. Furthermore, even if the level of violations is low, all organisations face challenging dilemmas and, as such, any management framework needs to be flexible and be able to develop the most appropriate responses rather than dismissing and/or denying that there is a problem within the sport.

If such an approach to developing a system of integrity management fails to deflect negative attention away from a sporting institution, there may develop a lack of trust within the organisation and be counterproductive. This, we suggest, is myopic. While exposing fraud and corruption within an organisation, it has the potential to reduce future scandals by dealing with them; if downplayed, future acts of fraud and corruption that can damage the integrity of the organisation increase even more.

Furthermore, there is perhaps an arrogance that sporting bodies have so little trust in the public's ability to distinguish between violations that are uncovered and stopped due to a management integrity system and those that are exposed by the media because of a failure by management to deal with obvious corruption. A further potential barrier to reducing the incidence of fraud and corruption in sporting institutions is the downgrading of the importance of organisational integrity. No system will completely stop fraud and corruption, but to dismiss the effort is to encourage inappropriate behaviour. For example, an organisation could have a code of conduct but not implement it or enforce it, and as such its own members see the integrity management system as 'window-dressing' (Trevino and Weaver, 2003; see also Chapter 6 on football).

The 'instruments' of integrity management – risk analysis, analysis of ethical issues, consultation of employees and stakeholders, a code of conduct, training, counselling, a whistleblowing policy, and investigation and sanctioning – are thus important. Rather than review all of these instruments here we focus on a few of the more important aspects that are integral to understanding organisational acts of fraud and corruption.

In risk analysis vulnerable parts of a business are mapped and analysed. This in itself is of little use as risk analysis, depending on how it is used, can be both a preventive measure and have damaging outcomes. For example, risk analysis can provide a clear framework which employees know they have to adhere to; however, if it is too restrictive it might be seen as signifying a lack of trust by management and thus undermine employees' work ethic and capacity for innovation.

Developing a code of ethics or conduct is a useful way forward, but it is best to involve all employees in a sporting body; if not, the code can be seen as the property of management rather than owned by all. A code of conduct, however, is very different from a code of ethics. A code of conduct is rules-based and starts with the assumption that people are primarily self-interested, and only behave with integrity if under threat of some sanction. A code of ethics, by contrast, is a values-based approach and views people as capable of moral reasoning (Maesschalck and Vanden Auweele, 2010).

Then there are those specific measures that we refer to as structural, such as a policy on accepting gifts and hospitality, which in the world of sport can present difficulties. While it is obvious that managers, coaches and referees should not accept gifts under any circumstances which may be seen as to influence a decision, such as picking a player for a match/event even though he is not suitable, it is difficult to achieve in practice. For example, a parent might offer a sports coach a gift of limited value for training their son or daughter as a token of appreciation rather than a bribe. If refused the parent(s) might be offended, but if accepted the coaches' integrity might be questioned. Separating and rotating roles could avoid some of the issues above. For example, it would be advisable to have one person prescribing and dispensing nutritional supplements to an athlete, and a personal manager dealing with sponsorship, rather than one person arranging all aspects of an athlete's career. Furthermore, it is wise to rotate people in positions in an organisation, because if an employee performs the same role for years the risk will increase that they acquire 'undesirable' routines (Gill, 2005; Gobert and Punch, 2007; Gill and Goldstraw-White, 2010). Developing an anti-fraud and corruption culture via ongoing instruction, updating all employees in an organisation and communicating such changes to potential sponsors might increase both commercial revenue and organisational and personal integrity. There is, however, a danger that once a code of conduct/ethics is announced the media might seek examples of where it has been broken and expose the organisation for any failures to sanction offenders.

Davies (2000) outlined the conditions in commercial and financial organisations that are conducive to and 'predictive' of fraud. For example, if the organisation has an autocratic management style where one person has substantial control with limited personal accountability and a weak and ineffectual board there is the potential for fraud. Attitudes are all important in an organisation and if those in a managerial position accept or actively promote a 'getting it done is more important than how it is done' ethos this will spread throughout the organisation and impact on behaviour. Employees can react to such a culture in many different ways; they can commit fraud, distance themselves from the organisation and do the minimum to stay employed or plan to leave when an opportunity arrives. The ultimate rejection of such a culture, though, is to expose the culture of fraud and corruption by 'going public' once all internal channels have been exhausted. It is useful to have a policy on such whistleblowing as part of an ethical working structure, but unless it is implemented properly, and then if a concern is raised it is not investigated correctly, it will leave the organisation open to criticism (Brooks, 2011). If a mere 'paper policy' is recognised and accepted by management, such an approach will discredit the organisation.

Even though acts of fraud and corruption are secretive and based on deception, and thus difficult to define and classify, there have still been attempts to construct a profile of characteristics and behaviour that might help identify potential corrupt individuals and fraudsters. There are no specific profiles of those in sport, but previous research has been of some use in highlighting common characteristics that occur regardless of the sector.

Conclusion

In this chapter we reviewed the individual, organisational and social and cultural explanations that account for the existence of fraud and corruption in sport and other sectors. Many of them are useful in helping our understanding of fraud and corruption. However, the theoretical and empirical literature we have drawn on has its limitations, too. This is not to dismiss it, but merely to recognise that we are still building on the useful and informative work undertaken to date. The search to understand why people commit fraud and acts of corruption in certain circumstances is ongoing, but research is also needed on keeping checks and balances in place that convince people to behave in an ethical manner. Even with measures in place to prevent fraud and corruption in sport and to deter 'unacceptable practices', it seems, as with other frauds and acts of corruption, that exposure of the individual and/or organisation is often due to the whistleblowing 'nuclear option' where information is leaked to the media, which has a record of exposing corruption and often seems a far more effective regulatory body than many sporting institutions' internal integrity processes in preventing fraud and corruption.

5
Internet Fraud, Corruption and Sport

Introduction

It has been claimed that the relentless expansion of the Internet is in the process of radically transforming the spheres of work, consumption, leisure and politics (Castells, 2002). Part of 'leisure' is the use of the Internet as a gambling medium. However, what is often referred to as cyberspace – the realm of computerised interaction – seems to offer a vast range of potentially 'new' criminal acts (Jar, 2006).

In this chapter, however, we primarily focus on the Internet and its association with money-laundering and its potential for victimisation. Often associated with crime, online gambling sites, particularly in unregulated jurisdictions, are seen as a 'conduit of crime'. We suggest here that depending on the location of the gambling site and jurisdiction and their commercial vested interests, *some* sites are in fact a 'conduit of information' for law enforcement (Brooks, 2012).

Then we turn our attention to the threats that online gambling sites face, such as denial of service, malware and phishing attacks (Furnell, 2002), blackmail from organised crime and how online sites deal with these threats, prevent breaches of customers' accounts and limit the potential for fraud. Each type of attack is dealt with separately here; they are, however, sometimes combined as part of the arsenal of online threats to a service(s). Cybercrime is therefore not so much a single, distinctive kind of criminal enterprise; instead it is a more diverse range of illegal and illicit actions that share in common an electronic environment (cyberspace) (Grabosky, 2001; Newman and Clarke, 2003) and which affect the services online gambling sites offer.

Old and tested methods of crime, such as fraud and money-laundering, that pre-date the Internet have been adapted to embrace the new technology. In this way the Internet can be an avenue for new, developing crimes as well as a vehicle for old crimes. Gambling has embraced the Internet as a new medium to reach people and offer a service; it can be, however, both a potential cause of crime and a victim, the latter of which is often absent in the online gambling literature.

Money-laundering and gambling websites

Information on money-laundering and fraud in the 'gambling industry' is limited. Apart from Blaszczynski and McConaghy (1994), Dohley (2000), Sakuri and Smith (2003) and Croft (2002, 2003) there is little reference to this association. Furthermore, the anti-money laundering, 'policing' literature (Sheptycki, 2002; Harvey, 2005; Sproat, 2007, 2009) rarely makes reference to the gambling sector, with the exception of Hugel and Kelly (2002) and Cabot and Kelly (2007) with the primary focus the USA.

While there is some currency to the condemnation of gambling, a 'psychological', negative approach has failed to see the contribution highly regulated gambling sites offer law enforcement and sporting bodies in preventing crime. Therefore, rather than simply condemning gambling websites as a 'conduit for crime', they should be viewed, depending on the jurisdiction, as a *potential* conduit of crime, a victim of threats, intimidation and fraud, and a line of defence protecting the integrity of gambling on sport, as it is in their interests to expose illegal acts, and prevent 'fixes' and 'frauds'. As a commercial private enterprise, gambling websites need sport to remain clean to attract future customers (Brooks, 2012). Association with money-laundering then is damaging to the commercial profile gambling online sites nurture.

Money-laundering is a term that is often misunderstood, as it covers wide-ranging circumstances. These circumstances comprise attempts to clean illegal funds by handling the benefit of acquisitive crimes such as theft, fraud and tax evasion. It is therefore a collective international problem. In response to this problem the Financial Action Task Force (FATF) was established. Its development, however, has been piecemeal; established in 1989 at a G7 summit, the FATF harnessed the commitment of 16 members (which included the European Commission) to draft national and international responses to money-laundering. Many directives followed with a focus on preventing the use of the financial system for the purpose of money-laundering (Mitsilegas and Gilmore, 2007). However, and perhaps somewhat surprisingly, it was not until a directive in 2005 that the FATF instituted due diligence measures regarding customers, and enhanced due diligence measures in respect of those people considered politically exposed and potentially dangerous (Egan, 2010).

Primarily seen by FATF as a crime committed by organised crime and/or terrorism cells/organisations, there is little reference made to new and emerging threats *to* and *from* online gambling. There is little information from FATF on the risk of money-laundering and gambling sites at the moment, but an old 'vice' is now available on a new medium. As with all 'services' online there are issues surrounding the jurisdiction, policing and legal sanctions (Jar, 2006) of online sites that are problematic. For example, in the USA gambling online is illegal across state lines. This is based on the Wire Act (1961), which was an attempt to deal with organised crime. The Act specifically wanted to stop the transmission of information across state lines (Schwartz, 2005). However, with the changes and advances in technology the Wire Act was seen as increasingly redundant. Due to the lack of clarity regarding this Act, Senator Jon Kyle (Republican) proposed the Gambling Prohibition Act in 1997. However, whilst the Act made it through the Senate it was not signed by the then President, Bill Clinton. A few years later Bob Goodlatte (Republican) proposed a Bill that criminalised US citizens if gambling online. This Act focused on the credit card sector rather than customers and 'encouraged', with threat of prison, US citizens not to make deposits on online gaming sites.

The Act, however, appears to be somewhat prejudicial. For example, it has a clause in it that still allows US citizens to go gambling in the USA. The Act therefore is not out to stop US citizens gambling, it is out to stop US citizens from gambling online on sites that are not based in the USA. The Bill was attached to the Port Securities Bill, which is seen as crucial against the 'war on terrorism', and it was therefore successful in passing the Senate, as senators might have feared appearing unpatriotic unless supporting this Bill. However, the relevant legislation is now under review, and it appears that all or some of the legislation regarding online gambling might be repealed.

Different systems of regulation and types of gambling, however, depending on the jurisdiction, are preferred elsewhere in the world with the matter complicated by varied historical, social and political structures – such as federalised ones – and local attitudes towards gambling (Horne and Zammit, 2010).

In Great Britain, however, with the promulgation of the Gambling Act 2005 and the subsequent development of the Gambling Commission, a different approach to online gambling has developed. Realising that gambling would occur even if made illegal, one of the primary objectives of the Gambling Commission, operational since September 2007, is to 'prevent gambling from being a source of crime or disorder, being associated with crime or being used to support crime' (Department of Culture, Media and Sport, 2005). As part of its remit it published *The Prevention of Money Laundering and Combating the Finance of Terrorism: Guidance for Remote and Non-Remote Casinos* (2007), which built on section 21a of the Terrorism Act 2000 and section 42 and 45 of *Money Laundering Regulations* 2007. The Gambling Commission is therefore limited to regulating those under its legal and geographical jurisdiction, with spread-betting under the remit of the Financial Services Authority (FSA) (Brooks, 2012). These types of bets constitute various ways of wagering on the outcome of an event, where the successful bet is based on the accuracy of the bet rather than a simple 'win or lose' outcome. A spread, then, comprises a range of outcomes and the bet is whether the outcome will be above or below the spread (see the discussion of point shaving in Chapter 9). The point spread is essentially a handicap where the wager is presented as 'will the favoured team/person win by more than the point spread?' If the 'books' are balanced a 'bookmaker' is unconcerned with the result of the match, as profits come from the commission (vigorish or 'vig' in the USA) charged by the gambling company.

Preferring a system of licensing to 'regulate' online gambling sites, the Gambling Commission hoped that customers would trust licensed 'sites' in a respected jurisdiction rather than those in 'suspect' offshore locations.

A 'Remote online gambling' licence, however, is subject to the condition, if based in Great Britain, that the 'gambling equipment' must be physically placed in the country and that this can be verified (unless this stipulation is waived by the Gambling Commission). The Gambling Commission is able, if it so wishes, to establish standards in respect of the manufacture, supply, installation and adaptation of software, and it is considered a criminal offence if these standards are breached. The Gambling Commission therefore has extensive powers to ensure compliance with the terms and conditions of a licence; it can impose financial penalties, and suspend and/or revoke a licence if it is breached. It can also request information or records – paper and electronic – and has the power to apply for a search warrant and inspect and seize 'assets', such as a computer, if an offence has been committed under the Gambling Act 2005. The Gambling Commission then plays an important part in checking; verifying and keeping under surveillance British-based online gambling sites. Its role(s), however, are primarily dealing with those employed in the gambling company rather than those who might use it as a conduit for money-laundering. The role the Gambling Commission plays in preventing this crime is therefore limited, unless it is committed by the company itself or some of its employees. Online sites, rather than the Gambling Commission, law enforcement bodies and sporting institutions, are really the front-line defence against money-laundering in relation to gambling in sport.

The international gambling sector is aware of the negative view held, particularly by sections of the media, about the 'service' they provide. Seen as a conduit for money-laundering, the gambling sector is seen to be complicit in crime, incompetent or lacking a proper anti-money-laundering strategy, and rarely the victim of crime. It is, however, perhaps misleading to view the respected parts of the gambling sector in highly regulated jurisdictions in this way. They, unlike many other businesses, spend their time protecting the funds they have, which people wish to 'win' from them. A gambling company is from the outset concerned with 'winning' as much money as it can from people, or encouraging gambling and taking a percentage of winning bets as commission if it is a betting exchange. As with any business, unregulated gambling websites, or those in jurisdictions that have little 'regulatory oversight', are seen as damaging to the gambling sector as a whole. The tightly regulated and licensed websites felt that they were often categorised and portrayed as the same as those based in 'questionable jurisdictions'. Instead, 'respected' sites help prevent potential frauds by working closely with law enforcement (Brooks, 2012).

The role 'respected' online sites play in passing on information to law enforcement and sporting institutions is often downplayed or completely ignored. This is not to say that gambling sites have no legal and moral responsibility, but they also have a vested business interest in honest sporting competition. Gambling scandals damage the reputation of the sport, but also cast doubt on the integrity of a genuine contest and affect peoples' willingness to continue gambling. Therefore, respected gambling sites have a vested interest in keeping sporting contests fair and honest.

It is also suggested that sporting institutions need to do more regarding the 'policing' of sport. This is particularly the case when provided with overwhelming information from the gambling sector that suspicious activity had occurred in relation to an event. Often it is the sporting institution that is in need of investigation to expose corruption in their sport. This problem, however, is similar to those in other business sectors that discover internal frauds. Money-laundering is only one threat to the integrity of sport and online gambling; it is threats to online gambling sites that we now turn.

Under threat from 'organised' crime: fraud, corruption and online gambling websites

Presented as a form of 'entertainment', international attitudes to gambling have 'softened' – see the case of Singapore – and access to gambling is increasingly widely available. Online sites are based in Malta, Dutch Antilles, Gibraltar, United Kingdom, Australia, India and Native American reservations in the USA; these 'sites', however, function under different systems of regulation. Online gambling has therefore moved from a 'cottage industry' to a form of international commerce. The popularity of this business is evidenced by the continuous growth of online sites, which are estimated to now number 2,132 worldwide (Brooks and Blaszczynski, 2011). These sites, however, are a mixture of single, focused sites, such as poker or sports, to wide-ranging online sites that offer every possible type of gambling available.

This substantial growth, however, has also brought a new wave of cyber-criminals who have worked to develop specialised hacking tools to attack online gambling and sports websites. The new stream of malicious software is, in some cases, highly organised. The ability of cyber-criminals to infiltrate online websites and steal sensitive data has made site security a priority for online operators. There is a comprehensive threat from cyber espionage to online gambling and sports sites. This threat has increased as the online gambling market has increased and these developments, coupled with new dynamic concepts of managing global enterprise and advancement in technology, has created various new avenues for committing crime. The rapid development of online gambling on sports is a direct result of such technological transformations.

Microgaming and 'Cryptologic' launched the first online gambling software and encryption tool to enable secure financial transactions in the 1990s (McMullan and Perrier, 2007) and the online gambling sector has experienced attractive financial returns due to its ease of access for the public, the normalisation of gambling, celebrity endorsement and sponsorship.

However, this popularity and expansion has increased online gambling sites' chances of becoming victims of fraud and cyber attack. This, however, is a complex matter as gambling sites are seen as exposed to fraud and security threats and yet also regarded as capable of defrauding customers. For example, several online poker players have complained of poker bots (viruses) which allowed gambling site personnel to see their cards without their permission. American Gambling Association research highlights that 50 per cent of online casino players blame Internet gambling and sports sites for cheating and 46 per cent accused other players of rogue play (AGA, 2011). This research, however, could reflect players' negative attitudes to losing rather than being a genuine criticism of the site on which they were playing.

Gambling sites have also been victims of hacking attacks – cyber-espionage and phishing. Advanced software programming skills of hackers are increasingly being used to exploit sites that offer businesses or players little protection; sophisticated software simplifies the task of hacking gambling portals. For example, the malware 'Smoke Poker' helps poker players beat the other online player. It uses a Poker Programming Language (PPL), which senses other peoples' playing strategy and then produces a strategy to beat them by scanning an opposing player's gaming/betting pattern, if they have one.

Similar software is available that helps players to download advanced mathematical packages that help corrupt players see other player's cards without their knowledge (McMullan and Perrier, 2007).

However, of all the attacks against the gambling and sports betting sites, malware, denial of service and phishing are considered to be the most sophisticated and dangerous. For example, the production and distribution of malware is a highly profitable business; it is a low-cost, high-impact tool. The ready availability of malware is a serious cause of concern as anyone on the Internet is able to purchase and/or hire malware from illegal, underground markets. The cost, availability and technical sophistication of malware in the 'underground (hacking) market' have altered the way organisations are targeted.

The malware command system is simple to use and has the capability to launch simultaneous and technically advanced attacks well beyond the skill levels of cyber criminals. The sophisticated design of malware is a challenge for those keen to measure and combat the problem. It also very difficult to quantify the extent of the problem, as techniques to measure malware do not follow a standard process.

Malware not only infects personal computers, it also has the ability to disrupt corporations by affecting routers and attached servers. Due to the low cost associated with the development of malware, it has become a very common but useful tool to capture credit cards and bank account data and commit corporate espionage by launching distributed Denial of Service Attacks (DOS). Stealing usernames/passwords to break to in a company or personal account is a common problem regardless of the sector. However, with the growth in online gambling there is the possibility of malware attacks where multi-factor authentication is employed with a 'man in the middle', that is, a link is established between the customer and website portal, which allows the hacker to see all sensitive information required for the financial gambling transaction.

Furthermore, it is possible for hackers to access online gambling and sports portals for extortion and ransom purposes; the common procedure is to hack into the database system, gather the data and then encrypt it. It is therefore possible to encrypt data with a cipher to produce a complex encryption code, which is difficult to break down. The victim (the gambling site) is then requested via email or phone call to deliver the required ransom for the delivery of the key to decrypt its own data so that the site can function. Malware and malicious viruses can therefore be used to extort money by targeting specific online sports sites.

Not all the above attacks, however, come from cyber criminals; there have been a few incidences where attacks have been blamed on competing firms whose intent has been to cause financial loss.

In addition to malware as a potential threat, there is the Denial of Service Attack (DOS). This is one of the most frequently deployed attacks against gambling and sports betting sites. Several hundred 'bots' are sent to overload the website, consume all available disk space and choke down the bandwidth, thus denying services to legitimate customers. 'Botnets' are malware that infect a computer; computers thus affected are referred to as 'zombies', as they are triggered and remotely controlled by these 'botnets'. Botnets scan computers for known vulnerabilities on the Internet and once these are discovered, the computer is infected with a specific malware. In most of the cases the malware is hidden within an encrypted code format, which makes it difficult for anti-virus software to detect it. Controlled by a criminal network, the malicious code (part of the botnet programme) is programmed to remain dormant, but once triggered can be used to launch various DOS attacks on the victim's site.

It is thought that one person can control a number of botnets, which can be used in various cyber attacks in different sectors or across the same sector, disrupting access to 'services'. The gambling sites are thus unable to trade, and the attack(s)/is/are set up to disrupt 'services' for few minutes when demand is at its highest, for example, during an important football match or tennis final, followed by a threat of further attacks if 'insurance' is not paid. The financial impact of DOS attacks is difficult to estimate because of a reluctance to publicise the cost of the attacks and inform the relevant law enforcement bodies; action taken can depend on attitudes towards the police, the jurisdiction in which the site is located, and its own international reputation as a respected site.

In a typical DOS the three-way handshake process is exploited. For example, normal 'correspondence' between a customer and websites is when a customer sends a SYN (synchronisation/start) request to the destination host (website) that sends back a SYN, ACK (synchronization acknowledge) response. On receiving this, the customers' computer sends the ACK (acknowledge) back before the connection is established. This complete process is termed the 'Three-Way

Handshake'. In a typical attack the hacker makes the destination host (the online gambling and sports betting site) send the SYN, ACK message to an incorrect address or to a non-existent host. This results in the destination host waiting for the final ACK thus exhausting its memory pool. By generating a random address 'criminals' can block legitimate services offered by the destination source.

However, it becomes difficult when hundreds of malicious bots are involved. The task of differentiating the legitimate from the malicious is a difficult to handle problem. A typical DOS attack might involve the manipulation of thousands of bots to bombard the target site with false requests and blocking the site's services. In this type of attack legitimate customers have no knowledge of the attack.

Once a site is under attack the cyber criminals demand ransom in return for protection from further attacks. In an incident in 2010, a major online gambling site experienced a well-organised cyber attack, which resulted in the theft of 2.9 million usernames and approximately 90,000 account names, with bank account details. The company, however, had encrypted the data and the chances of hackers breaking the encryption code were slim. However, it shows the vulnerability of the online gambling and sports betting industry and the level of sophistication now employed by cyber criminals. Finally, DOS attacks can work in both isolation, such as by denying a company its ability to function, but they can also work in cooperation with other forms of cyber crime and help infect servers and launch 'phishing' attacks.

Phishing originated from 'fishing'; bait is thrown into water (the Internet) with the intention to trick someone into biting (taking the bait), just like a fish. This technique, however, is used to defraud online 'punters' rather than the gambling sites. A typical attack comprises deceptive emails trying to trick customer(s) into giving out sensitive details by directing them towards a fake site. Most of these attacks are triggered following a legislation change or change in the website, for example, sending emails to the customer(s) to highlight a new change to gambling laws and asking them to authenticate their details by confirming the link. The availability of software such as 'Dark Mailer' and 'Spam Manager' has facilitated bulk phishing attacks to online gambling and sports sites. This is because gambling websites offer concealed chat rooms where 'punters' exchange views on gambling matters.

Other technological advancement has led to the development of a range of new types of phishing attack. However, irrespective of the type of attack, the process is similar. The emails appear to come from a trusted and reliable source, with the most common requests being for a personal security update, a request to update incomplete account information, a request to update personal account details, and offers of financial incentives.

Two commonly employed methods are the 'spray and pay' and the 'rod and reel'/ 'spear-phishing' approach. The spray and pay method consists of sending bulk emails to individuals without any particular affiliation, while the latter method is more focused towards a particular organisation. Other variations include advance phishing, spoofing (forging an authentic website), smishing (SMS phishing) and spear phishing (targeting specific organisations).

Online attacks can also consist of embedding malicious script that is triggered when an email message is read. The malicious emails execute/edit the host files on the victim's machine, and as a result, when the customer attempts to access their favourite online gambling site, the computer automatically directs them to fraudulent websites for the sole purpose of stealing sensitive information. The growth of the Internet has allowed the development of a range of phishing tricks; one of the most common methods is to deceive people with syntax tricks such as, for example, Paddypower presented as Paddy Power.

Failure to identify legitimate links makes it simple for cyber criminals to carry out phishing attacks. Wu (2006) refers to this as a 'semantic gap' between the system's model and people's perception/understanding. The decision to open an email and websites is normally made in response to its presentation and appearance without much thought being given to potential dangers, especially if a person is eager to place a bet on a specific event.

An important feature of online gambling and sports sites is that they can be set up and accessed from anywhere in the world. For the majority of customers, an accessible interface and attractive odds are appealing, while 'security' is a potential hindrance. The use of Internet and mobile devices for gambling appears on the increase and this is a part of the world of sport that needs academic attention as sport sponsorship and increased advertising leads more and more to the normalisation of gambling.

Conclusion

This chapter assessed the limited information available on money-laundering and online gambling sites. As was discussed, this is a complex matter because gambling online is illegal in some jurisdictions and highly regulated in others. Rather than see all the online sites in the same way it was suggested that 'respected' sites might help in combatting money-laundering (Brooks, 2012).

Furthermore, we outlined the nature of cyber threats posed by hackers – individual or organised – to online gambling and sports betting sites, and also the challenges inherent in dealing with hackers.

It is important to recognise that all the threats mentioned in this chapter, however, will change with the passage of new technological developments. Making gambling illegal, as some sports have, has been an unsuccessful tactic, as will be seen in Chapter 9 on US college basketball. Both terrestrial and virtual gambling on sport are nothing new and nor are the 'fixes' that have and will continue to be associated with them.

Part II

Fraud and Corruption in Sport: Key Bodies: Enforcement and Governance

In highly competitive sports, with substantial financial rewards for success, the pressure to bend and sometimes break the rules of the sport is always a potential problem. However, it is the duty of regulatory bodies – national and international – and those involved in the sport such as players, referees/judges and owners to protect the integrity of its sport as well (Greenfield and Osborn, 2001). All are responsible and should dissuade and/or report those that break the rules and point out that it is unethical and illegal behaviour. This presents a problem for the governance of various sports and sporting institutions.

There are three principal approaches to the governance of sport (Henry and Lee, 2004). These are:

- *Corporate governance*: the ethical conduct of processes involved in the management and direction of organisations in the sports business
- *Systemic governance*: the competition, cooperation and mutual adjustment of aims and actions within and between sporting and other relevant organisations in such systems
- *Political governance*: the processes by which governments or governing bodies seek to steer the sports 'system' to achieve desired outcomes, by moral pressure, use of financial incentives, licensing, regulation and control.

The use of the competing theoretical approaches of governance in sport is evident (Michie, 2000; Henry and Lee, 2004; Hums and MacLean, 2004; Kluka et al., 2004; Henry et al., 2005; Michie and

Oughton, 2005; Forster, 2006) at the national and international level, particularly with regard to 'sport management'. This interest is cultivated by concern about the management of sport organisations in the light of principles of administrative structure, resources and management of sport, and seeks to explain how sport organisations are really managed (how power *is exercised* within them) and/or how they should be managed (how power *should be exercised*).

This is perhaps best reflected in how sporting institutions punish those that have breached codes of conduct and committed criminal acts. The potential sanctions employed are of considerable interest and should be of such a magnitude that they are a sufficient deterrent to wayward sport stars, managers, owners, trainers and officials by convincing them that fraud and corruption are not worthwhile. This, however, is far from the case in reality. Each chapter in this section provides examples of the types of fraud and corruption committed in sport and assesses the role(s) of the relevant sporting bodies in dealing with corruption. The sports are:

- Football
- Cricket
- Horse racing
- Basketball
- Baseball
- Boxing.

6

Fraud and Corruption in Football

Introduction

In this chapter we start by highlighting the types of fraud and corruption existing in the 'modern' commercial era of football in an international context. This is not to suggest that football had a halcyon period free from fraud and corruption; it is merely recognition that with increased commercial exposure (Freeman, 2000; Hamil and Walters, 2010) more cases of corruption have appeared in football.

Following on from this we review how football league structures can contribute to fraud and corruption. Reviewing two very different structures and approaches to the sport we focus on the German Bundesliga and Italian football; in both leagues there is a lack of regulatory oversight, creative accounting, conflicts of interests and outright corruption.

The penultimate section is concerned with the encouragement of disclosure and the use of sanctions to reduce incidents of fraud and corruption in football. However, those wishing to protect the integrity of sport and 'blow the whistle' are often discredited and dismissed as biased and/or incompetent, which is similar to how employees that come forward are treated in other public and private sectors (Winfield, 1994; Holdaway, 1994; Coffee, 2006; Board, 2011; Mostrous, 2011; Davidson, 2012).

In the conclusion we make some brief suggestions as to how national and international bodies could increase the integrity of their sport.

Types of fraud and corruption in football

There is excellent literature on the historical and social development of football (Taylor 1971; Critcher, 1979; Dunning and Sheard, 1979; Mason, 1980; Delves, 1981; Tischler, 1981; Wagg, 1984; Mason, 1989; Philips and Tomlinson, 1992; Taylor, 1992; Giulianotti, 1999; Vamplew, 2004; Foot, 2007; Norridge, 2008; Millward, 2011) and while 'cheating' in some form has existed throughout the game's history we are concerned primarily with more 'modern' forms of fraud and corruption, such as negotiated fees, contracts, international ownership and other avenues of corruption, to name a few. However, we start with one fraud that is, disappointingly, always with us: ticket fraud.

As a fraud, this is not particular to football, as it is associated with all sporting and popular cultural events, such as festivals and concerts. Ticket fraud, however, is damaging to the sometimes small profit margin of football clubs around the world and little appears to be done to protect this form of revenue.

Ticket sales

Ticket sales are considered the most important income stream for the financial performance of football clubs (PKF, 2011). As a percentage of income these sales are as important as TV revenue for survival, and protecting the revenue stream is therefore of paramount importance. However, tickets, particularly for major sporting events, are often bought and dispensed in return for 'business favours'. Furthermore, there are businesses that sell tickets to events and specialise in providing premium tickets or tickets for sold-out events. Such tickets are sold at market price rather than the actual face-value of the ticket, and while these businesses might not actually manufacture illegal tickets, they are willing to sell them on from dubious sources. The market price of the ticket is determined by the demand for a football match, so the price the ticket is sold for is often far higher than the price printed on the ticket. There are many businesses that sell football tickets, but only a few hundred of these are legitimate ticket brokers, and only a handful have experience in selling football tickets. As demand always outweighs supply, illegal websites appear to take advantage of gaps in the market, and then disappear before anything can be done about them.

Apart from the tickets not arriving on time for the match or at all, the main risk for football fans from buying tickets from these websites is where personal details are supplied to an online company. As we saw in the previous chapter, identity theft and impersonation fraud are among the fastest growing frauds in the world, and care needs to be taken when buying tickets online (Serious Fraud Office, 2011). High-profile examples of this type of fraud in football include: the Liverpool vs Milan UEFA Cup Final in 2007 in Athens, Greece, where some Liverpool fans with genuine tickets were unable to get into the stadium to see the match, because people with fake tickets had already entered the stadium, which was full to capacity; at the UEFA Cup Final between Manchester Untied and Chelsea in Moscow, Russia, in 2008 some of the tickets sold were discovered to be forged and, as above, fans were stopped from entering the stadium to watch the match. In an attempt to combat these and other frauds at the European level, UEFA sets the requirements for all its competitions for such things as ticket prices, deadline dates for sales, and the number of tickets made available to the two teams involved in the match and to the public. However, policing these requirements is down to a Local Organising Committee (LOC) that submits its 'arrangements' to UEFA on how it will organise the match.

Tickets are also sometimes dispensed in return for business favours in the name of 'entertainment' and given to officials and players for high-profile matches when they should not have been; in some cases these tickets have been sold on for a substantial profit through a registered company (Jennings, 2007). For example, Graham Bean was appointed in 1998 as the compliance officer for the FA. In 1999 he exposed a ticket scam for the Worthington Cup Final between Leicester City and Tottenham Hotspur. Each player had been allocated 20 complimentary tickets and also had the option of purchasing an extra 75 tickets. These tickets were not for sale; some players, however, resold the tickets and were fined by the FA (Bower, 2007: 251–252).

Football fans, like fans of other sports, are often willing to pay more than the face-value ticket price for major matches (Millward, 2011). This desire provides an opening for fraud and corruption. In this context, the LOC, players and officials have the opportunity to sell tickets to make a substantial profit. While this is not necessarily illegal (it depends on the jurisdiction), the sale of such tickets is definitely an abuse of privilege.

We now turn out attention to the role of agents, payment for players they represent and the paying of fees for 'services'.

Football agents, fees and potential tax evasion

Often described as 'parasites' and damaging to the interest of football, agents have faced much criticism in Europe. Before 1995, football agents had no form of registration or regulation and football players were assets owned by clubs (Antonioni and Cubbin, 2000). In 1995 the Bosman case at the European Court of Justice changed the restriction on player movement and the Court ruled that football players were allowed free transfers at the end of their contracts, removing them as assets from the club accounts (Simmons, 1997; Binder and Findlay, 2012). In the same year Fifa stipulated that all agents needed to be registered with them. By 2002 there were 179 licensed agents in England, 82 in Germany, 88 in France, 54 in Italy; however, many others were active though not registered (Bower, 2007). Despite the registration requirements, obtaining a licence is open to corruption.

Furthermore, it has been suggested that the Bosman ruling encouraged transfers, leading to a spiral in wages and the reluctance of clubs in many leagues across Europe to train young players (Banks, 2002). In such an environment agents have been accused of encouraging players to initiate transfers, and of offering 'inducements' to managers to 'persuade' football club chairmen and/or boards that certain players were an integral part of the club's future success.

While it is against FA rules for an agent to receive payment from a club in the form of fees, chairmen also seem happy to defend or keep quiet about agents, particularly if the agents had 'conned' them out of substantial sums of money in the transfer (Conn, 1997; Bower, 2007). No club or representative has so far made an official complaint about important agents with 'contacts' due to the influence of some of them to block the sale of a desirable player to a team. With football agents involved in buying and selling players and getting paid fees from players (and sometimes the purchasing clubs as well), the exact fees involved are often obscured.

The first 'modern' case of a football manager accused of accepting a kickback in England was that of Arsenal manager George Graham. At an FA hearing (not a criminal prosecution) in February 1995, Graham was charged with receiving money as part of a transfer deal to his club in 1995 from the Norwegian agent Rune Hauge to sign players Pal Lydersen and John Jensen. Graham insisted that he had received 'unsolicited gifts' and not an illegal bung from Hauge, but was eventually found guilty of accepting illegal payments (Football Association Inquiry 1995).

Even now it is still difficult to know how much some players are bought and sold for and how payment is made and to whom. Because of this, less-than-transparent transfer deals can provide opportunities for tax avoidance and/or evasion. This could occur with the tacit approval, or at least knowledge, of football club owners, major shareholders, managers and players. Although this type of fraud can be argued to be of benefit to football clubs, players or others involved in the game, it is nevertheless fraud and as such needs to be dealt with to protect the integrity of the sport.

In an attempt to uncover the depth of such practice the FA employed Lord Stevens, a retired Metropolitan Police Commissioner, to investigate transfer practices. In a nine-month investigation which examined 323 transfers from 2004 to 2006, the Stevens Inquiry concluded that there indeed was corruption in football. Lord Stevens reserved most of his criticism for the FA and stated that its accounting processes and monitoring of club transfers was a mess, there was a lack of FA forensic investigators, and an independent body needed to be established to audit transfers (Lord Stevens, 2006 ; Ellen, 2008; Weir, 2008).

It seems, then, that while agents appear to be necessary due to the access they provide to players, clubs and managers are possibly complicit in various murky 'arrangements' with them, with the FA under pressure to monitor and prevent such abuses. This problem is, however, overshadowed by match-fixing.

Match-fixing and its association with gambling

It is often thought that only players are involved in match-fixing; this is incorrect. Players are needed to fix a match, but not always. Referees (Pfanner, 2011), club officials, owners and players have all been involved (Foot, 2007). However, it is when players and referees conspire to lose a football match in order to receive illegal payments that most damage to the integrity of the sport is done. Such *losing to win*, and thus depriving fans of a genuine sporting event, ruins the integrity of sport, regardless of the level at which it is played. For example, a referee in Germany, Robert Hoyzer, admitted fixing matches in 2003 and 2004 by 'inventing penalties'. Hoyzer acted on behalf of three Croatian brothers who paid him to fix matches. The mastermind of the scheme, Ante Sapina, was convicted of fraud and sentenced to 35 months in prison for fixing or attempting to fix games. He started his prison term in May 2007. His brothers Milan and Filip were given suspended sentences. The scam earned them at least €2 million. Hoyzer was released in July 2008, after serving half of the sentence (Pfanner, 2011).

Hoyzer cooperated with the subsequent investigation and, as part of his cooperation, the Berlin Prosecutor's office in charge of the case investigated a further 25 people, including four referees and 14 players, for possible fraud. Due to the damage caused to the German Football federation (DFB) by this fraud and corruption he was sued for compensation for €1.8 million. In an out-of-court settlement Hoyzer agreed to pay the DFB a monthly sum of €700 for 15 years as compensation for damages to the DFB as well as to a club knocked out of the domestic cup competition because of his match-fixing. The above example shows that players do not have to be involved in match-fixing for it to be a successful fraud; but like most such frauds, the underlying motive for the match-fixing was to make an illegal profit from 'gambling'.

However, to illustrate the level and depth of match-fixing, the reach it has and range of people involved we need to examine match-fixing and the 'scandals of influence' in Italian football. *Calcio* has been embroiled in a number of major scandals in recent decades (Foot, 2007; Jones, 2007). Below we examine a few of them.

In 1980 Italian football suffered from what is known as the *totonero scandal*. Totocalcio ('football lottery') is a state-run football-betting system where bets are placed on the outcome of matches selected from Serie A and B. In the 1980s this system was limited in scope, for example, bets were placed on which team would win the match, with no opportunity to predict the scores, who would score in the match and so on. To fill this need, although it was illegal, the *totonero* ('black lottery') was developed; *totonero* 'sites' were even often located on Totocalcio premises. Because of the much broader range of bets that could be laid, there came a much stronger motivation to influence the outcome of matches. The 1980 scandal revolved around attempts to 'fix' both the results and final scores of matches. However, perhaps because of its blatant nature, those involved in the scam were quickly arrested, the football clubs involved were deducted points, and some players were banned from playing football for varying periods.

In a final twist, however, all those involved were later acquitted due to a technical failure in the legal system; it was ruled that the case failed to reach court in time to pursue charges against individuals and clubs for 'sporting fraud' (see the *Calciopoli* case below). The law was subsequently amended in 1986, after yet another gambling scandal (Foot, 2007) and again in 1989 in an attempt to prevent this type of match-fixing fraud. In 2004 another bribery scandal erupted, this time with evidence of the influence of organised crime, in which teams from different leagues were involved in accusations of match-fixing involving six players and two officials from the AC Siena club.

Match-fixing in Italy is nothing new. In fact, it appears to be a recurring problem. However, the most recent confirmed needs to be discussed in some depth due to the level of fraud and corruption and range of people involved.

On 14 July 2006, the Italian football association (Federazione Italiana Giuoco Calcio – FIGC) stripped the then champions of Italy, Juventus, of the 2005/2006 Serie A title and demoted them to Serie B. Several other clubs were also punished for their alleged involvement in a match-fixing and refereeing scandal. AC Milan were deducted 44 points after finishing second to Juventus, which resulted in them dropping out of the Champions League qualification positions at the end of the 2005/2006 season. However, on appeal, AC Milan had the points reduction reduced from 44 to 8, allowing them to claim third place in Serie A and secure a Champions' League place. All judgments were subsequently appealed and reduced. UEFA, as the governing body of European football, however, was unable to do anything to stop this, as under its rules, national football associations have sovereignty over which clubs are put forward for the Champions' League. In the midst of the investigations, on 9 July 2006, the Italian national team won the Fifa World Cup, with AC Milan, nearly a year later, on 23 May 2007, winning the 2006/2007 Champions League, beating Liverpool in the final. Juventus were relegated to Serie B and stripped of the 2004/2005 and 2005/2006 Serie A titles, and ACF Fiorentina, SS Lazio and Reggina Calcio were respectively sentenced to deductions of 15, 3 and 11 points. ACF Fiorentina and SS Lazio were also banned from the 2006/2007 UEFA Champions League (Foot, 2007).

In this scandal it was the level and reach of corruption that was eventually uncovered that is significant. As enquiries proceeded, and not as a result of firm leads, police stumbled on a complex network of 'relationships' between team managers, referees, football agents and club executives.

At the centre of the scandal was FC Juventus general manager Luciano Moggi. Transcripts of recorded telephone conversations suggested that Moggi spoke with a number of officials in Italian football with the aim of influencing referee appointments and decisions in matches that involved Juventus. Following the publication of the transcripts in 2006, Moggi resigned. A few days later, Juventus won the 2005/2006 Serie A league title. The FIGC president, Franco Carraro, and the vice president, Innocenzo Mazzini, then also resigned. Carraro was aware of the accusations against Moggi but failed to act and was also caught on tape trying to influence the head of FIGC's referee section, asking him to 'take action' in a forthcoming Lazio match. Initially banned from exercising any sporting responsibility for four and a half years, Carraro appealed his ban to the FIGC's arbitration body, which altered the decision to a warning and a fine of €80,000 for failing to conduct his self 'in accordance with the principles of honesty, fair play and moral integrity'. Dissatisfied with this outcome, Carraro appealed again to the conciliation and arbitration body of the Italian Olympic Committee (CNOI), which ruled that the previous decision had no legal basis and annulled it, leaving Carraro with a fine. Paradoxically, even though he was ousted from the FIGC, the rules still allow Carraro to continue in his roles as head of Fifa's Internal Audit Committee, a UEFA Executive Board Member, and as an active member of the International Olympic Committee (IOC) (Hamil et al., 2010).

Countering fraud and corruption in football: a structural problem for football leagues

In this section we focus on the attempts made by two national leagues, the German Bundesliga and the Italian FIGC, to counter fraud and corruption. Drawing on different approaches to managing a football league we discover that much needs to be done to prevent fraud and corruption. The reasons for choosing these two leagues is that while both have been particularly successful in producing teams with a history of national and international success, the structure of their leagues and the organisation and ownership rules for their football clubs have been open to and affected by fraud and corruption.

German football: broad involvement, limited regulation and incentives for financial window-dressing

The structure of the Bundesliga is very different from that of the Italian league. Until 1998 all German football clubs were solely owned by registered associations (known as *eingetragener Verein*). Even with a change in Bundesliga rules in 1998 that allowed German football clubs to have a professional football unit, the registered association (*Verein*) was legally required to hold at least 50 plus one per cent of the club. These *Verein* are non-profit organisations, managed by representatives and elected by the members who are usually the fans. The power of a German football club then lies with its members, as priority is given to the fans as members rather than stakeholders such as investors. The logic behind this approach is to ensure the integrity of professional football by preventing one person having control over one (or more than one) team (Dietl and Franck, 2007).

However, this restriction results in a rather peculiar structure. The elected representatives of the football club are not responsible for the assets for the club, unless they personally commit fraud. Liability is limited to the assets of the *Verein*, as neither members nor representatives are expected to pay for the liabilities of a *Verein*. As it is a non-profit body, the *Verein* is not allowed to distribute any of its assets to representatives or members or to sell individual membership rights.

This legal structure, however, creates dysfunctional incentives. As the proceeds of the *Verein* cannot be distributed, there are no incentives to generate and accumulate income. Instead, club representatives have strong incentives to reinvest all available funds and even borrow against the club's future because the only way to benefit is by winning matches and bringing success at the highest level of the sport. The Bundesliga thus is exposed to the general economic problems of overspending associated with winning contests (similarly to the English Premier League), but it also suffers from league-specific governance failures, too.

The German football governance structure may well be suited to preventing integrity problems resulting from multiple club ownership or ownership by 'undesired persons or entities'; however, this comes at a price. In the power vacuum generated by member associations, residual rights of control are de facto allocated to representatives who do not hold residual claims. Low accounting standards for members' clubs therefore encourage 'window-dressing' and, combined with 'soft' law-enforcement procedures, club representatives can hide financial problems until the clubs are insolvent (Dietl and Franck, 2007).

The structure of the Bundesliga and its licensing and enforcement procedures offer football club representatives the chance to engage in 'creative accounting' and 'window-dressing'. First of all, a club needs a licence to operate as a football club. However, the licensing procedure is operated by the clubs' own association, the DFL. The DFL has limited powers, which are controlled by its members, the clubs. The licensing statutes of the DFL then include the provision that exempts the entire licensing procedure from any form of external control. Furthermore, the DFL is not allowed to interpret the quality of the data provided by the football clubs when submitting their accounts.

The external standards imposed on the financial accounts of Bundesliga clubs are therefore limited. Even with the change in 1998 allowing professional football units to become part of a club, 19 Bundesliga clubs (as of 2010) are still pure members' organisations, and as such are not required to publish their accounts. Moreover, of the 17 clubs that did decide to have a professional football unit, the DFL seems toothless in relation to them, as company law has not been applied to them, with significant numbers of them failing to submit balance sheets without being prosecuted.

In conclusion, the German system of governance is open to abuse: Bundesliga clubs have a strong incentive to 'gamble on success' while hiding excessive spending as income through creative accounting, leading to the risk of demise for some clubs as they 'spend their way into debt' in the pursuit of future success.

The structure of Italian football: creative accounting in a family business?

League football in Italy is organised in a pyramid system of interconnected leagues (Foot, 2007). The *Federazione Italiana Giuoco Calcio* (FIGC) provides guidelines for the operation of League Championships, with Serie A and B organised by *Lega Calcio*. The lower Italian leagues, however, are organised by a variety of different sporting bodies (Hamil et al., 2010). As with the German Bundesliga, the FIGC dispenses licences to football clubs through its financial commission called Co.Vi.Soc. The FIGC delegates its inspection powers in respect of financial performance to Co.Vi.Soc, which is supposed to act autonomously and ensure that clubs are financially stable in order to maintain the regular running of championships. Its role, therefore, is to make sure all clubs adhere to its rules and regulations and refuse an application for a licence if the requirements are not met. Its responsibilities do not extend to issues of club payments and tax; these issues are to the responsibility of the auditors of the clubs. A clear and transparent system of regulatory oversight for Italian football is thus in place. The licensing system suggests that a high standard of club management should exist. There is, however, a substantial gap between rules and enforcement of them.

Unlike in Germany, Italian football clubs are primarily family-owned; the Agnelli family network own Juventus and control the Fiat motor company, and AC Milan, whose majority shareholder is Fininvest, is owned and controlled by Silvio Berlusconi. A distinct part of Italian football but also of Italian society is that businesses are owned and controlled by families that have direct and indirect relationships with major corporations and politicians. This can be both a benefit and a problem, particularly if the family company that owns a football club sees its businesses embroiled in fraud and corruption and accounting scandals.

A few other examples of interconnected 'family networks' are: Riccardo Calleri, son of the former President of SS Lazio and Torino, and Francesca Tanzi, daughter of Calisto Tanzi who was former head of Parmalat (a dairy and food company embroiled in financial scandals in the mid-2000s) and President of AC Parma; Andrea Cragnotti, son of Sergio Cragnotti, the former head of Cirio (a food business which collapsed in 2002 amid allegations of false accounting and nearly bankrupted Lazio in the process) and president of Lazio. Lazio were bought by Claudio Lotito, implicated in a the *Calciopoli* scandal, who with the daughter of Cesare Geronzi, Chiara Geronzi, was investigated in connection with the collapse of Parmalat; both were major shareholders in SS Lazio (Hamil et al., 2010).

An examination of the economic structure of Italian football reveals a high level of complacency and failure to anticipate the long-term consequences of its administration – financial malpractice, substantial losses, and resources and influences moving towards a few privileged clubs leading to competitive imbalance. In this context it should come as no surprise that a significant number of Serie A clubs have collapsed in the last decade.

Rather than address the core structural problem of Italian football, most of the focus here will be on its financial health, financial reporting and presentation issues of its financial position and performance. Perhaps due to the many powerful vested interests mentioned above, in response to a crisis of financial mismanagement in Italian football in 2002, Silvio Berlusconi as Prime Minister introduced the *Salva Calcio* ('save football') decree. This was in direct response to a situation when it appeared that many football clubs would not be able to secure clearance from Co.Vi.Soc, the FIGCs regulator, to play in the 2002/2003 season because of extensive debts.

Salvia Calcio allowed the clubs to amortise the asset of the players' registration rights over a period of 10 years, thus improving their financial position and performance. Importantly, the licensing criteria were based, in part, on balance sheet debt-to-income ratios. Given the importance of football in Italy, allowing clubs to continue operating was in the public and political interest. However, the EU Minister for Internal Markets challenged the decree and a compromise was reached allowing the assets to be written off in five rather than 10 years in 2005 (Hamil et al., 2010).

One club in particular benefited from this 'arrangement'; SS Lazio. They were facing imminent financial collapse due to unpaid taxes when a deal was brokered with the Italian tax office and with the direct approval of Prime Minister Silvio Berlusconi, which allowed SS Lazio to stagger payments of €140 million over a 23-year period. Hailed as a success by Berlusconi and Walter Veltroni, then Mayor of

Rome, home city to SS Lazio, both seem to overlook or ignore the fact that the deal conferred a major, state-subsidised, advantage to SS Lazio in comparison to those clubs who had paid taxes and diligently and efficiently managed their clubs' financial position.

This is only one method of 'adjusting' the balance sheet to make it look favourable. Another practice appeared of purposefully inflating the costs of players bought and sold. Rather than engage in this practice, known as *plus-valenza*, numerous clubs developed reciprocal relationships with each other. For example, in the case of AC Milan and Internazionale, between 1999 and 2002 six players were transferred between these two clubs, netting on paper €3.5 million in profit each time. However, not one of these players ever played in Serie A, all of them eventually playing in the lower leagues (Hamil et al., 2010).

Prior to this, however, all Serie A and Serie B clubs and some Serie C clubs as well as the offices of *Lega Calcio* and the FIGC were raided by the Tax and Finance Police. It appears that late payment or tax avoidance is common practice in Italian football, with the regulator, Co.Vi.Soc, limited in its power to change the situation. This issue has, if anything, increased in seriousness as power has shifted away from football's governing bodies towards clubs keen to prioritise their own interests and manage themselves without interference. This, in Italy as elsewhere, is due to the sale and distribution of television rights, with more and more income going to a diminishing number of teams.

These are a few examples of the types of creative accounting that football clubs in different leagues engage in. While some will attempt to delay or avoid payment of tax, engage in creative accounting and launder money using football players as assets, it is ultimately the overall structure of the respective leagues which contributes to rather than counters fraud and corruption.

Detecting, exposing and preventing fraud and corruption in football

The detection of fraud and corruption in sport is difficult in any circumstances. It is made harder, though, by the structure of leagues, the potential for money-laundering and tax evasion and avoidance, and ticket and vote-rigging scandals carried out by those entrusted with the commercial success and integrity of the sport, as well as by players, referees and officials involved in match-fixing. With such a range of frauds and corruption it would be plausible to suggest that they were detected by professional investigators with a background in and knowledge of fraud and accounting practices; this is far from the truth.

The majority of these 'cases' were uncovered by accident; for example, the *Calciopoli* scandal, or 'common practices' such as creative accounting or tax avoidance. The problem, we suggest, is not one of resources, as football as a whole is awash with billions from TV revenue (Millward, 2011), advertising, sponsorship and rich investors; however, most of these lucrative funds reach just a few, elite, clubs.

As with the following chapter on cricket, we suggest that if national and international football wants to reduce the incidence of fraud it needs to do more than rely on 'policing bodies' to investigate fraud and corruption. The police themselves, due to a variety of factors, are limited in the actions they can take (see Chapter 3). Instead of relying on the police, therefore, a clear counter-fraud strategy is needed that exists to both prevent and detect fraud and corruption. Using constant risk assessment of all aspects of 'football business', analysing data gathered and employing professional counter-fraud specialists will go some way towards sending the message that fraud and corruption are not welcome in both national leagues and in international football. Overall this is an international problem, and working in a range of national and international jurisdictions, as with all frauds, is problematic. This, however, is not a sufficient reason to do nothing.

The Football Association of England, as well as several international bodies, has made some headway in the battle against racism in football. A similar campaign, supported by national and international bodies, to develop an anti-fraud culture would be a start. This anti-fraud culture, however, needs to be backed by sanctions, without which it will lack credibility. For example, even when fraud is discovered the sanctions can be pitifully weak; in 2001 it was discovered that some Serie A players had used false passports to play in the Italian leagues. However, so many teams were involved in illegally importing players that prosecuting them would have left too few 'clean' players in the league (Jones, 2007) for it to function.

This, however, is nothing compared to the lack of checks made on visiting international sides; all international matches should be arranged through a Fifa-licensed agent. This should have been the case in a match between Bahrain and Togo in 2010 when, instead of facing genuine Togo internationals, Bahrain played a group of 'ringers' pretending to be the Togolese national team; Bahrain won the match 3–0 (BBC, 2010).

Both Fifa and UEFA, however, are aware of the dangers of gambling and match-fixing. Fifa developed an Early Warning System (GmbH) in 2004, but did not monitor Fifa competitions until 2007, with UEFA later developing its Betting Fraud Detection System. It is estimated that there are 2,132 Internet betting sites in the world (not all are sport sites, though) (Brooks, 2012) and that £350 to £400 billion is 'gambled' a year on sport worldwide. A problem here, though, is that roughly 50 per cent of this is 'black market' gambling and therefore will not register on any existing early warning systems.

This is further compounded by the fact that gambling on football is increasingly 'in-play', that is, bets are placed as the match is in progress. While Fifa's system monitors bets, odds, payouts to customers and 'irregular' in-play betting patterns, it is still limited in its application because 'irregular' patterns are difficult to detect. Moreover, at present, there is no specific EU legislation on sports betting; instead it is left to national legal systems to deal with what is an international problem.

A different approach to preventing fraud and corruption in football is to determine the character of various people involved in management (especially owners and directors) using a 'fit and proper person test'. This 'test' was introduced in 2004 in the English Premier League to allay concerns that convicted fraudsters could move into club management. Under rules established by the Premier League and the Football League, anyone who takes over as director of a football club, or owner of more than 30 per cent of a club's shares, must pass the test. The Premier League now asks its clubs to make public the name of anyone who owns 10 per cent or more of a club as well. The Football League asks the same question, but does not make the information public. The Premier League also seeks to establish where money to purchase a club is coming from, with the funds confirmed as legitimate known income. An investigation of how a club is to be purchased will then take place before a purchased is approved. The Football League, however, assesses the legitimacy of the purchase only after the deal has gone through.

There are a number of conditions that can lead to owner(s) or potential owner(s) being disqualified. These include convictions for a variety of fraud offences, becoming bankrupt, being prohibited by law from being a director, or being director of a club that twice goes into administration. Two people have fallen foul of the rules in the past six years; one because his club went into administration twice, and another because he had been banned from being a company director for 11 years after admitting in court to involvement in a £500,000 VAT fraud (Christian Aid, 2010).

In these cases the football clubs have suffered because of the owner's financial mismanagement and/or fraud that might have had nothing to do with football. Nevertheless, if football as a sport is going to protect itself it must put in place strategies to prevent or counter fraud and corruption; once a fraud is discovered the damage has been done, and trying to retrieve the assets is time-consuming and difficult. Football is a business and as such needs to protect all its assets, not only players on the pitch, if league status is to remain an ambition.

Conclusion

There are a number of reasons why fraud and corruption in football is committed, but there is no one solution to preventing and detecting the varied range of fraud and acts of corruption. We, however, suggest that the following at least need to be considered if football is to increase its resilience against fraud and corruption. As organisations within the most popular sport in the world, football leagues and individual clubs need to employ counter-fraud specialists, punish players, referees, officials and all others involved in fraud and corruption, and encourage people to disclose information without prejudice, for example through the use of a anonymous hotlines. They should also employ constant risk assessment of all parts of leagues' structures. These are, we suggest, part of standard-model counter-fraud strategy, and as such are necessary if fraud and corruption are to be dealt with effectively.

7
Fraud and Corruption in Cricket

Introduction

In this chapter we focus fraud and corruption in cricket, a national and international problem in Test matches, Twenty20 matches and One Day Internationals (ODIs) and for all major cricket playing nations – England, South Africa, Australia, New Zealand, the West Indies, Sri Lanka, Pakistan, Bangladesh and India, as well as elsewhere.

We highlight some historical and contemporary examples of fraud and corruption, such as paying players for information, match-fixing and spot-fixing. All the examples referred to in this chapter are established in the public domain rather than being founded on rumour or hearsay evidence, with most enquiries into them reaching a conclusion and official sanction.

This is then followed by an assessment of countering corruption in cricket and the 'power' and willingness exhibited by the governing body, the International Cricket Council (ICC) and local national boards, such as the England and Wales Cricket Board (ECB), to monitor, control and deal with fraud and corruption.

This is followed by a review of what is presently done to detect fraud and corruption in cricket and what more *could* be done beyond drawing on national police forces to combat fraud and corruption in cricket. Some suggestions are then made as to the best way to progress and prevent fraud and corruption in cricket by encouraging disclosure and the use of sanctions.

In the conclusion we make some suggestions as to how national and international cricket bodies could increase the integrity of their sport.

Types of fraud and corruption in cricket

There are almost too many books on the early historical origins of cricket to count, but more recent and relevant literature includes Birley (1995, 2003), Firth (1978), Guha (2003), Harte and Whimpress (2008) and Williams (2003). They often assume the reader is familiar with the sport. We too make this assumption; however, we recommend that for those unfamiliar with the historical development of cricket it is useful to read Norridge (2008). Matches in the earliest years of the game, despite being played as a social event between 'gentlemen', were often influenced by gambling. However, these have little to do with the professional, commercial sport that cricket has become, so we focus on more recent examples of fraud and corruption in the modern game.

Like all sports players, cricketers want to win, and will resort to unfair tactics (Firth, 2003), from breaching codes of sporting conduct to committing outright fraud and corruption. Below are a few examples of international corruption that include high-profile cases involving some of the most renowned and talented players that have played the sport.

All of the cases we discuss below reached the highest level of inquiry where the International Cricket Council and/or national boards interviewed players, sought legal counsel and produced damning reports on the management of individual players and national teams; some cases ended in criminal convictions. By reviewing the examples below it will become apparent that fraud and corruption in cricket is international; paying for information, which could be considered a form of bribery and gambling, is often the cause of that fraud and corruption.

We therefore present examples of breaches of codes of conduct, paying for information, match-fixing and spot-fixing. This is only a sample of the types of fraud and corruption in cricket; however, our focus is on those that ruin the sporting integrity of the game.

The ICC is, however, responsible for the organisation and governance of cricket's major international tournaments, appointing Test umpires and referees, enforcing the ICC code of conduct and dealing with and coordinating action to prevent corruption and match-fixing through its Anti-corruption and Security Unit (ACSU). It, however, is not in charge of domestic cricket in member nations, and does not compile the laws of the sport, which are controlled by Marylebone Cricket Club (MCC) (Radford, 2011).

Under the ICC *Offences under the Anti-Corruption Code* (2011) corruption is therefore considered as:

> fixing or contriving in any way or otherwise influencing improperly, or being a party to any effort to fix or contrive in any way or otherwise influence improperly, the result, progress, conduct or any other aspect of any International Match or ICC Event.

It is not an offence under the Anti-Corruption Code to 'fix' international matches for strategic or tactical reasons, such as when players perform to ensure their team loses a pool match in an ICC event in order to affect the standings of other teams in that event. Instead, such conduct is prohibited under the ICC's *Code of Conduct for Players and Player Support Personnel*. This distinction is understandable, but can blur the boundaries of what is acceptable conduct.

It is also perhaps telling that 'advice' or guidance on gambling is in the ICC's *Code of Conduct for Players and Player Support Personnel* in 2011 and states that:

> placing, accepting, laying or otherwise entering into any Bet with any other party (whether individual, company or otherwise) and soliciting, inducing, enticing, instructing, persuading, encouraging, facilitating, authorising or seeking, accepting, offering or agreeing to accept any bribe or other reward to fix or to contrive in any way or otherwise to influence improperly the result is a breach of code.

However, any potential offence that comes under the *Code of Conduct for Players and Player Support Personnel* is to be considered in relation to its own set of 'facts' and the particular circumstances surrounding relevant disclosure. For example, it may be an offence under this clause to disclose inside information: a) to journalists or other members of the media; and/or b) on social networking websites where the player or other personnel might be expected to know that disclosure of such information in such circumstances could be used in relation to gambling.

It is important, however, to distinguish between opportunistic and premeditated acts which might lead to acts of fraud and corruption (Smith et al., 2010). Those that are opportunistic do not seek out the chance to engage in fraud or corruption; they take advantage of the opportunity if it is available. This does not diminish the seriousness of the corrupt act; it simply has implications for the strategies needed to address it, which are discussed later in this chapter. However, attempting to engage in fraud and corrupt acts with premeditation calls for a far more comprehensive strategy to tackle fraud and corruption in cricket than exists at present.

In some of the cases below, the required level of evidence needed to secure a conviction was lacking, and so the case was dismissed. This is perfectly understandable, as gathering evidence for a fraud conviction is difficult. Furthermore, a 'code of conduct' has to be treated with respect and sanctions feared even if it is to be even partially successful and therefore more than a paper 'mission statement' of intent that is easily circumvented. A code of conduct, regardless of the sport, needs 'teeth' if it is to prevent and deter fraud and corruption; the problem for the ICC, however, is that it is not a police force. Possessing no powers of arrest or seizure, the ICC is essentially powerless to stop criminal elements within the sport; instead it must rely on persuasion and moral condemnation of players and national boards. In turn, national boards are unable to arrest suspects and must engage their national police to investigate, arrest and seize 'evidence'. With fraud and corruption in sport international in its orientation (a match is played in Dubai between India and South Africa and gambling on this match is available legally in Great Britain or illegally on the black market in India, for example), it encounters a whole range of obstacles surrounding jurisdiction, willingness of national police to investigate, the sharing of information with international 'police colleagues', and available resources in order to reach a successful conviction.

Paying for information

Documented by the King Commission (2000), the Qayyum Commission (2000) and the Condon Report (2001) it has been suggested that bookmakers bribe players to breach codes of sporting conduct to gain a 'gambling advantage' from a cricket match. Such information can include key players' fitness, playing conditions (which in this sport are very influential and advantageous to know if gambling legally or illegally, as many do, particularly in India) (Radford, 2011), the potential tactics the team(s) might employ in the match, and if the match, or part of it, is fixed. For example, during the international Singer World Series in Sri Lanka in September 1994, which involved Australia, Sri Lanka, Pakistan and India, two players from one nation received money from an Indian bookmaker in exchange for information about the state of the cricket pitch and how the weather might affect the flight of the ball. Neither player passed on information about team tactics or named the players involved in the matches beforehand (Qayyum Commission, 2000: Harte and Whimpress, 2008; Radford, 2011).

In 1997 the Board of Control for Cricket in India appointed Justice Y. V. Chandrachud to examine 'revelations' that Indian cricketers and management were involved in match-fixing. These 'revelations' suggested that an Indian player had been offered a 'financial incentive' by a colleague(s) to underperform in the Singer World Series in a match between India and Pakistan. Justice Chandrachud concluded that, based upon the information provided to him, there was no proof that Indian players or officials were involved in match-fixing; Justice Chandrachud, however, accepted that widespread gambling occurred in India (Radford, 2011), and this itself *could* potentially influence *some* players and officials.

In these cases we can see that some of the most talented players in the world had a 'lapse' in judgement and were willing to accept money in return for providing limited information. This is not to suggest that anything untoward happened beyond this exchange; it is to point out that the most talented international players sometimes make errors of judgement.

While paying players for information is one way to secure an advantage in a cricket match, teams will also make sure the pitch is prepared in a way that is suitable to them. This, however, is something teams often do as part of 'gamesmanship' to secure home advantage in an international match, and as such it is regarded as 'part of the sport' rather than corruption. Such tactics are obvious to see, pitch conditions are widely discussed before the match, captains make batting and bowling decisions on the basis of equal access to this information, all members of the team are aware of the state of the pitch, and therefore international teams in particular are expected to adjust to such 'home conditions' at the highest level of the sport.

However, the same cannot be said of match-fixing where only a few key players and/or officials are needed to fix the result.

Match-fixing

This is perhaps the most unwelcome development – though it is not a new one – in international cricket; international players willing to *lose to win* for the sake of extra income. It is also hard to secure evidence for, unless a confession is forthcoming, as there is always rumour, counter-rumour and analysis of the result of a match retrospectively when the integrity of the event has been questioned. This 'analysis in hindsight' is of little help in tackling fraud and corruption. With so many cricket matches now played around the world, it is tempting for players to underperform once in a while, as some matches have little significance for world rankings and international status. The volume of English county and other first-class matches now played is also a problem, as 'vested gambling interests' can focus attention on such relatively low-level matches if international cricket is exposed as corrupt (Mahmood, 2012).

However, in some respects the term 'match-fixing for profit' is misleading. In domestic leagues teams can work together to go easy on each other to obtain bowling and batting points in order to secure final league positions; more runs for teams secure more points. Players are not bribed but rely on mutual interest. If a match is of vital importance to one team and not to the other then an accommodation could be reached; this, however, can be said of all team sports that play in a league format. As a result, in a number of matches the ethic of winning at all costs is replaced by a pragmatic arrangement to divide points and/or agree in advance as to who will win. If, however, there is a financial benefit involved, such as if your final position in a league table determines the level of payment from the commercial sponsors of the league then this is tantamount to corruption even if the players and team officials and representatives of the respective teams exchanged nothing more than an 'arrangement' for one match. This example illustrates how financial advantage can 'creep' into sport and encourage 'fixes' which are then rationalised as 'sporting agreements' where no harm is seen to be done to the sport or its integrity. Securing evidence of such 'sporting agreements' is, however, difficult if not impossible.

The problems of providing such evidence are equally intractable on the international stage. In 1995 the Pakistan Cricket Board (PCB), under Chairman Justice Fakhruddin G. Ibrahim, responded to suggestions in the media and by an Australian international that a Pakistan player had offered him and other Australian players 'incentives' to control and 'affect' the final day of a Test Match between Pakistan and Australia, and also later underperform in a ODI match in Rawalpindi. However, Justice Ibrahim unearthed no evidence substantiating these 'suggestions' and failed to 'discover' any wrongdoing. He concluded the proceedings by saying that the information available lacked credence, and must be rejected as unfounded (Radford, 2011).

This lack of evidence is a constant problem when trying to deal with fraud and corruption. Without a confession prompted by overwhelming evidence, players' 'complaints' often do nothing more than damage the integrity of cricket. Unless there is willingness to provide evidence to support them, suggestions or 'rumours' that player(s) are corrupt are likewise of no use. This is not an attempt to excuse the Anti-corruption and Security Unit (ASCU), whose track record for preventing fraud and corruption is woeful, it is simply to point out that the ASCU, similarly to other policing bodies, lacks the knowledge and expertise to deal with fraud (Button et al., 2009, 2010) and that 'policing' players is primarily the responsibility of national boards (Kochan and Goodyear, 2010).

In 1998 rumours of match-fixing surfaced once again in Pakistan. A one-man judicial commission – Mr Justice Malik Muhammad Qayyum – investigated suggestions that members of the Pakistan national cricket team were involved in match-fixing, working with 'vested gambling interests'. Due to the difficult task of discovering fraud and corruption, Justice Qayyum reported that the allegation that the Pakistan team as a whole was involved in match-fixing was based on allegation, conjecture and surmise, without positive proof.

However, Justice Qayyum concluded that the evidence suggested was of value and that one player should be banned from cricket for life, with an inquiry into his personal assets and other players subject to a range of 'penalties' from a warning about personal conduct to a public censure, with some placed under continued investigation. In a series of recommendations Justice Qayyum advised the Pakistan

Cricket Board (PCB) to order players to declare their assets and, if it were thought necessary, investigate their accounts to as a means to establish the level of corruption in Pakistan cricket (Radford, 2011).

Pakistan, however, is only one international nation that has conducted such a high-level inquiry. In 2000 the United Cricket Board of South Africa (UCB) established an inquiry into match-fixing after Hanse Cronje, then captain of the South African cricket team, confessed to accepting money from an Indian 'bookmaker'. Chaired by Judge Ewin King, the King Commission discovered that Cronje had been involved in match-fixing for some years. The UCB banned Cronje from playing and coaching cricket for life, and two fellow cricketers were both banned from international cricket for six months (King Commission, 2000; Hughes, 2010; Radford, 2011).

As captain of the South African cricket team, Cronje was revered in South Africa. However, Delhi police, by accident, had acquired a tape recording of a telephone conversation of him discussing the possibility of fixing a match with a bookmaker. The Delhi police referred the matter to the United Cricket Board of South Africa (UCB). Cronje was approached by the UCB but denied that he (or his players) were involved in match-fixing. Once learning that there was a recording of his conversation with a bookmaker he admitted that he had not been completely honest to the managing director of the UCB. Cronje eventually admitted to accepting money from a London-based bookmaker for forecasting results during a ODI series in India. He also later admitted that a South Africa 'sports betting agent' offered him money for the charity of his choice to influence the result of the Fifth Test against England at Centurion Park in Pretoria in January 2000 (King Commission, 2000; Radford, 2011).

The King Commission found that the evidence that Cronje was involved in match-fixing was overwhelming. In the 1994/95 season, the year in which Cronje started playing Test cricket for South Africa, a fellow player, Pat Symcox, testified that he was approached by Cronje to lose a match against Pakistan. Symcox also claimed that Cronje offered money to players during a team meeting to lose an ODI in Mumbai in 1996. Furthermore, other players corroborated evidence that Cronje made an offer to them in a hotel room before the second test against India in Bangalore in March 2000. With the weight of evidence and witness statements building, Cronje confessed to having accepted bribes since 1996, but claimed that he had never fixed or thrown a match (Radford, 2011).

Many questions still remain unanswered, however. Cronje may have taken money from 'bookmakers' but what is unclear is what those people he dealt with did about the matter. Fraud and corruption are able to exist and flourish in any business if those tasked with preventing it are involved, ignore the fact that it is taking place or are somehow involved in the fix as well. In this case, while Cronje was accused of match-fixing, his corruption continued to flourish as other players and possibly officials ignored or denied his conduct.

Both the King Commission Report (2000) and the Qayyum Report (2000) revealed a picture of cricket that was open to corruption, with indications that 'gambling cartels' had interests in match-fixing. As we have already discussed, match-fixing is difficult to establish unless substantial evidence is forthcoming; this type of corruption, however, is possible to detect; the new development of spot-fixing and 'creative bets' in the gambling sector makes gathering evidence even more problematic (Horne and Zammit, 2010; Leitzel, 2008).

Spot-fixing

Due to the development of technology, gambling is now far more accessible and available. In addition to this there is now an array of creative ways in which bets can be structured. For example, it is now possible to gamble on: a set number of wides, or the number of no-balls in a designated over and/or match; bowled or caught out at a specific point in the innings; the total number of runs at which a batting captain will declare and the timing of a declaration; all of these are open to manipulation by players on the field. It is therefore of some concern that many players are approached to 'deliver' or inform others of these 'plays' so that vested gambling interests – individual or organised (Wilde, 2011) – can make a profit during the playing of a match.

These 'exotic' and creative ways of gambling are now on offer on legal gambling websites, but also illegally in black-market bookmaking, which appears to be predominantly based in India, particularly for cricket. Since every single aspect of a cricket match *can be* and *is* bet upon, it is possible that a match or any part of it can be pre-arranged or manipulated in order to secure a vast profit. The problem for international cricket, then, is not only presented by legal bookmakers, from whom a creative bet is available and open to manipulation by corrupt players and/or officials; it also arises from those illegal bookmakers based in Asia and the Far East who have access to inside information and are difficult to monitor. A perfect example of this manipulation is 'spot-fixing', which can be prearranged with a few players. We might assume this is straightforward; it is where players underperform for part of the match, and the opposing team wins, or no-balls or wides are bowled 'to order'. The problem here is that corrupt players can also satisfy gambling interests by bowling many wide balls in a match or series and thus giving away runs to the opposition while at the same time still going on to win the match or series overall (see Chapter 9 for a similar tactic of winning a match in basketball, where players manipulate the spread of points in a game).

On 29 August 2010, the *News of the World* published nine pages on spot-fixing and corruption in cricket, with Sky Television in the UK showing footage of a London-based businessman claiming he could 'guarantee' no-balls to be bowled 'to order' in a forthcoming Test match at Lord's. Posing as a fictitious Far East gambling cartel, the *News of the World* reporters allegedly paid a 'businessman' £150,000 to secure the delivery of no-balls in the match at a prearranged time. As promised, three no-balls were delivered at the 'right' time during the match. These allegations were passed on to Scotland Yard at the same time that the International Cricket Council (ICC) held a Anti-Corruption Tribunal in Dubai, where Salman Butt, the Pakistan captain, Mohammad Asif and Mohammad Amir were charged with offences under its anti-corruption code for 'irregular behaviour' and banned for a maximum of 10, seven and five years respectively by the ICC, with Butt and Asif receiving sanctions with a five-year and a two-year suspension period respectively. Furthermore, the Metropolitan Police in England also interviewed Salman Butt, Mohammad Asif and Mohammad Amir, and passed the case file onto the Crown Prosecution Service. The players were eventually found guilty of match/spot-fixing, with Butt sentenced to 30 months in prison, Asif 12 and Amir to six months in a Young Offenders Institution (Atherton, 2011; ICC Report, 2011; Mahmood, 2011).

While this is fixing in a particularly serious and lucrative form, corruption in cricket, as we have seen, can manifest itself in a variety of creative ways. It is important to note that for a fix to be successful not all the players on a team are required to take part. Often, as with other team sports (see the football, basketball and baseball chapters) only a few key players are required to fix a match or a result to satisfy bookmaker's or other vested interests. By result, we can mean, for example, a correct score in cricket, a number of red cards in football, a number of home runs in baseball, and so on. It is these creative bets rather than a bet on who will win that has allowed fixes to 'move below the radar' of the ACSU. To clarify, match-fixing is organising a predetermined result – win, draw or loss for one team – and spot-fixing is fixing events within a match. It is therefore obvious which 'bets' are easier to fix during a match; a few no-balls or a key batsman getting out below a score of 50 will hardly register as corrupt during a international Test Match.

Furthermore, since only a few players are required to fix a part of a match other players from their own team and the opposition may well be unaware that such a 'fix' is in progress. After all, to bowl so many wide balls it is only necessary for all the bowlers – of which there are generally no more than four in a team – to be corrupt (see the case below). (For those unfamiliar with cricket, bowlers are the equivalent of pitchers in baseball. In addition to this the wicket-keeper [the man behind the stumps, like the catcher in baseball] can miss a catch when it should be caught; his role is important because the wicket-keeper usually takes a substantial number of catches, and can be expected to drop one or two. Therefore, with a team of 11 on a cricket field (nine in baseball) perhaps only three or four players need to be corrupt to make sure that 'their' vested interests are fulfilled).

Mervyn Westfield, an Essex county bowler in the UK, pleaded guilty to accepting £6,000 to bowl in a way that 12 runs would be scored in his first over (six balls are bowled in an over) for Essex against Durham in September 2009. Westfield was charged under the Prevention of Corruption Act 1906 and the Gambling Act 2005 and was sentenced to four months in prison in the UK in 2012 (Hobson, 2012; Brown and Kidd, 2012). Once Westfield admitted his guilt, the England and Wales Cricket Board (ECB) offered players the chance to contact the ECB Anti-Corruption Unit hotline regarding knowledge of corruption and/or suspicions of corruption. To encourage players to contact them the Unit deferred punishment of players for not coming forward to report illegal approaches or acts that would have otherwise resulted in a fine and/or suspension for them.

Furthermore, the ECB claims that it has upscaled its anti-corruption education programme so players are well aware of the rules and responsibilities (Hobson, 2012). This, we suggest, is a standard part of a counter-fraud strategy, and it is perhaps worrying, particularly with its previous knowledge of match-fixing, that the ECB decided that such an approach needed updating after the event. However, if a player is tempted by bribery, no programme of education is going to dissuade him from a particular course of action.

Even though the ICC has a Memorandum of Understanding (MoU) with 'gambling organisations' where information is passed on to them if a suspicious activity is detected, they are dependent on the gambling organisations (Brooks, 2012) providing them with information to protect the integrity of cricket. The ASCU is limited in what it can achieve as it is difficult for it to obtain the required level of evidence beyond banning a player(s) for an infringement of its rules for a period of time and instead has to rely on outside help in the form of gambling organisations' evidence, and the police to secure criminal convictions. In this sense fraud and corruption in sport is hardly different to fraud and corruption in other sectors, as evidence and witnesses is limited.

As with all businesses there are many potential avenues for fraud, such as construction of a new stadium, security, ticket sales and selling commercial media rights (Lord, 2010; Leahy and Fontanella-Khan, 2010). With the sport of cricket, as with other sports, countering all types of corruption is a major problem. However, we focus on a few aspects of countering fraud and corruption in cricket rather than all, which is beyond our remit here.

Countering fraud and corruption in cricket: the role(s) of the ICC ACSU and national boards

The International Cricket Council (ICC) ACSU has attempted to control match-fixing in cricket while admitting that spot-fixing is a growing problem. Complete prohibition of spot-betting is impossible to enforce, as the majority of the money staked on cricket in India is informal and underground. Even if it were legalised and regulated, overseeing the huge number of transactions involved would be difficult.

Therefore, policing cricketers is an option. However, given the difficulty of identifying cheating and proving that it is intentional, this also seems limited. Improving the level of pay for those playing international cricket from such nations as Pakistan might help, but this will not stop corruption. This leaves deterrence as an option through giving the ACSU the legal authority to seek criminal sanctions beyond its code of conduct. Severe sanctions against those match-fixing and/or taking money for information seems a practical option. However, lifetime exclusion from the sport has little impact of those at the end of a career, yet perhaps seems harsh on young cricketers who may have been 'pressured' into corruption. A fixed-term ban might seem appropriate for such young wayward cricketers. Regardless of the punishment, some people will always find corruption appealing and help fix all or, more importantly now, part of a match. In this way match-fixing has evolved rather than vanished. Proving that one pre-arranged ball was intentional is impossible, but arranging such 'errors' is simple. A player might 'justify' his action(s) (see Chapter 4 and the discussion of techniques of neutralisation) by claiming that his conduct would not have changed the outcome of the match, yet still make money by knowing the outcome in advance. Furthermore, even though every player must undergo an educational programme before playing in an international tournament, education is only one approach needed to prevent fixing in cricket matches. This also fails to take into account that matches below international level are open to abuse and corruption; here the ICC has no presence.

However, cricket, like all sports, is a subtle game which is difficult to gauge and measure, regardless of the level at which it is played. From this stem the difficulties in defining, detecting and reporting fraud and corruption. Even with ICC guidelines, what is defined as fraud and corruption is sometimes open to interpretation. For example, a player gouging a cricket ball with an 'appliance' such as a coin to make it swing more dangerously and thus make it difficult for the batsmen to hit or defend is illegal according to the laws of cricket; but is this fraud? If this is done to gain an advantage on the field of play and nothing more, it can be seen as cheating; however, if this is used as a technique to 'manufacture' a score so individuals win a pre-arranged bet, then this enters into the territory of fraud and corruption. Furthermore, if a player is detected using an 'appliance' to alter the state of the ball to influence its movement, which is always a problem when it comes to fraud and corruption, it is necessary to sanction the offending players.

While the ASCU might have a visible presence at every Test match, ODI and Twenty20 International, this is based on the questionable assumption that suspicious play relating to match-fixing is observable, and it is likely to have a limited impact on corrupt players engaging in spot-fixing, which is virtually invisible. After all, spot-fixing made headlines when a sting operation by the then *News of the World* ensnared a 'businessman' rather than players indentified by an ICC representative at a Lord's Test match.

Perhaps of more use is the use of undercover informants, which the ICC claims is assisting them in preventing corruption (Radford, 2011). This is difficult to prove either way; if successful the fixing of a match will be prevented, if unsuccessful, it is impossible to know because of the nature of the fix is often invisible without corroborating information. The 'network' of informants will also need to have credibility with players, officials, managers and law enforcement if a case reaches a court of law, which is in any case difficult to achieve. Preventing such fraud and corruption is therefore complex.

If a governing body – national or international – is to show it is truly willing to take the matter of fraud and corruption seriously, beyond media 'soundbites' to head off criticism, players, officials and corrupt managers need to be punished. This, however, is not always the case. For example, it was not until the spot-fixing at the Lord's Test match in 2010 that the Pakistan Cricket Board decided to implement an anti-corruption initiative (Radford, 2011), with measures similar to those of other international cricket boards along with an anti-corruption education programme for players and officials. A 'new' code of conduct included a clause stipulating that players cannot take a mobile (cell) phone into the changing room, and that all 'unauthorised' people be prevented from entering the changing room, before, during and after the match. We would expect this to be standard practice at every national and international match. The problem here, though, is that of stopping certain 'official' members of a team working in close proximity to the players; these include potentially corrupt personal managers and assistants who are authorised to move around the cricket stadium. Security at a cricket match, as at any public sporting event, is limited if the people who have official passes are 'conduits of corruption' and 'manage' the fix and arrange the 'right' result while remaining in the background. Even the prohibition of telephones will have a limited impact if the fix is already prearranged.

A further problem encountered by the ICC is national boards ignoring guidance and/or punishing players' transgressions only for penalties to be overturned by them or other bodies at a later date. Actions can also be tokenistic. Intikhab Alam, the Pakistan national team manager, announced before the Cricket World Cup in 2011 that the Board was withdrawing five players from its squad. Three of these players – Salman Butt, Mohammad Amir and Mohammad Asif – should never have been selected anyway, as they were already suspended (and jailed) due to the 2010 spot-fixing scandal (Radford, 2011).

The ICC is therefore sometimes powerless to prevent national boards from clearing a player for an international tournament. While it is easy to blame the ICC, it is also at the local and national level that corruption in cricket needs to be dealt with. National boards have perhaps also protected corrupt players and/or imposed trivial punishments before reinstating them into the national team as soon as possible.

Preventing players from engaging in fraud and corruption, however, is necessary if cricket is to retain sponsorship and commercial revenue (Chadwick, 2012; Gorse and Chadwick, 2010); the ICC has limited power and can only suggest and/or threaten national boards with expulsion if they fail to deal with fraud and corruption in the cricket under their jurusdiction. The problem here is that cricket has a federalised structure where the ICC has to deal with national boards that are protective of their teams and players. The ICC should perhaps be less tolerant of national boards that are too willing to clear players before an investigation is complete; without the boards' willingness to take fraud and corruption seriously cricket will make headline news *again* in the future.

Detecting and exposing fraud and corruption in cricket: a need for special investigators?

The ACSU spent $0.9 million on preventing, detecting and investigating fraud and corruption in 2011. This might seem a reasonable investment; however, the total amount of revenue collected by the ICC in 2011 was $134.9 million, with a profit of $76.1 million (Pawar, 2011). Primarily concerned with organising and the governance of cricket's major international tournaments and appointing Test umpires and referees, the ICC appears to attach a low priority to funding its anti-corruption measures.

Furthermore, the ICC financial statements (Pawar, 2011) contain no measurement of successes in countering fraud and corruption in cricket. Given the awareness of the level of fraud and corruption in cricket, particularly since the Qayyum (2000) and King Commission (2000) reports, we suggest that this is an area in need of some attention. As elsewhere, though, preventing and reducing the incidence of fraud and corruption is often seen as a cost rather than a saving or investment and so organisations ignore and/or dismiss the utility of fighting fraud and corruption or refuse to accept that it exists in their 'sector'. This is an issue that the ICC and all the national boards need to address, as they more and more frequently have to defend the integrity of cricket once fraud and corruption has been exposed.

Employing former senior police officers, even with a background and knowledge of fraud and corruption, also appears to be of limited use (Brooks and Button, 2012). Even if those employed by the ICC in the ASCU are experienced and possess expertise in investigating fraud, which we suggest is needed due to the complex nature of the crime, their track record is difficult to assess. Even though the ASCU carried out an extensive investigation into corruption in cricket under former Metropolitan Police Commissioner Paul Condon (2001) they discovered nothing that had not been mentioned in previous investigations, such as the King Commission (2000).

Furthermore, due to the limited powers of the ICC, the ASCU is dependent on the police if the case is so serious that the suspects need to be arrested and/or charged with criminal offences. As we have already discovered, however, some national boards are protective of players and will do all they can to prevent a case being dealt with in the criminal justice system. This is understandable, if unethical; players are 'assets' to be protected if glory and success on the pitch is to be achieved.

However, perhaps it is time for the ICC to consider the use of dedicated counter-fraud investigators from 'other', non-police backgrounds. Fraud is complex, international and its investigation requires specialist technical knowledge. This is not to dismiss the work of the police; it is simply a recognition that the police do not consider fraud and corruption as a priority (Brooks and Button, 2012) unless it involves organised crime and/or terrorism.

As we saw in earlier chapters, most fraud and corruption is uncovered by disclosure rather than investigation. Even if investigation leads to evidence, which is essential if the case is going to reach a civil or criminal court of law, the success of a case also depends on the credibility of information, backed up by witness statements, and on the willingness of witnesses to testify. However, even if criminal behaviour is revealed, sporting bodies tend not appear to be willing to publicise it or even to become involved. Therefore, encouraging disclosure is only part of the challenge, as quality of information and evidence, including independent corroboration, and support from sporting bodies are needed to progress to legally sanction those involved in fraud and corruption.

The extent of fraud and corruption is therefore impossible to determine unless those involved in a fix are exposed by someone complicit and aware of the fix and/or with knowledge of the corruption through a personal contact or approaches by 'vested interests'. These approaches are rarely reported, as players, as with all those who expose corruption, are often subject to personal abuse and victimisation. This problem is compounded by lack of credibility, because those who step forward and expose the depth and reach of fraud and corruption in cricket are often themselves involved in acts of fraud and corruption (Radford, 2011).

Furthermore, if the sanctions employed to deter fraud, corruption or rule-breaking are seen as ineffectual, cheating players and corrupt officials will risk 'earning' extra income, because a small fine or brief ban is an insignificant punishment. With the development of online gambling (Brooks, 2012), 'creative bets' and brief professional careers, the lure of 'easy money' or a 'quick buck', where players can still win the match while making 'extra' money for a few misplaced balls or a dropped catch, now plagues international sport.

Conclusion

There seems to be a number of reasons why fraud and corruption in cricket exists. Many cricketers have brief, uncertain playing careers and seek to embellish official earnings with money 'earnt' from corrupt practices. Furthermore, cricketers play a high number of ODIs; referred to as 'soft' or 'dead rubber' matches, *some players* might treat these matches with indifference and underperform in return for some financial reward. When one side in a cricket tournament has already qualified for the next stage and the other failed, it is easy to justify why a team or player underperformed. Such matches provide attractive odds, and if the match is fixed, it will guarantee a handsome return.

In conclusion, then, explanations for fraud and corruption in cricket vary in emphasis, but we suggest that the following is a way forward to reduce the incidence of fraud and corruption in cricket: the ICC needs to invest more money from the revenue that is generated from international cricket to prevent corruption; a clear counter-fraud strategy above and beyond the rules and regulations mentioned in this chapter is needed, including regular risk assessment exercises carried out on the ICC and on national boards by independent auditors. Preventing fraud should be seen as a cost saving or an investment, all acts of fraud and corruption prevented should be publicised, specialist investigators with expertise in fraud and corruption should be employed to run investigations, and corrupt players, officials and administrators must be seriously punished. Only this will preserve and enhance cricket's local, national and international integrity and its ability to keep attracting commercial sponsorship.

8
Fraud and Corruption in Horse Racing

Introduction

In this chapter we focus on the 'modern' international development of horse racing. Rather than dwell on the historical change (see Reith, 2002; Miers, 2004; Cassidy, 2010) in horse racing from an aristocratic 'pastime' to a commercial sport, our focus is on the more modern, contemporary era and the codification of the sport. Intermittingly associated with fraud and corruption in it earliest form (Vamplew, 1976; Chinn, 1991; Dixon, 1991), and in particular gambling, horse racing was, and still is, vulnerable to different types of fraud and corruption. The most obvious is fixing a horse race; however, while we touch on this type of fraud and corruption, we also highlight under-researched types of corruption, in particular auction fraud, doping horses and running a horse when injured.

More than other sports, horse racing is dependent on gambling to survive (Forrest and Simmons, 2010). This puts it in a vulnerable position. Jockeys, trainers and owners are all in a position to manipulate the outcome of a horse race and we use international examples of fraud and corruption to illustrate this.

Furthermore, we assess the effectiveness of governing bodies in dealing with fraud and corruption in horse racing and the available power(s) of governing sporting bodies to investigate fraud and corruption and their willingness to counter it. Finally, we focus on the power (or lack of it) of sporting bodies to prosecute those caught committing fraud and how difficult it is to reach a threshold of evidence and establish that fraud and corruption has occurred.

Types of fraud and corruption in horse racing

In this section we start with purchasing a horse at auction. This is where fraud and acts of corruption can occur even before a horse has run a race, and illustrates the 'sharp practices' that are an accepted part of custom and 'doing business', particularly in the USA.

We then move on to consider the doping of a horse and fixing a race; doping a horse, however, is different to athletes' consumption of illegal substances such as steroids, as horses can be 'doped' to both win *and* lose a race. This, however, is only one way a race is fixed; stewards can fail to test horses for illegal substances after a race and owners and trainers can run a horse in a race under a false name and with fake documentation as part of a gambling coup.

Trading a horse or horse trading? Buying a horse at auction

For many years purchasing and selling horses privately or at auction was based on personal reputation, common familial experience and historical relationships. However, the world of horse racing has changed as 'new money' has come into the sport, shifting the nature of the business from a closed community insulated from risk by expertise and personal familial trust, to an open market with rich but novice interests lacking knowledge and racing custom(s) (Millar, 1986). In this environment fraud and corruption appears to have increased. However, the fraud and corruption we refer to below is not a new practice, but one that has perhaps increased as 'new money' became available.

There is a fine line between showing a horse at its fullest potential and fraud (Finneran, 1996). This deception often starts before a horse has even run a race. For example, before auction, horses are sometimes injected with steroids to make them appear more athletic and robust; sellers use agents to bid up the price of their own horses at auctions, resulting in a inflated purchase price; and agents hired to bid for prospective owners have been caught defrauding them by colluding with sellers in accepting undisclosed commission for an increased purchase price for horse(s) (Altier, 2006). Rather than focus on one country, however, we review acceptable and unacceptable practices at auctions in the United Kingdom and the USA, as they have a long and sometimes illustrious past of 'sharp practices' in horse trading, and have made changes to prevent and reduce acts of fraud and corruption.

Auction fraud in the United Kingdom and USA

From 1752 to April 2006, the Jockey Club regulated the conduct of horse racing in the United Kingdom. As the regulatory authority the Jockey Club required all jockeys and trainers who worked in the United Kingdom to be licensed by them, and all owners to be registered with them. As a result, the Jockey Club's *Rules of Racing* bound these participants to set conduct. However, in April 2006, the Jockey Club passed its regulatory powers to the British Horseracing Authority (BHA) with trainers and owners required to register with the BHA. While trainers and owners are therefore bound by the rules and regulations of the BHA, bloodstock agents are not licensed or registered, and therefore do not need to adhere to the BHA *Rules of Racing*. Instead a bloodstock agent is more of a consultant who offers a variety of services, including identifying a horse at auction for either racing or breeding. Unlike the disciplinary measures the BHA can take against corrupt trainers and/or owners, such as imposing fines and revoking licenses, the BHA's ability to penalise bloodstock agents is limited (Jeswald, 1999).

Perhaps due to a scandal in 2004, and the subsequent passing of regulation, the Jockey Club announced a review of the ways 'to increase transparency in sales transaction', developing into a code of practice governing future auction sales. For example, in 2004 a bloodstock agent was engaged to ensure that a promising horse would be sold to an American client. The bloodstock agent offered the trainer of the horse a £10,000 'sweetener'. The horse's owners, however, were already paying the trainer a five per cent commission and were unaware that he would also receive an additional £10,000 in connection with the sale. The bloodstock agent maintained that the additional £10,000 was simply compensation for the loss of training fees for the trainer for when the horse was sold and claimed that such payment is customary in thoroughbred transactions. Even though the bloodstock agent denied any wrongdoing he ended up paying £50,000 in damages and costs (Evans, 2004; Altier, 2006: 1071–1072), with the Judge of the Central London County Court calling secret commissions 'quite illegal'.

Due perhaps to this case, the Jockey Club published its *Bloodstock Industry Code of Practice* in 2004 and established that 'agents shall not use their position to obtain a secret profit'; s/he should disclose if working for more than one principal in a transaction and if offered 'luck money' – which is a financial payment or gift in kind made after the sale of a horse has been concluded – s/he must report this (Altier, 2006). This proposal, however, like all codes of conduct, is often ignored in practice. This is clearly apparent in auction in the USA.

Inspired by the British Jockey Club, in the summer of 2004 the Thoroughbred Owners and Breeders Association (TOBA) sought to minimise deceptive auction practices by increasing transparency at thoroughbred sales. They developed a *Code of Ethics* that requires agents to disclose who they are representing in a transaction, because 'dual agency' – representing the person/organisation selling and those purchasing the horse without disclosure to all concerned – is fraudulent. The *Code of Ethics* also 'suggests' full disclosure from owners; however, it also recognises the right to personal privacy and therefore an owner is under no pressure to reveal that they own the horse that is for sale. It is possible to make an inquiry regarding ownership, but if the owner's agent rejects the request for information, the only recourse open is to delete this horse from consideration (Bandes, 2003).

Furthermore, horses' medical records are usually available for viewing in the auction's repository. In some cases, however, access to the repository is restricted to medical professionals, so potential owners are encouraged to hire an equine veterinarian to review the medical records and provide insight into the horse's health and fitness. Such background work is important, for once the hammer falls in an auction, a client has limited redress (DuBoff, 1977). If, however, a client feels 'conned' in his purchase of a thoroughbred, there are two forms of redress. A clarification of what a thoroughbred is is useful before progressing here; a thoroughbred's official 'birthday' is 1 January of the year it was born. Once a horse enters its second calendar year, it is considered a 'yearling', regardless of when the horse was born. Therefore, a two-year-old thoroughbred is one that has entered its third calendar year. People purchasing horses are thus willing to risk substantial sums of money on a horse's potential rather than its actual form; this makes information on the horse all the more important, and it is here that fraud and corruption enter the horse-trading market.

A client that has purchased a horse may attempt to rescind the deal by rejecting the horse or revoking his acceptance. They can also sue for damages based on breach of warranty. Most public auctions have a warranty as part of the *Conditions of Sale*. An auction's *Conditions of Sale*, printed in the sales catalogue with other information regarding the horse, includes the contract terms for horses sold at that auction. The persons buying the horse and selling it and the sales company are all bound to these terms. As a general rule, a horse is sold 'as is' at a public auction. Of course, there are exceptions – certain physical conditions (see below) which are expressly named in an auction's catalogue must be announced before bidding starts or must otherwise be disclosed by veterinary certificates on file in the auction's repository. Under the *Conditions of Sale* at public thoroughbred auctions, the onus is on those wishing to buy a horse to review its veterinary certificates, x-rays and any other medical information that is on file in the repository before purchasing the animal (Waxman, 2008).

However, this is not as straightforward as it sounds. Eye defects, cribbing and wobbler syndrome are among the conditions that must be disclosed to potential buyers under the *Conditions of Sale*. In horse-racing terminology, a 'cribber' is a horse that sinks its teeth into an object (often a fence), arches its neck, and then sucks air into its stomach. It is considered a controllable behaviour, rather than a disease. However, wobbler syndrome is 'a neurological disease associated with un-coordination and weakness'. In order to rescind the purchase of an undisclosed 'cribber' or 'wobbler' a buyer must be able to prove that the behaviour or condition existed at the time of sale (Altier, 2006). This can sometimes be difficult to detect and later prove. For example, a buyer at an auction in Keeneland, USA, was unable to rescind the purchase of an allegedly undisclosed cribber because he could not prove that the horse was a cribber at the time of purchase. The person who bought the horse produced no evidence that this particular horse exhibited cribbing behaviour prior to the sale, and a veterinarian explained later in an affidavit that horses do not typically develop such behaviour until they are over one year old. This horse was only seven months old when purchased (Altier, 2006).

This is only one problem when buying a horse at auction. A person's ability to rescind is further restricted, however, as s/he must notify the sales company in writing within the limited right-to-return time-frame recorded in the auction's *Conditions of Sale*. These conditions give the buyer a very limited amount of time to rescind, often 48 hours after the auction ends, as a horse's physical condition is subject to change quickly and the previous owners and auction house want the sale completed as soon as possible.

These conditions pale into insignificance, however, compared to the failure to disclose surgical procedures a horse might have previously had. The Thoroughbred Owners and Breeders Association (TOBA) (2004) categorised some medical procedures as 'acceptable, but must be disclosed, while banning the use of other prohibited, unacceptable practices'. For example, procedures that permanently alter a horse's conformation, such as invasive joint surgeries, were deemed acceptable, but the TOBA *Code of Ethics* required that these procedures be disclosed at the sale. However, injecting internal blisters to temporarily alter a horse's conformation is prohibited within 90 days of the sale, with the repeated use of anabolic steroids to alter a horse's appearance discouraged. Blistering is a procedure to increase blood circulation in a horse's legs. It can be done by applying a caustic agent to the horse's skin or injected beneath the skin, increasing blood flow to an affected part of the body to hide internal and/or external damage the horse might have (Altier, 2006). Furthermore, there is also use of anabolic steroids to help present a horse as healthy and robust. Anabolic steroids, however, should be distinguished from corticosteroids, which are prescribed for legitimate medical purposes, such as treating inflammation. In contrast, anabolic steroids are primarily used to keep horses eating and training or to replace hormones lost in male horses after being castrated.

Although the *Code of Ethics* was welcomed, its positive reception was tempered by a pervasive lack of confidence that these new rules would change the way bloodstock transactions had always been conducted. TOBA did not possess legitimate power to discipline transgressions. With no official body to investigate violations, and no stated penalties for these violations, it is doubtful that the *Code of Ethics* could possibly correct fraudulent auction practices.

The rules do not address the frauds and acts of corruption that are part of many equine sales. Misrepresentation of horses at auction is discouraged, but owners and agents can still manipulate the horse's market value. This temptation to exploit people who wish to purchase a horse but possess limited knowledge is an obvious one. For example, an individual familiar with the world of horse racing approached a family and suggested that they purchase a thoroughbred. None of the family members involved in buying the horse had any experience with horses or racing, but were offered advice on which racehorse(s) to buy, how to care for them, and how to go about selling them. In exchange for such services the individual was to receive five per cent of the net profits from these horse transactions. However, without the family members' knowledge, arrangements were made with the sellers that the individual kept all money paid above a set price determined by those selling the horse and the individual offering advice. The corruption was eventually discovered and the person in question was sued for breach of fiduciary duty and fraud. Although he maintained that he was not acting as the families' formal agent, the US District Court for the District of Maryland disagreed, finding that he violated his fiduciary duty by failing to disclose the kickbacks he received (Altier, 2006).

While the BHA in the UK lacks direct authority over agents (assuming the agents are not licensed as trainers) and other unlicensed individuals, violating its *Code of Practice* could still affect careers since the BHA licenses all British racecourses. The *Rules of Racing* thus empowers the BHA to exclude any person from any of the BHA's licensed premises, even those people the BHA does not license or register. Even though the BHA cannot directly bar these unlicensed violators from working as bloodstock agents in the future, it can banish them from all British racecourses, making it nearly impossible for them to ever again obtain employment in horse racing.

The American thoroughbred system, however, lacks a regulatory body comparable to the United Kingdom's BHA. While TOBA is a respected association and has influence, it is still merely a trade association without licensing or registration authority. Membership in TOBA is purely optional for owners and breeders and thus developing a code of ethics or conduct is a useful way forward, but it is best to involve all employees in a sporting body; if not, the 'code' is seen as property of management rather than owned by all those involved in the sport. However, as we noted in Chapter 4, a code of conduct is very different from a code of ethics. A code of conduct is rules-based and starts with the assumption that people are primarily self-interested, and only behave with integrity if under threat of some sanction; a code of ethics, by contrast, is a values-based approach and views people as capable of moral reasoning (Maesschalck and Vanden Auweele, 2010).

It appears then that although the law prohibits 'secret commissions' and 'kickbacks', with courts mostly ordering agents to pay back illegal profits, lack of moral integrity, or common practice and simple mathematics, illustrate why it is difficult to effectively deter these 'sharp practices'. If a bloodstock agent takes a 'kickback' in several or all of his thoroughbred transactions, he is unlikely to be caught for each one. Therefore, even if his fraud was detected and prosecuted in a few transactions, requiring him to disgorge these profits, the deceptive agent is still likely to make a profit. A far more threatening sanction seems the way forward.

A code of ethics without means of enforcement is meaningless. In order to be effective, codes of ethics must be clear and detailed, with repercussions for transgressions. A code of ethics is an integral part of a unified system of self-regulation, but without anyone or anything to oversee this regulation, a code of ethics alone will never have much of an impact.

There are, of course, some drawbacks to self-regulation (see Chapter 10 on baseball). Self-regulation itself presents the risk that nothing will be done, or that self-regulation is merely a tactic to deter more meaningful regulation. Furthermore, those in charge of regulation might prevent change and/or modifying practices because the old system is economically beneficial to them, and therefore preventing such change, particularly if powerful vested interests are involved, protects the sport for the benefit of a few rather than running the sport with personal and professional integrity.

'Sharp practices' at an auction, while unethical, have the potential to change, as illustrated by the BHA in the UK; doping horses and fixing races in an attempted gambling coup discredits the entire sport. It is to these types of frauds we now turn.

Fixing horse races: doping and gambling in the name of profit?

Sport has long considered doping a recent phenomenon and one associated with performance enhancement. It also views the debate prohibiting doping to be one about safety, 'fair play' and the spirit of sport. However, in the world of horse racing doping is regarded as a threat to gambling, which horse racing is dependent on as a sport to survive. As Vamplew (2007) noted, however, gambling influenced the development of sports rules. Rules in horse racing developed to protect the equality of opportunity to win (races and wagers) and eliminate 'sharp practice'.

Furthermore, those who originally formalised the rules of competition were the owners of the horses racing in the competition and of gambling enterprises, and therefore sought a rule-bound sport. If one is familiar with the cultural and social forces that helped modernise sport, it is no surprise that horse racing was the first sport to adopt anti-doping attitudes and the impact that horse racing had on modernising sport is equally unsurprising (Adelman, 1990; Huggins, 2003; Vamplew, 2007). Indeed, long before the development and codification of other sports, horse racing embodied Guttmann's (2004) seven characteristics of modern sport: standardisation, rationalisation, bureaucratisation, quantification, equality, secularisation and the quest for records. As Holt (1989) noted, horse racing was transformed from a casual competition engaged in by 'noblemen' to perhaps the most highly organised of all sports. The degree of organisation – from standardised tracks to the detailed calculation of odds – meant that horse racing is one of the quintessentially modern sports. Perhaps it is not mere coincidence, then, that horse racing also was the first modern sport to address doping. With significant financial investments on the line, these 'noblemen' created rules, as they have for most of our modern sports such as football and cricket, in an attempt to ensure equality of sporting conditions in a competition. In this context of gambling and standardisation, those involved in horse racing perceived that doping – whether to increase or reduce performance – allowed 'insiders' to place wagers on fixed races.

This amounted to an unfair advantage, in both *winning* the contest and *profiting* from it (Altier, 2006). Those developing the codification of doping rules and concerned about the spread of doping in horse racing, however, remained primarily concerned about 'fair competition' in the utilitarian sense of equality of conditions of competition. The high-minded rejection of enhanced performances and allegiance to a spirit of sport – both core aspects of the current doping debate in human athletics – were not factors in the initial anti-doping movement.

However, what is doping? For Hoberman (2001) doping has two elements or themes. In colloquial usage, doping is the boosting of human performance with the use of artificial illegal substances such as anabolic steroids (see Chapter 10). The second and more complicated aspect of doping is that it represents an illegitimate strategy to secure success on the pitch and/or track. Doping in horse racing, however, is about both improving and reducing, if not ruining, performance. Athletes can underperform, slow down or throw a match in ways that are difficult to detect. Fears that doping might be employed by an athlete to fix a defeat are unrealistic since athletes have no need to dope themselves to underperform – instead they can fake a poor performance. Horses, however, are subject to illegal substances that both increase and decrease potential performance – beyond their will, in effect.

The world of horse racing developed a saliva test in 1912 in the hope that it could detect the use of illegal substances such as cocaine or opium employed in the hope of, respectively, improving or decreasing performance. While the intolerance and negative attitude towards doping hardened in the world of horse racing, it is worth noting that the International Amateur Athletic Federation (IAAF) did not consider doping a serious enough matter to prohibit it until 1928 (Dimeo, 2007). With advances in medicine, doping reflected a complex web of shifting cultural, political and intellectual forces, particularly in the western world with advances in medical knowledge, increasing use of experimental science, technological developments such as the hypodermic needle (introduced in the 1850s), and advances in pharmaceuticals (including the introduction of morphine and cocaine) that all coalesced into a newfound trust and expectation that 'science' and 'medicine' could alter biological function (Hoberman, 2001; Dimeo, 2007; Rosen, 2008).

Grounded perhaps in false optimism and the promise of modern medicine or the fear of potential addiction, physiology sought to quantify such performances, while some assumed that the power existed to modify them. Similar to the fear of genetic modification, or gene doping now (Miah, 2004), the fascination of the Victorian era with scientific and technological mastery convinced the horse-racing community that individuals, through doping, could modify a horse's performance. They were willing to believe it was possible regardless of the lack of empirical evidence.

With ongoing technological developments, as the case of BALCO signifies (see Chapter 10), doping is a far more sophisticated and elusive problem than anything encountered in the Victorian era. However, instead of running the risk that a doped horse is tested, it is possible to bribe the relevant person(s), depending on the jurisdiction, to 'forget' to test all the horses entered in a race.

However, even though the BHA has a clear policy and procedure on preventing gambling corruption there are those that perhaps consider 'putting in the fix' a worthwhile risk. In 2005, the Disciplinary Panel of the Jockey Club held an enquiry to consider whether a licensed jockey at the time of the events, and his contact, had breached of the *Rules of Racing*. For example, a jockey was providing private information to an individual who had been excluded (in 2003) from involvement in racing, and to others, for organising a corrupt 'gambling operation' where they were laying horses a jockey was riding to lose. During the investigation the jockey attempted to mislead Jockey Club investigators by denying he knew the individual who had been excluded. He (the jockey) claimed that he was calling a different person about the purchase of a car, when in fact all the calls were to the banned individual. The jockey was disqualified for five years and fined £2000 while the individual linked to gambling was excluded indefinitely. The other defendants involved in the 'gambling operation' were mostly excluded from all premises owned by the Jockey Club (British Horseracing Authority, 2012a).

This is only one example of fraud and corruption and its association with gambling. There are examples of suspicious gambling around the world, as every day substantial sums of money are placed on horse races. The problem for those tasked with monitoring and 'policing' the sport is the volume of gambling and the limited resources available to them to counter fraud and corruption in the sport. However, gambling and its association with corruption in horse racing is only one avenue of fraud and corruption. Rather than punish 'after the event', which still discredits the sport, it is to detecting, exposing and countering these types of frauds and corrupt acts that we now turn, as these methods protect the integrity of sport more than consequential punishment.

Detecting, exposing and countering fraud and corruption in horse racing

Every new racing scandal discredits the sport and often leads to demands that the sport is in need of harsh sanctions to deter acts of fraud and corruption. Present and future sponsorship is withdrawn and the individuals involved often apologise and return to the sports 'remade'. The BHA and the governing and regulatory body for horse racing works with the gambling sector in preventing malpractice and corruption and willingly exchanges information regarding 'suspicious' gambling. The BHA Integrity Services Department, therefore, works closely with the gambling sector and the Gambling Commission and is in contact exchanging information on gambling and pursuing, if possible, accurate audit trails of gambling activity. The BHA also works with the police and Her Majesty's Revenue and Customs, if relevant.

In 2002 the Jockey Club and the British Horseracing Board commissioned a review of race security and intelligence due to negative publicity arising from a number of alleged race-fixing scandals (Gardham, 2007). The 2003 review made a total of 36 recommendations, 35 of which were accepted by the BHA. These were broadly centred on establishing integrity as a strategic imperative, establishing an effective intelligence-gathering and analysis framework, improving investigative capability and developing working partnerships with other sporting and gambling bodies. While it identified many threats to racing's integrity, its main thrust, however, was to establish a capacity to confront and root out corrupt practice. Part of this approach was educational, and included a programme on 'Inside Information', designed to protect jockeys and others from corruption. Drawing on the Police National Intelligence Model (NIM) (John and McGuire, 2003), the BHA sought an organisational risk assessment, which balances organisational and operational demands. This approach would reveal threats beyond race fixing involving animal rights extremism and money-laundering, and the use of unidentified techniques or substances to enhance or depress equine performance. In 2007 a review – known as the Neville Review – of the security measures put in place after 2003 was conducted, with a view to identifying areas for improving security, and considered the implications and lessons learned from the collapse of the Rodgers, Fallon, Williams and Lynch trial into alleged race fixing in 2007 (Gardham, 2007).

The BHA Integrity Services Department conducted 110 investigations in 2009 for a range of alleged breaches of the *Rules of Racing*; these included suspicious gambling (including the misuse of inside information), running illegally 'fake' horses (see the Flockton Grey scandal), positive drug tests on horses and jockeys, financial irregularities, assaults and a number of other disputes. The examples below, which are sports hearings rather than criminal cases, illustrate the range of frauds and acts of corruption that horse racing has to contend with.

One example is that of Flockton Grey, a British racehorse that won a race at Leicester racecourse in 1982 by 20 lengths. The margin of victory provoked suspicion of fraud and an investigation ensued. It was uncovered that the horse's owner had switched the two-year-old Flockton Grey for a seasoned three-year-old 'ringer' (a substituted horse in place of another). Furthermore, the owner and trainer backed the horse with £20,000 dispersed over several betting outlets. They were both convicted of conspiracy to defraud, fined £20,000 and received long bans from horse racing (Ashforth, 2003).

A few years later, in 2008, the Disciplinary Panel of the BHA began an enquiry into two family members who placed a ringer at two point-to-point meetings in 2006 (a Point-to-Point Hunt meeting is a rural meeting rather than a race at a designated course). The case centred on substituting one horse (a ringer) for another in two races. The horse entered in the races was registered as Green Admiral, yet the horse that ran the races was Kings Crest, a far better horse. In this case, however, there was not enough evidence to suggest that a betting coup had taken place even though the BHA reviewed the odds of the horse on offer on the days of the respective races (British Horseracing Authority, 2012c).

Finally, in 2008, a registered owner and the manager of horses owned by a Racing Club was found guilty of fraudulently selling shares in horses he was not permitted to. The BHA panel found that he sold shares in the ownership of a horse that he had never owned and shares in two other horses over and above the Racing Club's holding, and that he had fraudulently advised potential purchasers of a horse with the wrong purchase price. The total penalty imposed was a fine of £2,500 and a period of disqualification totalling six years and three months (British Horseracing Authority, 2012d).

Aware that the BHA has been subject to criticism regarding the length of time some investigations had taken, its Head of Investigations recently suggested that 12 months should be the maximum period to conduct an investigation. The BHA has a fully resourced Intelligence Unit including two betting investigators to monitor markets in real time, seven days a week. They are in daily contact with established bookmakers and exchanges, sharing information on gambling matters. In addition to this the BHA has recruited a raceday integrity coordinator who works closely with the betting investigators. This raceday integrity coordinator is the link to raceday stipendiary stewards and handicappers, reviewing live racing and carrying out post-race analysis and working with weighing room security officers. These 'improvements' are to be commended; however, the raceday integrity coordinator, raceday stewards and handicappers, reviewing live racing and carrying out post-race analysis are still assessing potential fraud and corruption 'after the event'. This analysis is worthwhile; however, as we mentioned in Chapter 2, the gambling sector, depending on its jurisdiction, is also a potential bulwark protecting the integrity of horse racing which can carry out 'in-play' real-time assessment of gambling on horse racing.

Improving information-sharing across organisations and racing resulted in an increase in the number of intelligence reports received by the BHA. In 2009 a record number (4,297) of these reports were dealt with, resulting in a 59 per cent increase in the amount of intelligence from 2008 to 2009 (British Horseracing Authority, 2012a). However, is the increase in intelligence reports due to the system in place or is there more fraud and corruption in horse racing? This is difficult if not impossible to answer, as an increase in reporting is no reflection of fraud and corruption in horse racing or in any other sport. The development of Racestraight in conjunction with Crimestoppers – an independent charity that helps find criminal suspects – might affect the number of reports, as it is an anonymous reporting line for the public and those working in the world of horse racing to come forward with information regarding potential breaches in the rules of racing.

Furthermore, the BHA works closely with its Equine Science and Welfare Department and, in particular, now adopts an intelligence-led approach to testing in training, and pre-race and post-race testing of horses. This, we suggest, is part of a clear counter-fraud strategy. The BHA, in the space of a few years, appears to have learnt from mistakes it made with the 'Fallon trial' (Gardham, 2007) and its operational and strategic approach to preventing and countering fraud and corruption. As a sporting body protecting the integrity of racing, it thus appears prepared to be flexible and reflective in its approach. This is impressive as many of the other sporting bodies in this section of the book tasked with protecting the integrity of their sport are reluctant to change, to conduct strategic reviews as part of an internal exercise and/or are incompetent or some of its members corrupt.

Conclusion

There are a number of different types of fraud and acts of corruption committed in the world of international horse racing. These, as we have shown, are many and varied, and range from purchasing a damaged horse at auction, selling false share(s), entering a horse into a 'clean race' where all the relevant animals were tested, to running the 'incorrect' registered horse in a race. Individuals and/or groups committed these acts with the full knowledge that they were breaching codes of racing conduct and in some cases committing a crime.

The BHA has gone some way towards addressing these frauds and has invested in developing its strategic and integrity unit. This is to be commended. However, while we have not covered all other international jurisdictions' approaches to preventing fraud and corruption and maintaining the integrity of racing, which was impossible, in the space available in this book it seems at least that the BHA is in the vanguard of countering fraud and corruption. We have managed to highlight 'sharp practice' in auction sales in the USA and the difference with the Jockey Club and then the BHA in the United Kingdom. The BHA's approach is to be welcomed and is one that other sporting bodies in other sports should follow to counter fraud.

Perhaps the most significant part of this chapter is the development of betting exchanges and the potential they have for fraud and corruption. The temptation is obvious if we are in possession of 'inside knowledge' to lay a bet on a horse knowing it will not win no matter the standard of the field of horses entered for the race. After all, such knowledge could offer attractive odds, and if the outcome of the horses' performance is known beforehand it will guarantee a handsome financial return.

Preventing fraud and corruption should be seen as a cost saving and not a cost, all acts of fraud and corruption that are prevented should be publicised as the BHA presently do, and specialist investigators with expertise in fraud and corruption should be employed to increase resilience to fraud and corruption as horse racing is in need of commercial sponsorship if it is to survive if not flourish in a world where sports increasingly compete for our attention and income and engagement.

9
Fraud and Corruption in Basketball

Introduction

In this chapter we focus on fraud and corruption in both college basketball (the National Collegiate Athletic Association – NCAA) and the professional National Basketball Association (NBA) in the USA. Where possible we draw on international examples as well, but due to the popularity of basketball in the USA and its long-established college and professional leagues, most of the chapter covers fraud and corruption in the USA.

We start by briefly highlighting some of the types of fraud and corruption in basketball, such as point shaving, and the influence of gambling on basketball and how, because of the nature of the sport, it is open to fraud and corruption. In this section we also review referee bias and the practice of tanking, that is, losing end-of-season matches on purpose as a way to secure the following season's most talented players.

Then, we move on to the changes in allocation of players from intercollegiate to professional basketball in the USA, as this part of the management of the sport is a major obstacle in attempting to prevent fraud and corruption and thus the problem of ranking players and tanking in end-of-season matches.

Following on from this we review the use of data by basketball teams to improve a team's performance, but also suggest that such an approach is of use to detect tanking. The penultimate section is then concerned with the encouragement of disclosure and the use of sanctions to reduce the incidence of fraud and corruption in basketball.

In the conclusion we make some suggestions as to how the NCAA and NBA could increase the integrity of basketball.

Types of fraud and corruption in basketball

In all sports, players want to win (and sometimes lose), and will resort to unfair tactics; sometimes they go beyond this to committing outright fraud and corruption. However, we will not dwell on the numerous historical cases of match-fixing in college basketball that have been amply dealt with elsewhere: for example, in 1951, 35 players who played in 86 matches from 1947 to 1951 were accused of accepting bribes to fix matches (Figone, 1989); 50 players from 27 colleges in the 1980s were accused of corruption while playing matches across 22 states, as were colleges and universities in the 1990s (see also Kirchberg, 2006; Weinstock et al., 2007; Nelson, 2009; Walker, 2011).

We, however, focus on the structural and organisational issues in college and professional basketball such as point-shaving, referee bias and tanking in end-of-season matches. This is not to dismiss the significance of fixing the result of a basketball match, it is simply a recognition that 'vested gambling interests', as with cricket, are far more sophisticated now in 'putting in the fix'. Therefore, 'putting in the fix' in college basketball is not a historical anachronism which would not happen in the highly commercialised world of college basketball; in fact it thrives in the context of the naive attitude of college administrators, coaches and the NCAA, and is a powerful symptom of the depth and pervasiveness of gambling in college basketball.

Furthermore, the issue of illegal substances is also a problem in basketball, as players, until recently, were not tested in the off season from July to September for performance-enhancing substances. This has now changed, with players tested no more than twice in the off season; players, however, are not screened for cannabis, and it is unclear if testing will occur for Human Growth Hormone as well; this is currently under review.

Point-shaving

Point-shaving occurs when a basketball team that is favoured to win a match still wins but fails to cover the point spread of the estimated margin between the two teams competing. Initial evidence suggests that point-shaving is potentially widespread (Wolfers, 2006). This practice by teams 'attempting' to win basketball matches by less than the point spread in order to yield profits for those involved in the fix, which needs only a few players on the team, is thought to be pervasive throughout college and professional basketball (Gibbs, 2007). The incentives for such corruption derive from the structure of basketball betting.

For example, team A is expected to beat team B by more than 8 points. Therefore, if a bet was placed on Team A and they covered the spread of points it would be a winning bet. If, however, they lost the game the bet would be lost. However, when team A beats team B, but by less than 8 points, the opportunity for fraud and corruption can come into play. For example:

Team A scores 98 points
Team B scores 95 points

Team A wins the game, but fails to cover the spread, that is, they did not win by 8 points or more, and thus if you backed Team A to cover the spread of 8 points, it would be a losing bet. Team A, however, still won the game. Team A, or some key players in it, could have controlled the game, as they were the far superior side, to make sure that they still win, and thus satisfy the coach and fans, college and/or owner(s), but also make money from 'gambling connections' who place bets on Team A *not covering the spread*.

With a big enough point spread, say ten to thirteen points, a small group of players, or even one star player, could 'control' the outcome of a game and manipulate the spread to their and others' advantage with little fear of detection by coaches and other players. Due to the high-scoring nature of the sport, the regularity of scoring throughout a game, the closeness of scores right up to the end of the game, and the fact that team scores are often dominated by single players, superstars can score or miss a lot of shots without arousing suspicion. This is the case even at college level.

A player putting in the fix could offer a piece of the profits to one or more players on the favoured team by shaving or dumping points. In this way the favoured team could win the match, but fail to cover the spread. But this type of fix is not foolproof; a team could lose the match outright and the fix would fail, uncorrupted team-mates could spoil the fix by having a very good game and cover the spread, or the opposing team might play so poorly that it would become obvious if the opposing team was shaving points.

The two sides of the equation are players, who care about winning the match, and people 'gambling', who care about whether a team beats (or covers) the spread. Gambling, however, exists if there is no fix in place. We do not consider it gambling if the outcome of the event is known in advance or if players involved are paid if they fail to cover the spread (as it is easy for players to reduce effort in response to financial incentives). Wolfers (2006) provided some empirical data to substantiate this suggestion. The favoured team beat the spread in a little over 50 per cent of matches analysed with strong favourites (those favoured to win by more than 12 points) covering the spread approximately 48 per cent of the time. While point-shaving may affect whether a strong favourite covers the spread, it should have no effect (or minor effects) on the team's chances of winning. It was also noticed that teams that win increasingly fail to cover the spread as the spread widens.

Furthermore, a clear favourite is more likely to shave points than a weak team. For example, when the spread is three points, an attempt to win by only one to two points, especially in basketball, may backfire, either leading the player(s) to lose the match (raising the cost of point-shaving) or those involved in the fix to lose the bet (lowering the benefit). By contrast, a team that has to shave down a wide spread of points encounters very little risk.

As for match-fixing, *losing to win* is not a simple task. A potentially confounding factor is that players may reduce effort or coaches may use lower-rated players when the result of a match is not in doubt. This, however, is no guarantee of success, as the losing team, especially if it is in on the fix, will also reduce its effort and the result will possibly be unaffected. There is some anecdotal evidence to support this from college sports, but as 'running up the score' is typically regarded as poor sportsmanship in college basketball, this collusion is difficult to prove (Bernhardt and Heston, 2010) (see also the section on referee bias for a discussion of keeping the score 'under control').

While the discussion so far has proceeded as if point-shaving reflected a conspiracy between players and 'gambling interests', the outcomes and results of matches might equally reflect selective manipulation by coaches of playing time for star players. Further, players are able to fix matches without the need of 'gambling interests' offering them bribes, as they can use family members or friends to place a bet.

The key incentive driving point-shaving is that players can win both matches and money by failing to cover the spread. If this spread were not available the incentive to offer bribes to players would be sharply reduced, as they would be expected to win or lose a match outright; this however would not affect illegal gambling where a spread could still be set. While referees may also be corruptible (see below) they do not (or should not) have a vested interest in either team winning and are therefore unlikely to be the source of the systematic patterns previously identified (Gibbs, 2007; Wolfers, 2006).

One way of assessing potential corruption is to focus on the opening and closing point spread (the spread of points can change as matches progress). Betting lines or spreads move to reflect information on the amount of money placed on the teams in a match. If far more money is bet on the underdog than the favourite – as is likely when a team is point-shaving – the closing line will be less than the opening line, that is, the price of a bet on the underdog will rise.

The bookmakers will balance bets on each side to reduce exposure to risk (as would bookmakers on any sport). Players and 'vested interests' that fix basketball matches profit by betting significant amounts on the underdog; this drives the point spread down (Bernhardt and Heston, 2010). However, the opportunity to gamble on college basketball is limited, since Las Vegas sports books are the only legal commercial US market for college basketball betting. But this will not stop people gambling illegally, and with the development and 'internationalisation' of online gambling other jurisdictions can offer spreads on US basketball that are beyond the respective sporting bodies' control (Horne and Zammit, 2010).

Bernhardt and Heston (2010) raise a note of caution regarding gambling, corruption and college basketball. While historical and contemporary examples of point-shaving are numerous, as there are documented cases of point-shaving by NCAA basketball players (McCarthy, 2007) and a recent example of gambling by an NBA referee (Donaghy, 2009), corruption is not endemic.

Referee bias

In all sports that require a referee, umpire or judge there is the potential for fraud and corruption. However, while there is little documented evidence of referees in basketball committing such acts, there is evidence of referee bias (Anderson and Pierce, 2009; Gilovich et al., 1985; Greer, 1983). While not technically corrupt, a referee can, and does, affect the outcome of a match due to personal relationships and such in a set of matches can increase commercial revenue (Donaghy, 2009; Pedowitz 2008; Rodenberg and Choong, 2009).

However, such conduct appeared of less importance when Tim Donaghy (2009), an experienced NBA referee, admitted to laying bets on basketball matches in violation of his contract of employment. Donaghy maintains that he did not bet on any matches that he officiated in and only gambled on those he watched where he knew the referees' bias. In a widely read report on the Donaghy issue and referee gambling, Pedowitz (2008) confirmed that 52 of 57 referees interviewed during his investigation acknowledged that they had engaged in some form of impermissible gambling while working as an NBA official.

In the wake of Donaghy's exposure, the NBA made a number of changes to its referee 'oversight' programme. First, it created a new position of referee operations; secondly, it developed a 'system of recruiting, training, monitoring, managing, and developing' its referees, and thirdly, it created the Office of League Operations and Officiating to 'help coordinate wagering intelligence and screening' (Pedowitz, 2008: 113–114). All of these measures came several years after the NBA started using digital technology in its review of matches to monitor individual referees and assess specific calls (and non-calls) made. Regardless of these changes it is still thought that there is a 'substantial number of [NBA] team representatives that consider that referees make calls, on occasion, based on personal bias' (Pedowitz, 2008: 56; Thu, 2002).

Donaghy suggested that he could predict, within reason, based on his position as NBA referee, how his fellow referees would 'control' a match. He suggested that one referee would keep a match 'tight' by making sure the superior team did not secure a double digit lead over the opposing team. He would therefore frequently blow the whistle on the team playing the better basketball. With such inside knowledge Donaghy could bet on matches knowing that the spread would be close (Donaghy, 2009: 93; Thu, 2002).

Sports governing bodies such as the NBA should avail themselves of every reasonable, feasible and permissible resource in the course of monitoring the performance and objectivity of their referees, as should all sports. While the NBA has promised to implement changes to stop such bias, it is difficult to determine bias all the time (Lehman and Reifman, 1987), and as such this situation needs to be kept under constant review.

Tanking: losing to win?

In some instances, sporting bodies can contribute to the potential corruption in their own sport. In basketball teams are ranked according to the final position in the league at the end of the season. In the spirit of competition the worst-ranked team picks the upcoming best players in a draft in an attempt to balance the competition. However, getting to pick the best young player in your team for the following season can lead to individuals or teams trying to lose contests rather than to win them (Frick, 2003; Preston and Syzmanski 2003). This system of distributing players in a reverse order into the NBA created a climate where some teams expended effort to win and others in the same league expended effort to lose ('tanking'). The NBA is aware of this problem and has made a number of changes to the format of its draft system over the past 20 years, in part because of real or perceived tanking.

Taylor and Trogdon (2002) noted that teams face an incentive to lose if having a poor season. Supported by Balsdon, Fong and Thayer (2007) evidence was produced that NCAA men's basketball teams perform poorly in conference championships to improve opportunities to draft the best new talent for the following season. Past research in sports economics has provided empirical strategies for highlighting corruption among Sumo wrestlers (Duggan and Levitt, 2002), Olympic judges (Zitzewitz, 2006), and evidence of biases on the part of sports officials (Parsons et al., 2007; Price and Wolfers, 2007; Price et al., 2009) as well as in basketball. On a positive note, though, this type of research can suggest changes that can reduce the opportunity for corruption (Dietl et al., 2009); the NBA has changed its ranking system countless times to rectify the tanking problem. Tanking, however, is mostly associated with college basketball rather than the professional NBA (or at least more research has been completed on the college league).

There are two categories of teams that receive NCAA tournament invitations (to play in a prestigious tournament once national league positions are confirmed); first, teams that are declared conference champions receive what is referred to as an automatic bid. Conference champions are decided either in a conference tournament that follows the regular season or by the final regular season standings (with no conference tournament) (Balsdon et al., 2007).

Secondly, teams that do not qualify by winning a tournament or league are considered for 'at-large bids', which are made by a selection committee based on a set of criteria (relative national ranking, overall won-lost record, record in the last 10 games, and a performance ratings index). Since 1990, the number of at-large bids for a specific conference in a specific year has ranged from zero to six.

The burden of success, however, might cause a problem here. A successful team might win its own conference or tournament depending on the structure of the league and consume physical energy before a NCAA tournament. Therefore, teams might tank in one of two ways: they lose depending on their position in the league to secure a superior player draft pick; or play a weak team to preserve players for the prestigious NCAA tournament. However, tanking in a conference can involve a real cost in terms of a team's seeding in the NCAA tournament, as a poor showing against a weak conference rival a few days prior to the NCAA tournaments can understandably influence the selection and/or seeding committee.

There is a problem here; conferences are ranked – minor, mid-major and major, based on the level of skill and standard of play of the colleges involved. A mid-major conference team therefore should be far more confident of an invitation to the NCAA tournament than a team in the lower leagues. In major conferences, the cost of tanking a match near the end of the season once qualified for the NCAA tournament is small because even if they lose the conference tournament they are almost always invited to play in the NCAA tournament.

There is also the incentive to tank if it helps fellow teams from the same league qualify. For example, revenue is shared among teams in a conference. A college keeps a proportion of the television and other revenue from each NCAA tournament match played and the remainder is shared equally among the other teams in the conference. Revenue to athletic departments in a year depends not only on the success of its own team in that year's tournament, but also on the success of its conference rivals (Zimbalist, 1999). With such revenue sharing an athletic department has a financial incentive for its conference competitors to receive an NCAA tournament bid (though not at the expense of their own team). The prize for tanking in this situation is the prospect of an otherwise non-qualifying team winning the tournament and the accompanying automatic bid increasing local conference revenue. However, the financial gain derived from the success of a conference rival, and therefore the incentive to tank, is diminished when revenues are shared among many teams. Furthermore, historical and institutional factors (tournament site, design of revenue sharing, rivalries) may influence the outcome of conference tournaments.

Balsdon, Fong and Thayer (2007) found that it was not the major conference teams that appeared to be involved in tanking but mid-major teams. An explanation for this is that although the winner of a major conference tournament would receive (be guaranteed) attendance at a NCAA tournament, so would other high-ranking teams in the conference. The contenders for the conference tournament title in a major conference therefore might secure a place for an NCAA bid simply because of the league in which it plays, and thus it would be more difficult to increase the number of NCAA bids in a major conference than in a mid-major conference where an 'at-large bid' to play in the NCAA might be available.

This situation of 'invitations to play' in an NCAA tournament appears unsatisfactory. The NCAA are aware of this. They have over the years also attempted to reduce the incidence of the end-of-season tanking aimed at increasing chances of picking up the basketball star of the future.

Detecting, countering and exposing fraud and corruption in basketball

Players come into the NBA from amateur/college leagues such as the NCAA, or from interscholastic sports leagues. The NBA originally awarded the team with the worst record the pick of the first-draft player, allowed teams to select players based on territorial considerations, and to select college players from their local region. This was to help teams build local fan bases in then new leagues. This format was in essence a reverse draft pick. This consists of a number of rounds with each round containing a number of picks corresponding to the number of teams in the league. The team with the worst record has the first draft pick in each round and can select any player eligible in that year. The team with the second worst record received the second pick in each round and selected from the remaining eligible players, and so on.

Following the 1984–1985 season the NBA changed the format as it was thought that the system was unfair and that this change would help reduce the incidence, or alleged incidence, of tanking. Under the structure at that time, a number of teams did not advance to the prestigious postseason tournament. Under this format, these unsuccessful teams would be randomly assigned a ranking. Therefore, the first team randomly drawn was awarded the first pick in the draft; the second team drawn was awarded the second pick, and so on. Each team eliminated from the postseason had an equal probability of getting the first pick in the draft. This was done to stop teams tanking and it was hoped the uncertainty of this lottery-type system would reduce the benefit of finishing lower in the standings. This format, however, met with resistance as it was felt that it produced unfair outcomes and failed to distribute new talent to the teams that needed it the most (Taylor and Trogdon, 2002).

In 1989–1990 the NBA changed the format again, this time to a weighted lottery. The teams that did not make the postseason playoff were assigned a set of numbers between 1 and 66. The amount of numbers that each team received decreased according to their win–loss percentage. The worst team was assigned 11 numbers, the second worst team 10 numbers, and so on. This lottery mechanism assigned only the first three picks of the NBA draft. After three draws, the next draft picks were assigned in reverse order of win–loss record. If the worst team did not receive the first, second, or third pick, then it would automatically receive the fourth choice. Some NBA team executives believed that this format was the best way to balance deterrence of tanking with competitive balance (Soebbing and Mason, 2009). Taylor and Trogdon (2002) and Bernhardt and Heston (2010), however, found evidence that teams eliminated from the postseason were more likely to lose matches.

In 1992–1993 the league voted to accept the idea of increasing the weights. The number of lottery balls was reduced from 66 to 14, and each team received a certain allotment of combinations of four numbers ranging from 1 to 14. The first team whose combination of numbers was selected (without respect to the order in which the numbers were drawn) received the first pick, and so on.

The introduction of uncertainty about the awarding of the first overall pick in the draft led some to question the fairness of a team such as Orlando Magic in 1993, who almost qualified for the postseason, receiving the number one pick. Soebbing and Mason (2009) discuss the conflict within the league regarding the different draft formats and describe how the NBA, with various stakeholders, attempted to balance tanking (or the perception of tanking) with league-wide competitive balance to protect the integrity of the sport.

Tanking is appealing, as the first-pick player is generally outstanding. Such a star player also has an impact on gate revenue, even controlling for the number of wins. Additional revenues also come from licensed merchandise sales, advertising revenues and concessions. Therefore, getting the first pick in the draft has a positive impact on all aspects of running a basketball team. One potential pitfall, however, is that the costs of tanking could offset the potential benefits of securing the number one draft pick; as teams lose matches they lose revenue.

As with all sports perception and rumour rather than fact was enough to force the NBA to institute changes (Soebbing and Mason, 2009). Uncertainty, though, is a core characteristic of sports leagues (Mason, 1999) and this must be protected if spectators are to see the sport as a genuine contest and not as something manipulated by vested interests.

While changes can and have been made to counteract tanking at end-of or postseason in basketball by changing the draft pick system, this has not completely eradicated the incentive to lose on purpose (or its perception) to help a fellow conference team and increase revenue. However, as suggested by Balsdon, Fong and Thayer (2007) there are other ways in which the NCAA can discourage tanking in conference tournaments. A simple solution is to eliminate conference tournaments altogether and grant automatic bids to the conference champions.

An effective anti-tanking policy must address two issues – the security of a team's NCAA bid and revenue-sharing. A more fundamental problem, however, is that of vested interests. Postseason basketball contests generate a substantial and increasing proportion of revenue from ticket sales and television revenue, which has encouraged not only the proliferation of conference tournaments but also the expansion of the NCAA tournament. Any solution to the current problem, therefore, that reduces the number of postseason matches would no doubt meet with resistance from those who benefit financially from the current system.

Furthermore, the NCAA needs to address the role of revenue-sharing in corruption. Several conferences, notably the Atlantic Coast Conference and the Metro, did not share revenues from first-round NCAA tournament games prior to 1991, at which time the NCAA established new rules for distributing prize money (McClure and Spector, 1997). It may be time for the NCAA to have another look at those rules with the aim of reconciling the need for fair competition with incentives for postseason effort.

However, other changes are possible to help counter fraud and corruption. Sports are a good source for data. All kinds of statistics can be collected. The National Basketball Association (NBA) produces abundant statistics of its approximately 1,200 matches played throughout the season. Members of the NBA's Game Stats Program enter these 'play' statistics into a computer, which gets a universal time stamp based on the play clock. All this data is then uploaded to a hosting centre. This 'play data' is available to all basketball teams to download and use. Teams download the data to integrate into their own databases and mine the data for meaningful patterns and relationships about plays and players in an attempt to incorporate them into successful plays during games (also see Lewis, 2004 for influence of statistics on baseball).

In the 1997 NBA Finals, the number-four-seeded Orlando Magic used this technology to their advantage. They were losing two matches to zero in a seven-match series against the number-two-seeded Miami Heat. The coaches used data mining and discovered that certain combinations of players worked better than others; the players scored more points and played better together in defence.

The coaches gave more playing time to these players, which almost turned the series around against superior opposition.

Such an analysis of data can also detect patterns of tanking (see Bernhardt and Heston, 2010; Soebbing and Mason, 2009; Taylor and Trogdon, 2002). This approach is akin to a risk assessment where vulnerable parts of the NBA format can be kept under constant review. Even if the existence of tanking is based on perception rather than data, the advantage of gathering and analysis of data is twofold; first, it sends a signal to players and coaches that the NBA is aware of the potential for fraud and corruption, and that it is gathering information in order to protect the integrity of its sport; second, if tanking is noted (or at least suspected) the NBA can speak to the owner(s) of a team officially or unofficially, deal with a problem if suspected or detected, and if it is then proven punish the team accordingly.

Punishment could take the form of a fine, or it could modify the ranking of team when it comes to postseason placement of players. This, of course, would depend on the type of corruption, such as tanking to secure better players in the forthcoming season or point-shaving in individual matches.

Collection and analysis of data is one of many ways to detect and perhaps even prevent some (but not all) players and teams from engaging in certain types of fraud and corruption. It is more of a starting point, but since all plays are recorded, it comprises a useful body of knowledge.

However, it is also useful to encourage players to disclose information. As we saw in earlier chapters most fraud and corruption is uncovered by disclosure rather than investigation. But even in the case of an investigation, successful pursuit and/or prosecution still relies on credible witnesses being willing to come forward and give evidence in an unofficial or official capacity.

The case of Donaghy (2009) is enlightening here, as he was a respected official. However, once he 'confessed' and was banned, the NBA and fellow referees disowned him and questioned his credibility. So encouraging disclosure from players, coaches, owners and officials, while desirable, can also face problems, because once someone is involved in a fraud or corrupt act, he or she loses credibility.

Furthermore, if sanctions are seen as ineffectual, players and corrupt officials willingly risk 'earning' extra income as a fine or brief ban is an insignificant measure. This is a problem for those involved in sport, as much research on disclosure in the USA has shown how those willing to come forward and expose corruption are treated by organisations and fellow employees (Hannigan, 2006; McDonald and Ahern, 2002; Near and Miceli, 1985; Verschoor, 2005). There is much for an individual to consider before disclosing fraud and corruption: reputation, effects on health because of stress, ostracism at work and future consequences for one's career. In the USA, however, offering substantial rewards for disclosure might be successful in encouraging those 'blowing the whistle' to consider these negative outcomes as acceptable and worthwhile risks (Johnson, 2003; Hesch, 2007).

As was illustrated by Glazer (2002), whistleblowers fall into three types – unbending resistors, implicated protestors and reluctant collaborators. While it is useful, we suggest that this typology is limited. While it attempts to explain the characteristics of the whistleblowers, it does not address the motivation of the persons involved. Often those who 'blow the whistle' can have (or be accused of having) a ulterior motive, they can be or be characterised as incompetent employees (Westin, 1981), may expose corrupt practices in order to avoid justified sanctions, may act from motives of revenge (Gobert and Punch, 2000), while some may be purely altruistic.

However, point-shaving and tanking are just the end product of a generally corrupt system; abuses in collegiate sports reflect commercialisation (Wetzel and Yaeger, 2000), subsidisation, pressure for elite recruitment and a multitude of academic abuses (Thelin, 1994). College administrators doctor high school transcripts, and coaches openly bid for the services of athletes by offering gifts and/or financial rewards in the form of nonexistent jobs. Fraud and corruption thus have reached beyond the basketball court, and compromised the credibility of the academic institutions that players represent (Roberts and Olson, 1991); offences of forgery, false documentation, enrolling of athletes in perfunctory courses (Figone, 1989) and bribery by players and coaches have all flourished in an attempt to secure success on a basketball court.

Despite coaches' salaries, scholarships, cost of travelling, basketball equipment and promotional expenses, basketball is a business venture well worth the investment to college administrators because sport provides prestige and publicity to a college. It appears then, that players are only one part of the problem in intercollegiate basketball;

college administrators and coaches are involved in the corruption either as accomplices in fixes or for simply ignoring and denying the practice and influence of gambling. The players then are perhaps nothing more than symptoms of the disease.

Due to the nature and difficulties in investigating fraud and corruption, the NCCA and NBA, even if they are so inclined, will find it hard to prevent corruption. Even if caught, corrupt players and coaches have already damaged the reputation and integrity of the sport. For both officials and players, it might seem easier to maintain a system that lends itself to fraud and corruption than disclose such practices and find themselves excluded from the sport and its rewards.

Conclusion

There are a number of reasons why fraud and corruption in basketball occurs: the influence of gambling; key individual players controlling a match; failing to cover point spreads; tanking in all its manifestations; and a system of ranking and future player picks that encourages manipulation.

The most worrying aspect of fraud and corruption in basketball, however, is point-shaving. A team might tank to conserve players for forthcoming rounds of a tournament once qualified (as with other team sports in a league format), or to help more teams from its division reach the tournament to increase conference revenue – a relatively altruistic form of corruption.

College basketball, however, has suffered a major gambling scandal each decade since 1951. Banning gambling on college basketball has not worked; it has failed to stop people 'putting in the fix'. Gambling will continue, especially illegally and/or legally in remote jurisdictions; this makes it harder to detect and monitor and potentially increases dangers for those foolish enough to get involved, especially if organised crime becomes involved and threatens the integrity of the sport.

In conclusion, explanations for fraud and corruption in basketball vary in many ways, but we suggest that the following need to be considered if the NCAA and NBA wish to increase their resilience against fraud and corruption: use all available data to analyse patterns in basketball; employ counter-fraud specialists to detect fraud and corruption; punish players and all those involved in fraud and corruption proportionately; encourage people to disclose through, for example, anonymous hotlines; and carry out constant risk assessment of all parts of the league structure. These are, we suggest, part of a standard model counter-fraud strategy, and as such are necessary if fraud and corruption are to be dealt with.

10
Fraud and Corruption in Baseball

Introduction

In this chapter we focus on fraud and corruption in baseball. We start by reviewing the different types of match-fixing in baseball around the world; these consist of match-fixing for 'vested gambling interests' (Ginsburg, 1996), state corruption and manipulation of Little League Baseball (LLB) in Taiwan and playing ineligible players to win national and international matches (Junwei, 2007).

We then consider how Major League Baseball (MLB) is dealing with the use of illegal performance 'drugs' in the USA. In particular, we focus on the use of steroids and Human Growth Hormone (HGH) and the assessment of the Mitchell Report (2007) of MLB inaction and the Major League Baseball Players Association (MLBPA) reaction to and perhaps knowledge of players' use of steroids and HGH for personal and commercial interests. This leads to a discussion on the detection and 'policing' of the use and abuse of steroids and HGH (Abrahams, 1998). The tests presently in place to detect the use of banned substances are limited because players and MLB control the policy and procedure of testing players. We suggest an independent body would be far more appropriate for this role.

We then assess the potential for recourse to the law and the Mail Fraud statutes in the USA as a way to prevent the use of steroids and HGH by players. This, rather than match-fixing, is the true contemporary scandal in baseball (Hart, 2010; Ventresca, 2011) and so it is the focus of much attention in this chapter. This is not to suggest that match-fixing is not occurring (see the scandal in Taiwan in 1997) but it is a recognition that the most pressing issue in baseball, particularly in the USA, is its lack of integrity as players consistently break records, seemingly with the assistance of banned substances.

In the conclusion we make some suggestions as to how MLB could increase its resilience against the different types of fraud and corruption it is experiencing.

Types of fraud and corruption in baseball

Match-fixing *for money*: a justification for poor pay and restrictive contracts?

Baseball has a long and disappointing association with 'putting in the fix' (Asinof, 1963; Ginsberg, 1995) in association with 'vested gambling interests'. Baseball was originally an amateur sport, played by 'gentlemen clubs', until the professionalisation of the sport in 1903 (Asinof, 1963). As with other sports, such as football, it was thought that a sport played by 'gentlemen' and for pleasure, companionship and physical exercise was immune to corruption and far from the reach of dishonest influences. This was far from the truth, but as professionalism in baseball increased, so did scandals. Professional players were targeted by vested gambling interests, and managers of teams also solicited and accepted 'kickbacks' and attempted – sometimes successfully – to bribe officials (Ginsburg, 1995). Some matches were even disrupted by bookmakers who feared a substantial financial loss. For example, on 16 June 1917 the Chicago White Sox were visiting the Boston Red Sox when the pitch was occupied by bookmakers in the hope of the cancelling the match, making the result void and all bets cancelled. This was not to be and the bookmakers were forced to pay out (Ginsburg, 1996: 85).

The most famous match-fixing scandal in baseball, and perhaps sport, is the Black Sox scandal of 1919 (again involving the Chicago White Sox). Described (at the time) as unthinkable, the fixing of the 1919 Baseball World Series was considered a scandal of such magnitude (Ginsburg, 1995) that all the players involved were banned from playing professional baseball for life. This lifetime ban, though, has been suggested as inappropriate, as each player's involvement in the fix varied (Carney, 2006). The entire affair was characterised by confusion and deception (Gropman, 1979) and, as with most frauds, it was difficult to determine who was involved (although for something as sophisticated as a nine-match World Series to be fixed a number of major players on the team needed to be involved: Cottrell, 2002).

However, it has been suggested that low wages and the reserve clause, which was implemented in 1879, was partly responsible for the players' involvement in the Black Sox scandal. The reserve clause was implemented as a system to control the movement of players (Asinof, 1963; Calpin, 1996) (also see the discussion of the Bosman Ruling in football in Chapter 4). With complete control over players' salaries because of the clause, the club owner(s) would employ the players' services for one year, holding in reserve the right to renew a contract. If players did not wish to accept the contract, they could not play anywhere else and they would be out of the Major League (Carney, 2006). The clause allowed owners to pay the players whatever they wanted and created a monopoly that was nevertheless regarded as perfectly legal. Legal challenges to the reserve clause failed as the courts ruled that organised baseball was not considered as interstate commerce, and therefore not a trust (Martindale and Lehr 1997; Cottrell, 2002; Carney, 2006). In other words, baseball was big business to the owners, but to the courts it was a sport (Willisch, 1993; Nathanson, 2008). While the reserve clause allowed the owners to continue to reap significant financial rewards from the players' efforts and vast profits were made from the growing popularity of baseball, the players were excluded from partaking of this increased revenue. However, long before the 1919 World Series, there were many documented instances of players willing to fix matches (Ginsburg, 1995).

Since this 'fix' other scandals associated with 'gambling' have plagued baseball in minor and major leagues (Ginsburg, 1995). Recurring gambling scandals, however, have appeared to have had little effect on the commercial success of the sport.

Those investigating the recent use of steroids by players have noted similarities to the Black Sox scandal, especially that much of the initial evidence was ignored. As Nathan (2003: 139) points out, 'acts of corruption remind people of previous acts of corruption'. The problem for baseball is that these acts keep recurring and damaging the integrity of the sport.

Match-fixing *for glory*: Little League Baseball (LLB) and state corruption in Taiwan

The island of Taiwan fell under Japanese control in 1894. It was under this occupation that the notion of 'modern' sports such as baseball was introduced to the island. With Japan's defeat in the Second World War, however, Taiwan was handed back to the Chinese. In late 1949 the Kuomintang (KMT) were defeated in a civil war in China and ceded control of the country to Chairman Mao's People's Republic of China. Those loyal to General Chiang Kai Shek of the KMT escaped to Taiwan and took control of the island. Military rule lasted for 38 years, all vestiges of Japanese occupation were eradicated and Chinese culture and tradition were imposed.

It is in this context that Little League Baseball was developed by the KMT to enhance its international credentials, national identity and success in Little League Baseball World Championships (Junwei, 2007). This brief historical background to the development of baseball in Taiwan is important, as the context in which baseball develops has ramifications for the fraud and corruption that follow. Under military rule baseball was a 'tool' to be manipulated by the KMT rather than a 'pastime' and/or a commercial enterprise as it was in the USA (Morris, 2011). While the manipulation of a sport in the service of national pride is nothing new, in Taiwan it led to young players being used to commit sporting fraud.

Little League Baseball (LLB) is a competition held in Williamsport, USA, for children aged 5 to 18. There are different age ranges and classifications, such as Senior League (age 13–15) and Big League (16–18). Local teams from around the world can enter and represent their 'community' as well as nation. To reach the LLB tournament in Williamsport, teams have to win local, 'regional' tournaments in their respective country with players in a set age range. Japan joined LLB in 1966 and a team then went on to win the LLB tournament in 1967. In this year Japan also sent a young team to Taiwan to play the Taiwanese Provincial Children's Cup champions – Hongye. Hongye defeated the Japanese team and much political capital was made of the victory. The problem was that six of the Hongye team were older than 12 and were therefore ineligible to play in this tournament. Many of the squad players were registered under assumed names or used the names of students under 12. The principal coach and the administrator of Hongye were each sentenced to one year in prison, with a two-year suspended sentence, for producing fraudulent documentation regarding the players' names and ages (Junwei, 2007).

This practice of playing ineligible players in Taiwan, however, was regularly sanctioned by schools in local tournaments. This had a positive effect on baseball in the country, with extensive TV coverage of matches; Taiwanese baseball became increasingly popular and the KMT saw in its success the potential for international prestige.

In 1969 Jinlong represented Taiwan in Williamsport in LLB and returned to Taiwan as champions. Two years later another Taiwanese team, Juren, won the series, with a pitcher – Xu – who had represented a different team from Taiwan the year before. The then LLB President could not understand how the same player represented two different geographical regions of Taiwan (Junwei, 2007).

The answer was straightforward; Taiwanese baseball officials picked a national team from the best players in Taiwan instead of sending a community team to represent them in the USA. With unofficial acceptance of such a practice, players were moved around Taiwan. This practice contributed to Taiwan amassing 17 Little League Baseball (LLB) championships in 27 years, with success in Senior League (age 13–15) and Big League (16–18) as well. This practice was so prevalent that the winning team of the Senior League in 1973 was registered at a school in Taipei, the capital of Taiwan; however, 14 of the players came from the south of the island. Furthermore, they also registered names of players who were not even playing baseball, and made up the names of teams so as to increase player registration and increase the pool from which Taiwan baseball administrators picked players for the LLB teams (Junwei, 2007).

There were two methods of playing overage players in Taiwanese baseball. First, a players' age is/should be determined by his age on 1 July to play in the tournament. In the case of LLB it is no more than 12; however, if aged 13 after 1 July players are still eligible if enrolled in elementary school. However, many of those playing in the LLB had left elementary school and were in junior high school. The second practice is less corrupt and more cultural; delayed birth registration. Officially the child's age in Taiwan is counted from the date of registration rather than birth and hence a player could be older depending on the speed with which the child was registered.

However, the most common violation of the rules was in Big League Baseball, which stipulated that a district must have a league with at least five but no more than 10 high school baseball teams. From the outset Taiwan (as a country) never had more than 10 high school teams and thus chose an all-star national team from them.

In 1974 Taiwanese teams won the world championships at all three levels. The LLB suspected 'foul play' and banned all foreign teams from competing until they were reinstated in 1976. Even though Taiwan was far more careful in international tournaments after the ban, parents, schools and the KMT continued to accept playing ineligible players as 'part of the sport' in Taiwan. With corruption accepted at this level of the sport it is hardly surprising that the same type of corruption existed in national Taiwanese baseball.

Playing ineligible players at the local, national and international level of baseball in Taiwan appears to have been 'common practice'. It seems that 'bending the rules' to secure an advantage and win was part of the culture of Taiwanese baseball. However, this was nothing compared to the match-fixing scandals in youth and professional baseball that followed. While unacceptable and unethical, 'cheating' to win was tolerated; *losing to win*, on the other hand, is seen, in any sport, as undoubtedly corrupt.

Match-fixing *for organised interests*: bribery, threats and intimidation

Following the coming to power of the nationalist Kuomintang Party (KMT) in Taiwan a single-party state was established. Enjoying a monopoly of economic and political privilege, the KMT regime constructed alliances with local factions, sharing political power and material benefits in exchange for allegiance (Brown et al., 1998; Hood, 1996; Kau, 1996; Kuo, 2000; Wang, 1994; Wu, 2001, 2003). Factions thus arose to mediate between the 'Chinese' KMT state and the local Taiwanese population (Bosco, 1992). Such an arrangement was successful in that 'the system of sharing economic and political interests…provided the foundation of…political stability and the legitimacy of the regime' (Hung, 1989: 26–27).

Organised crime had been an accepted and often courted 'agent of power' when the KMT had been in power in China (Bosco, 1992; Hood, 1996; Kuo, 2000). These links with organised crime continued to develop in Taiwan (Brown et al., 1998; Reaves, 2002). This specific political phenomenon undermined Taiwan's political and economic system, resulting in the creation of a corrupt political elite and a reduction of people's confidence in judicial independence.

With the end of martial law in 1987 and developments in political and economic 'freedoms' (Wu, 2003), and the national baseball team's impressive performances in international tournaments (including the bronze medal at the Olympic Games in Los Angeles in 1984), governmental, sporting and business interests became convinced that Taiwan could sustain baseball at a professional level. The Chinese Professional Baseball League (CPBL) was thus established in 1990, with a rival professional league, the Taiwan Major League (TML), set up in 1997. The legitimacy of professional baseball, however, was undermined in 1997 with revelations of bribery, gambling and the involvement of criminal elements (Kao, 1996).

Despite these scandals, cases of bribery continued. On 20 June 1997, nine players from the China Times Eagles and one player from the Uni-President Lions team were 'interrogated' by the public prosecutor and subsequently released on bail. During this period, there were only two domestic players of the China Times Eagles team available for selection since players who were under suspicion were suspended and could not play in the CPBL. The China Times Eagles finished the rest of the season by using other clubs' bench players, and on 2 August 1997, seven Mercury Tigers players were kidnapped along with four players in Kaohsiung in an attempt to 'persuade' them to lose upcoming matches (Junwei, 2007).

Due to the monopoly of economic and political privilege and alliances with local factions (Brown et al., 1998; Hood, 1996; Wu, 2001, 2003) it was hardly surprising that organised crime, with political support, should become involved in gambling in professional baseball. The independence and influence of baseball and the sports organisations such as the TML and the CPBL, the Republic of China Sport Federation and the Chinese Taipei Baseball Association were thus open to question. Even as the sentences were passed in 2003 for the 1997 scandal, match-fixing and corruption persisted. In 2005, the chief prosecutor in charge of investigating gambling and match-fixing was detained for alleged corruption, along with nine 'runners' working for 'baseball–gambling interests' who were thought to have sent bullets to CPBL players in an attempt to threaten them to fix matches.

Detecting, countering and exposing fraud and corruption in baseball: the role(s) of Major League Baseball (MLB)

In this section we focus on the attempts made by MLB in the USA to deal with the problem of players' use of illegal substances, particularly steroids and Human Growth Hormone (HGH). The use of illegal substances, rather than match-fixing, appears to be the major problem in baseball in the USA. In this section our main concern is the structure and organisation of MLB's testing policy that allows baseball players to 'cheat' the public of a real spectacle of sporting endeavour and claim record-breaking home-run tallies (Emory, 1992; Lavelle, 1995; Reinsdorf, 1996; Nathanson, 2008).

On 17 June 1991 the MLB Commissioner's Office released a memorandum acknowledging the harmful effects of steroids. In the document, it stated that players' use of steroids 'are subject to discipline by the Commissioner and [players] risk permanent expulsion from the game' (Vincent, 1991: 1). No provision, however, was made for testing players for steroids or other banned substances. It was not until the 2002 MLB Collective Bargaining Agreement (CBA) that the MLB addressed the problem of steroid use. This, however, came about because of substantial public pressure that forced both MLB and the players' union to accept testing on a trial basis in 2003 (Staudohar, 2002).

This public pressure was due to a variety of factors; however, perhaps key was Grand Jury testimony in 2004 regarding the Bay Area Laboratory Co-Operative (BALCO) investigation, which suggested that MLB stars had used tetrahyrdogestrineone (THG), a then-new synthetic steroid. This revelation was then followed by the release of Jose Canseco's (2005) autobiography, which alleged that famous players such as Mark McGwire and Rafael Palmeiro had also taken steroids.

The BALCO investigation, coupled with the other allegations, 'forced' the US House of Representatives to announce a hearing regarding MLBs anti-doping policy. However, unlike the National Football League (NFL) and the National Basketball Association (NBA), prior to 2002 MLB had no official anti-doping policy. As a result of high-profile exposés, MLB and the Major League Baseball Players Association (MLBPA) agreed to conduct random provisional testing.

During the 2003 season provisional testing was conducted in order to gauge the level of banned substance use in baseball. While MLB and the MLBPA agreed to anonymous tests, these were for 'standard' steroids rather than synthetic steroids like THG. The latter were impossible to detect using the type of test the MLB administered, and players were informed as to when the tests would be administered. Furthermore, once tested, players knew that they would not be tested for the rest of the year.

Despite drawing the ire of both the House of Representatives and the Senate in September 2005, MLB owners and players could still not agree upon a new testing policy. When the World Series ended in October of 2005 without a new testing policy in place, several anti-doping bills were introduced into Congress. In November of 2005, MLB and the MLBPA relented to congressional pressure, and banned substances were expanded to include all steroids and masking agents. This, however, was probably more to do with the intervention of the US Congress, which 'forced' MLB to test its players and punish offenders. Unannounced mandatory testing of each player was thus now to be conducted over the course of the season, along with random testing of selected players and random testing during the off-season.

However, despite the pressure from Congress, and the move to mandatory testing, we suggest that it still would have made financial (rather than ethical) sense for MLB to continue with a 'limited' testing policy. Increasing home runs (Fort, 2006) increases public demand for the sport: increased offence, or run production (Schmotzer et al., 2009), is desirable to fans and MLB owners, as it has been shown to boost attendance (Domazlicky and Kerr, 1990; Winfree et al., 2004). As Haugen (2004) suggests it is also completely rational for players to cheat if those tasked with running the sport are happy to ignore the use of steroids (Yilmaz et al., 2001: 181). It follows that if steroids increase runs, and therefore attendance, owners and players both benefit from the consequent increased fan interest.

This is not an attempt to provide a defence for MLB and the MLBPA; it is simply an attempt to perhaps understand that there is a possible financial incentive for avoiding implementing a 'proper' testing policy, especially if steroid use is widespread as it is in professional baseball.

In an attempt to clean up the tainted image of baseball and its stars' use of illegal substances, Senator George Mitchell, at the request of MLB, was appointed to conduct an investigation: '...to determine...whether any Major League players associated with BALCO or otherwise used steroids or other illegal substances banned by the CBA.'

Released on 13 December 2007, the Mitchell Report identified substantial numbers of players who had taken steroids and other suspected substances in violation of federal law over several years. Mitchell (2007) concluded that the signing of the 2002 CBA was of limited value. Before this time it was clear that certain substances were illegal and prohibited and this prohibition applied to steroids. No player, however, was disciplined for steroid use before the prohibition was added to the CBA in 2002.

The report noted that although the MLB Office lacked the power to issue warrants and subpoena players, it could conduct investigatory interviews and compel them to attend. MLB, however, rarely requested its players to attend an interview regarding alleged substance violations. The report noted that, if it wished, MLB could work with state and federal law enforcement agencies, which have warrant and subpoena power, and coordinate investigations through the indirect use of these powers. However, prior to the investigation undertaken by Senator Mitchell, MLB made little use of this avenue.

Without the legal threat MLB had no incentive to comply with a tough, 'proper' testing policy. The Mitchell Report (2007) exposed the vested interests of MLB and the MLBPA and, despite the machinations of MLB to deflect attention away from itself and on to individual players, there have been too many instances of abuse to ignore or dismiss the problem as one of 'rogue', unethical individuals, as is often the case regarding acts of fraud and corruption.

As we have seen so far, baseball is used to gambling scandals in both the USA and Taiwan, substance abuse by professional players, individual and cultural explanations of corruption and fraud, and organisational issues and selective blindness relating to codes of conduct transgressions and outright fraud. Like other organisations we have examined in this book, baseball bodies are strongly concerned with the commercial success of their sport. This focus, however, often leads to those tasked with running the sport and protecting its integrity damaging it instead.

The current MLB policy calls for a 'three strikes and you're out' approach to the use of illegal banned substances. For example, a first positive test would result in a 50-game suspension; a second positive test in a 100-game suspension, and a third positive test in a lifetime ban. This might seem overly punitive, but there are 162 baseball games in a season and a first-time offence means a player misses less than a third of a season. It is not until the offender is caught for a third time that they face a possible lifetime ban. However, banning substances is only one part of the process; the detecting of illegal substances needs to be comprehensive and applied rigorously to catch those players using any of the range of substances banned.

Although the use of Human Growth Hormone (HGH) has been banned by the current steroid policy, the current testing policy, at the time of publication, does not test for HGH. Furthermore, MLB players can only be screened for HGH through the use of a blood sample, and the MLBPA refuses to allow its players to submit to any type of test besides ones using a urine sample. The MLBPA cites 'invasion of privacy' as the reason for why it does not allow its players to submit to blood tests, and has therefore undermined the policy regardless of how tough it claims it is.

The current policy for detecting professional baseball players' use of illegal substances then has limited reach. If MLB is unable (or reluctant; this is not clear) to implement a sound testing regime similar to those in other sports, it is perhaps worth considering passing the testing procedure to an independent body.

Presently, the MLB testing agency is controlled by MLB and the MLBPA. The testing programme administrator, who is responsible for overseeing the integrity of the entire testing programme, can be removed at will by MLB or the MLBPA. A testing agency that is not fully independent of MLB and the MLBPA raises a conflict of interest issue and undermines the integrity of the testing process.

Furthermore, MLB and the MLBPA have retained exclusive control over the administration of tests, what they test for, and the actual collection process for the tests. Despite attempts to establish random, unannounced testing of players, it has already demonstrated that the current policy is incapable of random testing. By telling team officials of impending visits, the element of surprise is undermined and, due to the advances in pharmaceuticals, players are free to use this time to mask and/or clear their systems of illegal substances.

Unless there is a change in the approach to testing players, MLB will continue to see scandals occur. If MLB officials and players are reluctant to allow an efficient, robust policy to be implemented the prevention of such substances is bound to be hindered. However, recurring scandals do nothing to protect the integrity of the sport, and if players destined for the Hall of Fame are found to have 'cheated', fan loyalty, commercial revenue and sponsorship might be affected (Gorse and Chadwick, 2010).

Recourse to the law: getting MLB attention?

The proliferation of MLB players who have tested positive for banned substances has tainted nearly every recent major statistical achievement in MLB and left baseball in a compromising position (Nathanson, 2008). If MLB is unable or unwilling to 'police' the players and protect the integrity of baseball then recourse to the law is a possible avenue to prevent fraud and corruption.

The Mail Fraud statute allows the United States Attorney's Office to bring MLB players under federal jurisdiction. The threat of indictments might place MLB players on notice that the use of banned substances is illegal. Furthermore, the US Attorney's Office can use the threat of an indictment to 'encourage' MLB to adopt a tough testing policy. As a result, a private employee, such as an MLB player, could be indicted if it is proven that he deprived an employer, a baseball club owner, of 'honest services'. The use of such a statue is worth considering, but without the assistance of MLB officials, which appears doubtful, such action will remain difficult (Manfred, 2008). Nonetheless, clear sanctions that players fear and that threaten the financial interests of clubs and the reputation of MLB is a step in the right direction.

To be convicted of a mail or wire fraud offence, the Attorney's Office must show beyond a reasonable doubt that the defendant committed the scheme:

- to defraud that includes a material deception
- with intent to defraud
- while using the mails, private commercial carriers, and/or wires in furtherance of that scheme

- that did result or would have resulted in the loss of money or property, or the deprivation of honest services.

A scheme to defraud including 'material deception' could refer to a player defrauding his employer. If a player admits to taking or tests positive for steroids, the player has deprived MLB, the employer rather than baseball club owner(s), of his honest service. Players who use banned substances knowingly and on purpose break the established rules of baseball. Furthermore, they are deceiving their employer if they participate in competitions, and this deception is material because an MLB player who is 'on' such substances is gaining an unfair competitive advantage over other players who have followed the rules.

Intent to defraud is established by intent to cheat, mostly for the purpose of financial gain and causing financial loss to others. The intent is proven when a player tests positive for use of banned substances and gains an illegal, unfair competitive advantage. Furthermore, if a player uses a banned substance to secure a roster spot that he otherwise would not have had he has caused financial harm to 'clean' player(s).

Posting illegal substances through the mail or by courier is one of the easiest methods for athletes to receive steroids and HGH; however even if a MLB player attempted personally to avoid the US mail system by having a third party, such as a friend, order and receive them, the player would have caused the mail to be used and would still be culpable under the statute.

The final part of the statute is the requirement that the mailing was for the purpose of executing the 'fraud'. The statute stipulates that comprehensive use of the mail system for 'posting' banned substances is illegal.

In the light of this statute MLB would have a choice; either adopt a demanding testing policy, which calls for the blood tests that HGH can be detected by, or continue with the current policy with the understanding that, if caught, players will face criminal prosecution for violating the 'intangible right of honest services' doctrine of the mail fraud statute.

The adoption of these more demanding standards would result in more organisational enforcement, which would reduce the need for the use of criminal sanctions. If, however, baseball players are caught using steroids and nothing or little is done to deter or detect them, MLB puts at risk both its credibility as a sport and its commercial revenue (Gorse and Chadwick, 2010).

Conclusion

Baseball is considered America's national sport. It connects the past and the present through statistics, but those numbers are losing the inherent value that makes baseball unique. Record numbers will become devoid of any meaning if players attain such records by using illegal substances.

The rules of MLB clearly state that using banned substances in competition is not allowed, and MLB players who continue to use them defraud both fans and the sport. To rely on MLB and the players to willingly and internally change the system of testing for steroids and HGH is perhaps naïve. It appears, then, that the power of prosecution is the last threat left to MLB and MLBPA.

While this chapter has shown that gambling scandals in baseball are nothing new, it is the problem of banned substances that has damaged contemporary baseball the most in the USA. To counter this problem, a demanding testing policy is needed, along with risk assessments of all MLB commercial activities. Like many of the other sporting bodies we have reviewed in this book, MLB has been found wanting, and needs to protect not only its own interests, but also the integrity of baseball itself.

11
Fraud and Corruption in Boxing

Introduction

Rather than dwell on the long, and sometimes, corrupt nature of boxing, which is established elsehwere (La Motta, 1997; Lazaroff, 1990; Sammons, 1990; Neiman, 2008; Norridge, 2008) our focus is on the more 'modern' version of the sport. We therefore focus on the different types of fraud and corrpution found in 'modern' boxing. This is done by examining the roles of the main 'participants' involved in the sport, such as boxers, managers, promoters and sanctioning bodies and how they have contributed to and committed acts of fraud and corruption.

This is followed by an assessment of the evolution and regulation of boxing, particularly in the USA, which for most of the 20th century dominated the sport. Therefore, this is where most of the examples of fraud and corruption in this chapter originate. We futher highlight the limited and inadequate structure of some of the Boxing Commissions and their association with corruption.

We then make some suggestions on how to prevent acts of fraud and corruption (or at least minimise them) by improving contracts, developing a database of boxers and employing credible referees and judges.

In the conclusion, as with other chapters, we make suggestions on how the sport of boxing can reduce the incidence of fraud and corruption.

Types of fraud and corruption in boxing

The best way to see the reach and extent of corruption in boxing is to examine those involved in the sport and the avenues that are available to them to commit fraud and corruption. Since detecting fraud and corruption is difficult, particularly for a sport that is international, there is ample room for fraud and corrupton to occur. Below are a few examples of international fraud and corruption in boxing which have included the involvement of organised crime: they include bout-fixing; the use of false documentation to hold a fight; breach of contracts and influence of different sanctioning bodies on boxing commissions; and the arranging of international 'title fights'. With a range of different sanctioning bodies and commissions, no one agency appears to have a overarching role in running the sport of boxing. Vested interests have prevented the development of an overarching sporting body, which, if free from corruption, could document fraud and corruption and banish those committing such offences from the world of boxing. The existence of a single body, however, is no recipe for success, as we saw in the chapters on football, cricket and baseball.

The participants

Most elements in the world of boxing – sanctioning bodies, trainers, managers, promoters, boxers – have been involved in fraud and corruption in some way, but it is the boxers who appear to be the group that has attracted most attention. It is useful to break this down into individual acts of fraud and corruption, even though they are often a combination of acts by and collusion between organisations and individuals.

Boxers

There are approximately 8,500 licensed professional boxers in the USA, and while a few enjoy financial success, most are exploited. Boxing is structured in such a way that a 'fighter' has to pay managers', trainers' and licensing fees from his share of the 'purse' (prizemoney from the match). Corrupt individuals therefore can make substantial sums of money from often uneducated and exploited individuals, with little of the commercial revenue available beyond a select few.

Although many boxers are often the victims of fraud and corruption (see the sections below) some also ignore and breach signed contracts. A contract is signed with a promoter to organise the fight, secure television deals and increase exposure of the fight to increase revenue. It appears, however, that a contract can be open to interpretation. For example, a heavyweight boxer signed a contract with a promoter for the right to promote a fight with Gerrie Coetzee of South Africa, with a 90-day right of refusal. The promoter learnt that the boxer had completely ignored the contract and scheduled a fight against Coetzee without consulting him. The promoter brought an action against the boxer and was granted an injunction stopping the fight with Coetzee and preventing the boxer signing a contract with anyone but himself. However, the fight then fell through due to lack of financing and the injunction was dropped (Foreman, 1996).

There is also a range of 'minor' in-fight techniques that boxers use to gain an advantage in a fight; these include removing padding from the gloves, and applying foreign substances to the gloves that irritate the opposing boxers' eyes and blur his vision. For example, in a fight between Billy Ray Collins and Luis Resto in 1983, Resto had removed the padding from his boxing gloves. Due to this he gave Collins a savage beating and caused him permanent eye damage, which resulted in the end of his career. In a criminal trial, evidence showed that Resto, his trainer (Carlos 'Panama' Lewis) and second (Pedro Alvarado) all conspired to remove padding from Resto's gloves. Lewis and Alvarado had their boxing licences permanently revoked and Resto was suspended indefinitely (Department of State, Division of State Athletic Commission, 1985) .

The reason such a case could occur was that no one could enter the dressing room except those involved in the fight. The promoter, Top Rank, had a duty to deliver the gloves in an unadulterated state to the contestants, but no duty to monitor gloves prior to the match. The referee only had to inspect the outside of the gloves prior to the fight. As the Boxing Commission in New York stated, it was required to inspect the gloves once delivered to Madison Square Garden, to approve Resto's bandages before his gloves were put on, and to adjust and inspect gloves after they were on his hands. The regulations called for an inspection of the exterior of the gloves and boxers' bodies by the referee to make sure no 'foreign substances' were attached, but there was nothing in the rules to require anyone to watch as gloves were placed on the boxer's hands (Foreman, 1996).

Managers

A manager (or managers), as there can often be more than one, represents his fighter in all business transactions. The manager's 'services' are paid out of the 'purse', the total sum of money that boxers make from a fight. The managers should also select an appropriate trainer(s), a promoter for the 'event' and negotiate the promotional contract, and, in part, help choose the opponent. Managers are licensed by the states in the USA, but each state has different procedures. Therefore, a manager could represent his fighter in one state, but not another, unless also licensed by that state. This lack of regulation is an oversight.

For example, former junior welterweight champion Aaron Pryor came out of retirement to fight Jerry Strickland. Pryor was blind in his left eye and Strickland had a fight record of 11 wins and 74 losses. Pryor's manager, Diana Lewis, failed to organise the fight when state commissions in New York, California, New Jersey and Nevada all refused a licence because of Pryor's blindness. However, Wisconsin, which did not have a boxing commission or athletic commission, allowed the fight. Following the fight an investigation revealed that Pryor had submitted forged mandatory medical and insurance forms (Neiman, 2008.)

Usually paid around a third of the purse in exchange for their services, managers are in a profitable position. However, due to corruption, successful boxers such a Oscar de la Hoya have set up their own company to negotiate bouts, commercial revenue and help manage both upcoming and established boxers.

Furthermore, a manager should not represent two boxers in the same contest, or be both manager and promoter of an event, as this represents an obvious conflict of interest. This rule, however, is not always observed.

A manager is therefore in a powerful position; it is both prestigious and lucrative to handle a fighter, particularly one of high ability. It is perhaps for this (and other) motives that organised crime has long had links with the international world of boxing. Jake la

Motta ('Raging Bull') testified that in the 1940s he purposely lost two fights in return for a promise to fight for the middleweight championship of the world; he got his 'shot at the title' by promising organised criminal interests that he would lose to satisfy 'gambling interests' (la Motta, 1997). Such links, however, are not just a part of history; there are many more recent examples of organised crime involvement in the world of international boxing (Neiman, 2008).

Promoters

Apart from the boxers, promoters are probably the most important people in any fight. Promoters negotiate with managers to arrange a fight, making sure that the match is exclusive so that all television rights are controlled by his company and, more importantly, the boxer(s) are contracted to fight only those people the promoter is willing to sanction. A boxer is thus paid a lump sum for a minimum number of bouts per year at the professional level, with a minimum purse for each match. While the promoter pays all the expenses incurred in promoting a fight and assumes the financial risk of staging an 'event', if the fight is successful the risk is worthwhile as a company will secure substantial revenues from ticket sales, television rights and advertising and merchandising income.

However, managers and promoters can, and do, work in collusion and manipulate and sometimes defraud boxers. Some states even prohibit promoters from having a financial interest in any of the fighters they are promoting; however, such 'rules' are not always successful (Brubaker, 1993).

Promoters of big 'marquee' fights also have to take out insurance against the fight being cancelled due to unforeseen circumstances. This is expensive as boxing is a dangerous sport and during training 'accidents' can and do happen. There are also matters of personal illness, promoting contests in 'unstable' political places, such as Zaïre in 1972 for the 'rumble in the jungle' between George Foreman and Muhammad Ali, and the sometimes reckless behaviour of boxers that can all stop a fight going ahead. For example, it is possible to have a insurance policy that would pay certain expenses if the fight was cancelled and a fighter was injured during a training session and had to withdraw from the fight. The promoter could request costs incurred as non-refundable training expenses. It is, however, possible that the contract submitted is fraudulent, with some details amended and/or the injury to the fighter is 'manufactured' (Foreman, 1996; Harbison,1995).

Promoters can also control a boxing championship through what is known as 'multiple option contracts'. In such a contract, a promoter of a champion can make sure that the challenger signs a contract that allows the promoter to promote his next fight if he beats the champion. The promoter can therefore prevent the fight if the boxer refuses to sign such a contract or make sure that he has the opportunity to promote the next championship fight, regardless of the outcome. James 'Buster' Douglas signed such a commitment with Don King after he won the world heavyweight championship from Mike Tyson in Tokyo on 10 February 1990. The 'contract' signed was for three years, that is, for the duration that Douglas was champion and a further two years after losing the title. Douglas brought a suit in federal court claiming the option was void due to its intention to run for an unlimited period of time. The court reasoned that it was excessive, but also that it did not suffer from indefiniteness and an 'unlimited period' of time.

Promoters can thus control access to important championship fights, and prevent worthy challengers coming up against 'their' champion. As a result, we often see meaningless, one-sided and even dangerous fights that should never have taken place. Promoters, however, are unable to set up such a fight without the ignorance, compliance or collusion of a Boxing Commission.

Boxing commissions

Unlike most sports in the USA, professional boxing is not governed by a single, central organisation that establishes rules; regulation is left up to each state. In some states the commissioner is politically appointed; in Iowa it is the labour commissioner, while in Georgia it is the secretary of state who is in charge of regulating boxing. The commissioner need have no knowledge of boxing, yet still establishes the rules and licensing requirements and also appoints judges and referees; it is thus a vehicle open to political influence (Hauser, 2003).

There is also a inherent conflict of interest when a state has to regulate a boxing match. If they are 'too demanding', promoters and sanctioning organisations might take the fight to another state which is more accommodating in its approach (as seen above in the Pryor case). With potential state revenue to be made from a championship fight, states do not want to see the fight promoted elsewhere. The same can be said if a fight is stopped to protect a fighter. In Las Vegas during a four-month period in May-September 2005, two boxers died and two others suffered life-threatening brain injuries. Nevertheless, neurologists and the ringside physican were criticised by promoters for stopping these fights too soon. The ringside physican was replaced on the board shortly afterwards by a non-physician who had donated money to the then governor's campaign (Neff, 2006).

Until 1997, there was no formal communication between the various commissions. A boxer could fight in one state and receive a health-threatening knockout, then fight the next day in another state. Boxing is filled with examples of fighters travelling from one state to the next if denied a licence to fight. For example, Ramon Zavala was listed as having fought in six states between 1989 to 1991. However, the six states' commission reports listed Zavala with different birthdays, social security numbers and residences; Eddie Flanning was knocked out in a fight in New York in 1982 and under New York rules was not allowed to fight again for 45 days. However, six days later, Flanning, under the name Raheem Tayib, fought in Charleston, South Carolina (Neiman, 2008).

However, even though some fighters are willing to use false documentation and names to 'earn' money, they are not alone in such forgery. Boxing Commissions have been embroiled in accusations of corruption after issuing fraudulent licences for fights. The Department of Labor in Oklahoma suggested that fraud and corruption in boxing was rife and went on to reveal that racketeering schemes, tax evasion, social security fraud, harbouring of fugitives and transportation of fugitives across state lines, 'bout-fixing' and false documentation were commonplace in boxing (McElroy, 1999).

This is probably possible because boxing commissions seem to 'work in isolation' rather than as a coherent national body protecting the integrity of the sport. This working in isolation has made them vulnerable to explotative sanctioning organisations looking to hold championship fights in compliant states.

Sanctioning organisations

Sanctioning organisations are national or international bodies that rank boxers and license championship and elimination bouts. These organisations do not regulate the sport of boxing in the USA; this is down to each state. There are many sanctioning organisations ranking fighters, which work independently of each other, competing to promote their 'champion' or contender. The ranking of fighters is important as it determines who can fight for a championship and which fights have the largest purses available, and confers champion status on the winning boxer who can then defend his title. These organisations are largely funded by a fee levied on the boxers in exchange for the opportunity to compete for a championship title.

There is no oversight of these organisations, and prior to 2000, they did not follow published, objective criteria in establishing rankings. The legitimacy of these ranking organisations is thus questionable. They have been criticised for basing ranking on financial 'agreements' rather than a boxer's ability or form, and several promoters have admitted bribing sanctioning organisations to raise the ranking of boxers contracted to them (Neiman, 2008).

Futhermore, there has been criticism of some promoters exerting 'control' over some sanctioning bodies by agreeing to have their most marketable boxers fight in bouts for a particular organisation in exchange for preferential rankings and treatment of a 'stable' of boxers under contract. This practice has many implications; it can lead to a mismatch between boxers, jeopardising their safety. For example, in 1982 in Las Vegas Duk Koo Kim, a 23-year-old Korean boxer, undefeated in 13 fights, challenged Ray 'Boom Boom' Mancini for the World Boxing Association (WBA) world lightweight championship belt. Kim had only fought once outside of Korea and all of his fights were against obscure, unknown opponents. However, he was designated the 'number one challenger' by the WBA, even though he was not even listed amongst Korea's top 40 boxers by the Korean Sports Foundation, which is the government's supervisory organisation. In contrast Mancini was a proven fighter. On 13 November 1982 the two fighters met at Caesar's Palace in Las Vegas, where Kim was counted out in the 14th round. Within minutes of the count, Kim was found comatose, and although he underwent brain surgery to remove a hemorrhage, he died five days later (Walsh, 1994).

The lack of a national regulatory organisation in the USA contributed to the fact that these mismatched boxers were allowed to fight.

Boxers can also have their rights and talents exploited by commissions and sanctioning organisations. For example, state commissions have sole responsibility for selecting officials for fights held in their state. Due to competition to hold fights, however, it has been suggested that sanctioning organisations and promoters influence the selection of judges and referees. A state boxing commisioner claimed he was willing to overlook criminal behaviour in order to ensure a fight occurred in (his state) and that the sanctioning organisation's referees be used instead of those authorised by the state (United States Congress, 1994).

Furthermore, sanctioning organisations often require that their own rules govern the fight rather than those endorsed by the state commissions. New York Boxing Commissioner Randy Gordon testified before the US Senate that he was approached by the WBA regarding a world lightweight championship and told that for the fight to go ahead the WBA's selection of judges had to be used (Neiman, 2008).

The competition to hold a fight is so considerable that some states are willing to pay 'site fees' for promoting attractive high-profile boxing matches. The most notable are Nevada and New Jersey, as both have legal gambling that attracts substantial revenue above and beyond the boxing match.

The sanctioning body also requires a champion to pay a fee every time they defend a title. It seems, then, that sanctioning bodies exist for the sole purpose of extracting as much money from boxers, managers, promoters and state commissions as possible. With such a disorganised 'structure' and no overarching body to protect the interests of boxing, these competing individuals and organisations appear to be willing to engage in fraud and corruption to secure an advantage by cheating in the ring, breaking contracts, accepting bribes and manipulating rankings. The types of fraud and corruption illustrated in this section show that all those involved in boxing are capable of and willing to commit acts of fraud and/or corruption. However, the way the sport of boxing is organised in the USA also lends itself to such corrupt behaviour.

Detecting, exposing and countering fraud and corruption in boxing: the evolution of federal regulation of boxing

There are many athletic state commissions in the USA; however, we mainly focus on the New York State Commission as it is one of the most well known and became the first state to make boxing legal.

New York State attempted to regulate boxing when it was first recognised as legitimate sport in 1911; it has a state athletic commission, as well as an advisory board. Rather than focus on all the regulatory roles that the New York State Commission has, we examine its attempts at dealing with acts of fraud and corruption and on controlling the illegal element in boxing.

New York State has made it a crime for a boxing contestant to be paid before a fight, and any licensed individual who participates in a sham or collusive fight will have their licence removed by the commission. The commission also has the right to withold payment if it has 'reasonable grounds' to suppose that an honest exhibition of boxing was not given. In addition the commision has the right to revoke the licence of anyone associated with bookmakers, convicted of a crime or who is associated or consorting with any person who has been convicted of a crime (Altschuler, 2002).

However, as illustrated throughout this chapter, having a commission and regulatory powers have a limited effect if sanctioning bodies can 'suggest' that certain referees and judges should be used for a boxing contest on pain of the bout being held elsewhere. Furthermore, rules appear all too often to actually be 'guidelines' which can be ignored depending on 'business relationships'. Apart from the responsibility to protect boxers (see the case of Aaron Pryor) it appears that state commissions are otherwise held to ransom if they wish to hold a boxing championship bout. Due to the federalised structure of the USA boxing system and the lack of any overarching body protecting the integrity of boxing this situation is probably inevitable. Since the states are in competition with one another to hold prestigious championship bouts, Federal regulation is needed, particularly in relation to criminal elements ruining the integrity of boxing.

The detection of fraud and corruption, regardless of the sport, is difficult. However, in boxing, which is open to abuse due to lack of regulation from a sporting body that has the integrity of the 'whole of the sport' rather than individual boxing bouts as its remit, the difficulty of detection is compounded by competing vested interests that are both national – state commissions – and international – sanctioning bodies. Given the examples seen in this chapter so far, it is hardly surprising that federal involvement in boxing finally took place; however, it *is* surprising that it took so long, particularly with the known influence of organised criminal elements in the sport.

The first federal intervention into professional boxing did not occur unitl the 1950s when the Department of Justice investigated organised crime within the sport. The US Supreme Court found that boxing utilised the channels of interstate commerce and therefore the sport was subject to anti-trust laws. These laws are primarily concerned with policing the channels of interstate commerce. The Supreme Court found that although a boxing match is a intrastate event, the revenues, endorsements, ticket sales and broadcasts were interstate and thus came under the anti-trust laws. The Senate Subcommitte on Antitrust and Monopoly conducted a four-year investigation of the effects of organised crime on boxing; however, before 1963 it was not illegal to bribe a contestant in a sporting contest!

Furthermore, promoters negotitated contracts and leased venues using such interstate commerce channels. For example, the Federal Bureau of Investigation (FBI) instituted an investigation with the Department of Justice into the International Boxing Club. The IBC was organised in 1949 for the purpose of promoting boxing, and for the following decade, with the assistance of organised crime, gained exclusive control of the best boxers of the 1950s, and of the best venues. The IBC was used as a shell corporation through which organised crime fixed fights and bribed boxing judges, whilst using the IBC as a front to also launder money and engage in gambling (Sammons, 1990). The FBI eventually managed to successfully prosecute the 'corporation' for acting as a shell for organised crime.

However, many years later the situation appeared to be little changed; on 8 February 1992, International Boxing Federation (IBF) middleweight champion James Toney fought an unknown challenger named Dave Tiberi in Atlantic City. The fight was of little significance in the boxing world and in 1992 there was little oversight or accountability demanded of sanctioning organisations. After 12 rounds of the fight, most thought that Tiberi had won, yet Toney was awarded a split decision by the judges. Senator Roth of Delaware – Tiberi's home state – ordered an investigation into practices surrounding the world of boxing. A subcommittee received testimony from 130 witnesses and made three important findings: private sanctioning organisations such as the WBC and the IBF operated with practically no oversight or accountability; the current state of the system of regulation was open to manipulation – for example, a fighter could fight in several states even though banned from fighting for life in other states for medical reasons, and credible evidence existed that organised crime was influential in the world of boxing (Walsh, 1994).

Evidence of widespread corruption was cited and it was found that boxers were being exploited by the Association of Boxing Commissioners (ABC), which was orignally formed in 1985 with executive directors from state boxing commissions to establish uniform state regulations for staging boxing matches.

As a result of the findings of the subcommittee the Professional Boxing Corporation Act (PBCA) was put forward; this proposed a self-funded national governmental body to set minimum standards for bouts, and a national registry system that would scrutinise fighters, managers, physicians and promoters.

The bill failed primarily because of the criticism that the federal government would have too much control over the sport of boxing. In response to this, in 1994 Senator John McCain introduced a competing bill which eventually became the Professional Boxing Safety Act (PBSA) in 1997. This required state commissions to share information about fights and fighters. However, no action was forthcoming, and so McCain reintroduced the bill in 1995; it then passed Congress and was signed by President Clinton in 1997. The PBSA also suggested:

- protection from coercive contracts between boxers and promoters
- a rationale for sanctioning organisations' fighter rankings, to be provided upon request
- mandatory disclosures by sanctioning organisations to state commissions
- all costs and payments to boxers related to a match, and all fees and benefits the promoter provides to the sanctioning organisation holding the match to be disclosed
- judges and referees to provide the boxing commission in the state where the match is held a statement of all the remuneration received for participating in a bout (Howard, 1997).

The provisions in the PBSA are enforcable by the US Attorney General and violation of the act can lead to a prison term or fine. However, the relationship between boxers, managers and promoters is little changed and was perhaps best summed up by a District Court Judge in New York in 1991:

> Prior to the development of common law courts, our ancestors hired fighting champions to resolve their legal disputes in trial by battle. Today, it is not unusual to find fighting champions hiring heavyweight legal counsel to resolve disputes in court over the lucrative rights to championship battles. (Foreman, 1996: 101)

The problem is that with so many powerful vested interests in the world of boxing, particularly in the USA, it appears that those tasked with regulating the sport of boxing have limited control of what is acceptable in its state, and thus the sanctioning bodies, which decide where a lucrative championship bout is held, are in fact able to control and/or influence the state commissions. What, then, can be done to protect the integrity of boxing, and if an 'event' occurs before, during or after the fight, which organisation is held accountable?

The following section on the prevention of *some* fraud and corruption is an attempt to answer some of the intractable issues of fraud and corruption that seem to be part of international professional boxing.

Preventing *some* fraud and corruption in boxing: improving contracts, developing a database of boxers and employing credible referees and judges

Boxing attracted much attention in the USA in 1977 when the American Broadcasting Company (ABC) joined Don King Productions to produce what is known as the US Boxing Championships. It was discovered that numerous fighters who particpated in sanctioned fights in this event had fabricated records. For example, Ike Fluellen had claimed two wins in Mexico, was ranked third in tournament rankings for his weight division and was given an honourable mention as the 'most improved boxer'; in truth he had not fought a single round that year. It is impossible, though, to know who fabricated the records.

However, as a result, the Subcommittee on Communications of the House Committee on Interstate and Foreign Commerce (1977) conducted oversight hearings into the scandal. However, no legislation was produced. Two years later, as a result of fears of organised criminal influence, the Subcommittee on Labor Standards of the House Committee on Education and Labor (1979) proposed a bill that would require all boxers to register with a federal agency and would regulate safety measures in the sport. The hearing took place in 1979, but again there was no action on the bill.

Three separate bills were introduced in 1983 in relation to boxing in the USA: one sought to attract interest from state commissoners, promoters, physicians and professional boxers in an advisory commission focusing on health issues and ranking guidelines; a second bill had the same aim but suggested a different composition of people on the advisory board; the third sought to create a commission within the Department of Labor that focused on compensation, working conditions and safety equipment; Congress took no action on any of the bills (Neiman, 2008).

Two more bills were then introduced in 1985 that sought to regulate boxing through the use of a non-profit body. These were designed to oversee state commissions by setting minimum standards for rules and regulations. A similar bill was introduced in 1987. Yet again, none were passed by Congress. The legislative process appears doomed to fail, and therefore it is perhaps down to the boxers, without whom the sport would not exist, to organise and protect their interests and those of boxing against the various other elements in the sport.

It has been suggested (Nieman, 2008) that if boxers were to form a union (similar to those in baseball, basketball and American football) they could influence the use of standardised contracts on a single fight-by-fight basis and prevent signing long-term contracts with a promoter. The latter contracts are open to corruption because they restrict a boxer to fighting only boxers the promoter and sanctioning body make money from. A committee was created to form a boxing union in 1999 with the purpose of giving all professional boxers the opportunity to receive and enjoy the benefits of collective bargaining; however, little progress has been made on this matter. Boxers could also combine to set a limitation on fees charged by managers to prevent exploitation.

It is also perhaps time to revisit Senator John McCain's suggestion of a United States Boxing Administration (USBA). This would have a centralised confidential database of boxers' medical information to be used by any state commission in making fight/bout decisions. The

USBA, would also and perhaps more importantly hold information on promoters, trainers, referees and judges and would have the power to license boxers, promoters, managers and also sanctioning bodies. The USBA would thus have the power to suspend or revoke the licence of any participant in the case of any violation. It was also suggested that referees and judges should receive mandatory training/education and be required to pass a test to show that they are competent; if found incompetent they should be removed or suspended from the USBA list.

Without the monetary power of certain interest groups, a majority of boxers might enjoy better health and better living standards. As it is, only a few earn vast sums of money, and a federally controlled boxing administration would be a logical step towards bringing in the necessary reform to end the exploitation of boxers, but also to rein in the corruption that appears, at least sometimes, endemic in the world of boxing.

Finally, the Muhammad Ali Boxing Reform Act 2000 sought to make changes that were not dealt with in the PBSA. It stipulated that fighters should be ranked according to objective measures of skill or form rather than by a sanctioning organisation that has been paid by a manager and/or promoter to push his fighter up the ranking system for a championship fight. A pension system is also suggested; currently boxing is the only major American sport that fails to provide health benefits or compensation if the boxer receives a life-threatening injury; in this sport, of course, the chances of this happening are substantial (Groschel, 2002).

Conclusion

In this chapter we have given a sample of the frauds and corrupt practices that plague the world of boxing. Unless some of the suggestions mentioned above are enacted, fraud and corruption will continue in the world of boxing. We are not suggesting that all fraud and corruption can be prevented, nor that legislation alone is the answer to reducing the incidence of fraud and corruption; we recognise that powerful vested interests in boxing want to maintain the present 'system' that works to their benefit.

It therefore falls to those most successful boxers to work against the exploitation of their fellow fighters. All boxers are vulnerable to fraud and corruption as both victims and transgressors, and many, if not most, need protection.

To protect all those involved in the sport, an overarching body, with the integrity of the sport rather than increasing commercial revenue as its focus, is needed if boxing is to progress beyond the manipulation of men, and now women, for the pleasure of spectators and the profit of promoters and regain its noble beginnings.

12
Overview and Final Reflections

In the Introduction we claimed that this book is a pioneer of the subject of the depth and range of fraud and corruption in sport and a contribution to debates in the sociology of sport. As we have illustrated, sporting institutions have appeared to either be unable to prevent most fraud and corruption, are involved in it, or simply ignore the problem. There are numerous articles explaining and highlighting the key elements of a counter-fraud strategy (Brooks et al., 2009, Button and Brooks, 2009, Button et al., 2012; Brooks and Button, 2012) in other academic 'disciplines', and these were referred to in this book, where relevant. There is also growing body of work (see Brooks et al., 2009; Button and Brooks, 2009), on fraud and corruption in the public and private sectors around the world; it has, however, yet to reach the world of sport to the same extent.

The focus of this book was to highlight the significant issues of corruption presently facing sport and the limitations of the bodies and individuals tasked with managing them. Key recurring issues in this book included: the use of illegal substances to increase performance; the fixing of matches or parts of them for financial gain; the investigation by sporting institutions of fraud and corruption; and the need for international legislation to counteract the power of unregulated sporting institutions.

The use of illegal substances in sport, as we have shown, is a complex matter. Athletes are often banned, if caught, for a period of time, and then return to the sport. Some of the sports we reviewed here that have a problem often compound the matter. Both the athletes and those tasked with 'running the sport', and sometimes the proprietors of teams, franchises or individuals, defend the use of illegal substances by either denying the sport has a problem or asserting that it is an invasion of personal privacy to test a sportsperson for illegal substances. In the USA, and in baseball in particular, for a real change to take place, players, administrators and owners need to work together for a testing policy to work (this is the case in any sport – see Chapter 4 on codes of ethics). At present, the process of testing is controlled by MLB and MLBPA. For baseball and basketball (as well as professional cycling, to name another sport not discussed in this book), we suggest an independent body is required; one that is under the control of an elected body funded by contributions from professional players, sporting institutions and owners of teams. Furthermore, random testing rather than prearranged 'appointments' is required. Finally, significant sanctions on highly paid players and team owners – rather than insignificant fines, which players and teams can easily afford – are well worth considering.

Many of the sports discussed in the book have a structural problem; that is, they are designed in a way that contributes to the corruption. These structural matters range from: organisational corruption (for example, vote-rigging and influence-peddling); selective myopia regarding the use of performance-enhancing substances, or a naive view that sport is 'clean'; a belief that if gambling is made illegal then the sport is free from its influence; and limited powers to 'police' a sport beyond breaches of a 'sporting code of conduct'. In relation to the last point, most sporting institutions condemn corruption, but in actuality turn out to be virtually powerless, with their actions resting more on persuasion rather than the imposition of serious sanctions on both those caught committing technically legal but corrupt acts and those engaged in criminal actions. Furthermore, powerful vested interests often oppose change that might encroach on their power and authority.

A high-profile criticism of sport rests on its association with gambling. This association, as we illustrated, is nothing new, and in the case of horse racing, the link is fundamental and the sport could not function without betting. However, the development of technology, and in particular online gambling sites, raises a new level of concern, especially in relation to issues of national sovereignty in the regulation of legal sports gambling (Humphreys, 2011). There is a need for an international legal agreement on issues of jurisdiction. We are aware that this is a major task, and that in some sports – the NCAA opposes all forms of legal gambling – this fails to deal with the problem; opposing all forms of gambling, the same as any prohibition, simply pushes the 'service' towards illegal gambling and organised crime.

Furthermore, due to the 'internationalisation of gambling', sporting institutions, law enforcement bodies and gambling organisations need to form a triumvirate to 'police' both legal and illegal gambling. Although this is difficult to achieve, it is also imperative. Sports fans enjoy the talent, flair and histrionics of players on a pitch, field, course or in the ring, but players gaining an unfair advantage for their team, *losing to win* and depriving fans of an honest contest under the influence of gambling pressures is, we argue, unacceptable to all.

Preventing match-fixing is the responsibility of all. However, the struggles of the anti-corruption units of many sports have shown how difficult it is to deal with the problem. The solution is not to accept the situation, but to assert that current practices and present systems in most sports need to be reviewed.

Sport is primarily self-regulated, with no democratic culture. As this book has shown, it has so far failed to prevent corruption at all levels, from sports institutions and organisations right down to individual 'sports stars', amateur athletes and officials. Examples of corruption at the organisational level are: personal demands made for accommodation and transportation; lifting or bending visa rules for executive members; and the willingness of host nations that want to hold a major sporting event to comply with these 'requests'. One way of reducing the power of heads of sporting institutions is to have a set period of time in office. As this change has to come from the 'inside', there is little hope of this happening as sporting institutions often refer to their sport as a 'family', which all too often comprises a network or 'republic of cousins' that 'manage[s] sport on a personal and informal basis' (Bures, 2008).

Institutional corruption, then, is a major problem for the world of sport. If bodies appear to be complicit in allowing corruption, by, for example, denying the sport has a problem when it is obvious, abusing positions of influence and committing outright acts of corruption (fraudulent ticket sales, selling of executive votes for personal gain, soliciting for gifts and 'donations'), the integrity of the sporting body is cast into doubt. Much of the fraud and corruption literature has illustrated that leadership is important in shaping the attitude to fraud and corruption within an organisation. For effective change to take place, however, an organisation must genuinely want to reduce and prevent the incidence of fraud and corruption, rather than engage in media soundbites and condemn 'gambling' as the sole problem facing its sport. As we have shown, the range and types of fraud and corruption are legion, and fraud relating to gambling – legal or illegal – is only one of them.

Part of a counter-fraud and corruption strategy, regardless of the sport, is to carry out an ongoing risk assessment of all those employed by the organisation/institution/clubs. As with every business, those on the 'inside' can and often commit fraud (Gill, 2005). Such 'internal' employees who are familiar with the organisation and its practices and methods of operation are often seduced by internal influences and a culture of corruption. As suggested elsewhere, vigilance should apply regarding risk assessment regardless of employees' contractual position, and it should be ongoing (Brooks et al., 2009).

An independent disclosure ('whistleblowing') process is also an important part of developing a culture of prevention and detection of potential frauds (Winfield 1994; Davidson, 2012) in sports. While we would expect a company to have some type of whistleblowing procedure in place where employees can raise their concerns, the reality is that whistleblowers' motives and integrity are often impugned by employers and professional colleagues (Nichols, 1991); they can also become the target of verbal abuse, demotion, termination of employment and even threats of physical harm and violence (Glazer and Glazer, 1989; Brooks, 2009).

As we also mentioned in this book, fraud and corruption can damage the commercial success of a sport. Confronted with the loss of integrity in a sport, commercial interests might seek new avenues for advertising and withdraw and/reduce sponsorship (Gorse and Chadwick, 2010). Any organisation that takes fraud and corruption seriously and has, or is in the process of developing, an anti-corruption strategy is to be commended. However, the development of such things as anti-fraud and corruption ethics committees is of limited value if there is no clear understanding of what fraud and corruption is. Sets of guidelines regarding risk, ethical behaviour, conduct, response plan(s) and anti-fraud and corruption policies alone are insufficient. A strategy needs direction and leadership, and codes of conduct need to be vigorously enforced if they are to have any chance of success. Furthermore, if those tasked with running the sport are corrupt, then the sport itself has little chance of preventing fraud and corruption. The important collective social, political and cultural role that sport plays in national and international life will then be damaged, and its integrity will be cast into doubt.

Final thoughts: sport, fraud and corruption

We began this book by suggesting that there is a wealth of literature on the sociology of sport in general. We also referred to a number of scholars who have helped expose the limits of research on fraud and corruption in sport; many of these have focused on specific sports.

We hope that we have demonstrated that there is a vast array of frauds and acts of corruption in sports that still require attention and produced a book that has attempted to navigate the complex world of fraud and corruption in sport beyond specific areas of interest. There is still much research to do on a variety of sports, and we think this is simply the start of new work in the field, drawing on a whole range of disciplines.

Bibliography

AAPPG (2006) *The Other Side of the Coin: The UK and Corruption in Africa, A Report by the Africa All Party Parliamentary Group (AAPPG)* (London: AAPPG).

Abrahams, R. I. (1998) *Legal Bases: Baseball and the Law* (Philadelphia: Temple University Press).

Adelman, M. L. (1990) *A Sporting Time: New York City and the Rise of Modern Athletics* (Urbana: University of Illinois Press).

American Gaming Associaation (2011) *Online Gambling Five Years After UIGEA* (Washington: AGA).

Agnew, P. (2007) *Forza Italia* (London: Random House).

Akindele, S. T. (2005) 'A Critical Analysis of Corruption and Its Problems in Nigeria', *Anthropologist*, vol. 7, no. 1, pp. 7–18.

Albrecht, S. W., K. R. Howe and M. Rommey (1984) *Deterring Fraud: The Internal Auditors' Perspective* (Altamonte Springs: Institute of Auditors Research Foundation).

Aleem, A., S. Wright and J. Wilson (2010) *Convergence – Addressing the Security Dilemma: Threats Report* (London: PWC).

Allison, L. (2005) *The Global Politics of Sport: The Role of Global Institutions in Sport* (Abingdon: Routledge).

Altier, C. (2006) 'Putting the Cart Before the Horse: Barriers to Enforcing a Code of Ethics For Thoroughbred Auctions in the United States', *Brooklyn Law Review*, vol. 72, no. 3, pp. 1061–1099.

Altschuler, D. (2002) 'On the Ropes: New Regulations and State Cooperation Step into the Ring to Protect Boxing from Itself', *Vanderbilt Journal of Entertainment Law & Practice*, vol. 4, no. 1, pp. 74–91.

Anderson, K., J. and D. A. Pierce. (2009) 'The Effect of Foul Differential on Subsequent Foul Calls in NCAA Basketball', *Journal of Sports Sciences*, vol. 27, no. 7, pp. 687–694.

Anderson, C. and Y. Tverdova (2003) 'Corruption, Political Allegiances, and Attitude towards Government in Contemporary Democracies', *American Journal of Political Sciences*, vol. 47, no. 1, pp. 91–109.

Andvig, J. C. (2006) 'Corruption and Fast Change', *World Development*, vol. 34, no. 2, pp. 324–340.

Antonioni, P. and J. Cubbin (2000) 'The Bosman Ruling and the Emergence of a Single Market in Soccer Talent', *European Journal of Law and Economics*, vol. 9, no. 2, pp. 157–173.

Arlidge, A. J. and J. Parry (1985) *Fraud* (London: Waterlow Publishers).

Arlidge, A., J. Parry and J. Gatt (1996) *Arlidge and Parry on Fraud* (London: Sweet and Maxwell).

Ashforth, D. (2003) *Ringer and Rascals: A Taste of Skulduggery* (Compton: Highdown).

Asinof, E. (1963) *Eight Men Out: The Black Sox and the 1919 World Series* (New York: Henry Holt and Company).
Atherton, M. (2011) 'Why the Sport Is Vulnerable when in a Fix', *The Times*, 2 November, p. 78.
Bakre, O. M. (2006) 'The Spoil of Oil: How Multinationals and Their Professional Advisors Drain Nigeria of Much Needed Resources', *Tax Justice Focus*, vol. 2, no. 3, pp. 4–5.
Bandes, A. I. (2003) 'Saddled with a Lame Horse? What State Consumer Protection Laws Can be the Best Protection for Duped Horse Purchasers?', *Boston College Law Review*, vol. 44, no. 3, pp. 78–83.
BBC (2010) 'Fake Togo Football Team at Bahrain Match To Be Investigated', at: www.bbc.co.uk/news/world-middle-east-11304208 (accessed 10 April 2012).
Bamfield, J. (1998) A Breach of Trust: Employee Collusion and Theft from Major Retailers', in M. Gill (ed.), *Crime at Work* (Leicester: Perpetuity Press), pp. 123–143.
Banks, S. (2002) *Going Down: Football in Crisis* (Edinburgh: Mainstream).
Barnett, J. and C. Kirchberg (2006) *Hoop Lore: A History of the National Basketball Association* (Jefferson: McFarland & Co Inc).
Barney, R. K., S. R. Wenn and S. G. Martyn (2002) *Selling the Five Rings. The International Olympic Committee and the Rise of Olympic Commercialism* (Salt Lake City: University of Utah Press).
Balsdon, E., L. Fong, and M. A. Fayer (2007) 'Corruption in College Basketball? Evidence of Tanking in Postseason Conference Tournaments', *Journal of Sports Economics*, vol. 8, no. 1, pp. 19–38.
Bennett, M. (2008) *Football Dynamo: Modern Russia and the People's Game* (London: Virgin Books).
Binder, J. and M. Findlay (2012) 'The Effects of the Bosman Ruling on National and Club Teams in Europe', *Journal of Sport Economics*, vol. 13, no. 2, pp. 107–129.
Birley, D. (1995) *Playing the Game* (Manchester: Manchester University Press).
Birley, D. (2003) *A Social History of English Cricket* (London: Aurum Press).
Board, J. (2011) 'In Praise of Whistleblowers', *Financial Times*, 14 March, p. 3.
Bosco, J. (1992) 'Taiwan Factions: Guanxi, Patronage, and the State in Local Politics', *Ethnology*, vol. 21, no. 2, pp. 157–184.
Bernhardt, D. and S. Heston (2009) 'Point Shaving in College Basketball: A Cautionary Tale for Forensic Economics', *Economic Inquiry*, vol. 48, no. 1, pp. 14–25.
Blaszczynski, A. and N. McConaghy (1994) 'Criminal Offences in Gamblers Anonymous and Hospital-treated Pathological Gamblers, *Journal of Gambling Studies*, vol. 10, no. 2, pp. 99–127.
Blitz, R. (2011) 'Fifa Clears Blatter of Approving Bribes to Voters', *Financial Times*, 30 May, p. 30.
Boisjoly, R. M. (1995) 'Commentary on "Technology and Civil Disobedience: Why Engineers Have a Special Duty to Obey the Law"', *Science and Engineering Ethics*, vol. 1, no. 2, pp. 169–171.

Bower, T. (2007) *Broken Dreams* (London: Simon and Schuster).

Bowman, D. and G. Gilligan (2007) 'Public Awareness of Corruption in Australia', *Journal of Financial Crime*, vol. 14, no. 4, pp. 438–452.

Box, S. (1983) *Power, Crime and Mystification* (London: Tavistock Press).

Braithwaite, J. (1985) 'White Collar Crime', *Annual Review of Sociology*, vol. 11, pp. 1–25.

British Horseracing Authority (2012a) Appeal Board decisions regarding the appeals of Maurice Sines, James Crickmore, Peter Gold, Nick Gold, Kirsty Milczarek, at: www.britishhorseracing.presscentre.com/Press-Releases/Appeal-Board-decisions-regarding-the-appeals-of-Maurice-Sines-James-Crickmore-Peter-Gold-Nick-Gold-and-Kirsty-Milczarek-299.aspx (accessed 21 April 2012).

British Horseracing Authority (2012b) Disciplinary Panel, at: www.britishhorseracing.com/inside_horseracing/about/whatwedo/disciplinary/disciplinary.asp?theDate=01/01/2012 (accessed April 2012).

British Horseracing Authority (2012c) Disciplinary Panel, at: www.britishhorseracing.com/inside_horseracing/about/whatwedo/disciplinary/disciplinary.asp?theDate=01/01/2012 (accessed April 2012).

British Horseracing Authority (2012d) Disciplinary Panel, at: www.britishhorseracing.com/inside_horseracing/about/whatwedo/disciplinary/disciplinary.asp?theDate=01/01/2012 (accessed April 2012).

Brooks, G. (2011) *Whistleblowing: Following a Procedure in the Internal Betrayal: A CIFAS Report on Beating the Growing Threat of Staff Fraud* (London: CIFAS), pp. 12–14.

Brooks, G. (2012a) 'Challenging the Myth of Urban Regeneration: Raising the Profile of Problem Gambling with a Media Campaign', *Journal of Gambling Issues*, vol. 28, no. 4, pp. 741–751; available online at: DOI 10.1007/s10899-011-92767.

Brooks, G. (2012b) 'Online Gambling and Money Laundering: Views from the Inside', *Journal of Money Laundering Control*. vol. 15, no. 4, pp. 304–315.

Brooks, G. and A. Aleem (2010) 'Cricket, Corruption and Gambling', *Spectrum: The UK's Fraud Prevention Service Newsletter*, October, pp. 16–17.

Brooks, G. and A. Blaszczynski (2011) 'Judicial Decisions on Cases Involving Problem Gambling and Crime in England and Wales', *International Gambling Studies*, vol. 11, no. 1, pp. 81–92.

Brooks, G. and M. Button (2012) 'The Police Commitment to Investigating Fraud: Is a Hybrid Solution the Way Forward?, *The Police Journal*, vol. 84, no. 4, pp. 305–320.

Brooks, G., M. Button and K. Frimpong (2009) 'Policing Fraud in the Private Sector: A Survey of the FTSE 100 Companies in the UK', *International Journal of Police Science and Management*, vol. 11, no. 4, pp. 493–504.

Brooks, G., J. Lee and H. Kim (2012) 'Match-fixing in Korean Football: Corruption in the K-League and the Importance of Maintaining Sporting Integrity', *International Journal of Contents*, vol. 8, no. 2, pp. 82–88.

Brown, D. and P. Kidd (2012) 'Westfield Had Global Glory in His Sights, but Opted for the Quick Fix', *The Times*, 13 January, pp. 82–83.

Brown, D. A., E. P. Moon and J. A. Robinson (1998) 'Taiwan's 1998 Local Elections', *Asian Survey*, vol. 38, no. 6, pp. 569–584.

Brubaker, B. (1993) 'Grand Jury, FBI Probe Don King; Boxing Promoter's Finances Is a Focus', *Washington Post*, 18 March.

Bukovansky, M. (2006) 'The Hollowness of Anti-corruption Discourse', *Review of International Political Economy*, vol. 13, no. 2, pp. 181–209.

Bulmer, M. (1982) *The Uses of Social Research: Social Investigation in Public Policy-making* (London: Allen and Unwin).

Bures, R. (2008) *Why Sport Is Not Immune to Corruption* (Czech Republic: Transparency International).

Button, M., L. Johnston and K. Frimpong (2008) 'The Fraud Review and the Policing of Fraud: Laying the Foundations for a Centralised Fraud Police or Counter Fraud Executive', *Policing*, vol. 2, no. 2, pp. 241–250.

Button, M. and G. Brooks (2009) '"Mind the Gap", Progress towards Developing Anti-fraud Culture Strategies in UK Central Government Bodies', *Financial Journal of Crime*, vol. 16, no. 3, pp. 229–244.

Button, M., J. Gee and G. Brooks (2012) 'Measuring the Cost of Fraud: An Opportunity for the New Competitive Advantage', *Journal of Financial Crime*, vol. 19, no. 1, pp. 65–75.

Cabot, A. and J. Kelly (2007) 'Internet, Casinos and Money Laundering', *Journal of Money Laundering Control*, vol. 2, no. 2, pp. 134–147.

Cadot, O. (1987) 'Corruption as a Gamble', *Journal of Public Economy*, vol. 33, no. 2, pp. 223–244.

Caplin, M. (1996) 'It Ain't Over 'til It's Over: The Century Long Conflict Between the Owners and the Players in Major League Baseball', *Albany Law Review*, vol. 60, pp. 205–238.

Carney, G. (2006) *Burying the Black Sox: How Baseball's Cover-Up of the 1919 World Series Fix Almost Succeeded* (Washington, DC: Potomac Books).

Cassidy, R. (2010) 'Gambling as Exchange: Horserace Betting in London', *International Gambling Studies*, vol. 10, no. 2, pp. 139–149.

Castells, M. (2002) *The Internet Galaxy: Reflections on the Internet, Business and Society* (Oxford: Oxford University Press).

Cavico, F., J. and B. G. Mujtaba (2010) 'Baksheesh or Bribe: Payments to Government Officials and the Foreign Corrupt Practices Act', *Journal of Business Studies Quarterly*, vol. 2, no. 1, pp. 83–105.

Chambers, D. (2009) *Race against Me* (Libros International).

Chan, J. (2003) 'Police and New Technologies', in Tim Newburn (ed.), *Handbook of Policing* (Cullompton: Willan), pp. 655–79.

Chinn, C. (1991) *Better Betting with a Decent Feller: A Social History of Bookmaking* (London: Harvester Wheatsheaf).

Christian Aid (2010) *Blowing the Whistle: Time's Up for Financial Secrecy* (London: Christian Aid).

Christensen, J. (2006) 'UK, US and Co Are Most Corrupt…Not African Nations Says British Economist', *Public Agenda*, 1 September.

Clarke, G. R. G. and Lixin Colin Xu (2004) 'Privatization, Competition, and Corruption: How Characteristics of Bribe Takers and Payers Affect Bribes to Utilities', *Journal of Public Economics*, vol. 88, no. 9–10, pp. 2067–2097.

Coffee, J. C. (2006) *Gatekeepers: The Role of the Professions in Corporate Governance* (Oxford: Oxford University Press).

Cohen, G. M. (1994) 'The Fault Lines in Contracts Damages', *Viginia Law Review*, vol. 80, pp. 1225–1349.

Coleman, J. W. (1999) 'Motivation and Opportunity: Understanding the Causes of White Collar Crime', in M. Levi (ed.), *Fraud: Organisation, Motivation and Control (Vol 1: The Extent and Causes of White Collar Crime)* (Aldershot: Ashgate).

Coleman, C. and J. Moynihan (1996) *Understanding Crime Data: Haunted by the Dark Figure* (Buckingham: Open University Press).

Condon, Sir Paul (2001) *Report on Corruption in International Cricket. Anti-Corruption Unit* (London: ICC).

Cook, C. (2008) 'Blockley and McKeown Banned for Corruption', *The Guardian*, 24 October, p.11.

Cook, C. (2010) 'Reeder Banned Twice by BHA for Corruption', *The Guardian*, 16 August, p. 9.

Cook, P. and G. Zarkin (1985) 'Crime and the Business Cycle', *Journal of Legal Studies*, vol. 14, no. 91, pp. 115–28.

Conn, D. (1997) *The Football Business: The Modern Football Classic* (London: Mainstream).

Connor, J. M. and J. Mazanov (2009) 'Would You Dope? A General Population Test of the Goldman Dilemma', *British Journal of Sports Medicine*, vol. 43, no. 11, pp. 871–872.

Cottrell, R. (2002) *Blackball, the Black Sox and the Babe: Baseball's Crucial 1920 Season* (Jefferson: McFarland & Company).

CNN (2012) 'Four Players Suspended in NFL Bounty Scandal', at: http://edition.cnn.com/2012/05/02/sport/football/nfl-saints-suspensions/index.html (accessed 20 May 2012).

Cressey, D. (1973) *Other People's Money* (Montclair: Patterson Smith).

Critcher, C. (1979) 'Football since the War', in J. Clarke, C. Critcher and R. Johnson (eds), *Working Class Culture: Studies in History and Theory* (London: Hutchinson).

Croall, H. (1992) *White Collar Crime* (Buckingham: Open University Press).

Croft, P. (2002) *Gambling and Criminal Behaviour: An Analysis of Local and District Court Files* (Sydney: Casino Community Benefit Fund).

Croft, P. (2003) 'Problem Gambling and Property Offences: An Analysis of Court Files', *International Gambling Studies*, vol. 3, no. 2, pp. 183–197.

Cronin, M. and D. Mayall (1998) *Sporting Nationalism: Identity, Ethnicity, Immigration and Assimilation* (London: Frank Cass Publishers).

Crowther, N. (2002) 'The Salt Lake City Scandals and the Ancient Olympic Games', *The International Journal of the History of Sport*, vol. 19, no. 4, pp. 169–178.

Davidson, A. (2012) 'The Olympus Whistleblower who Risks Losing Everything', *The Sunday Times*, 12 January, p. 7.

Decker, W. (1995) *Sport in Greek Antiquity: From the Minoan Tournament to the Olympic Games* (Munich: C. H. Beck).

Delves, A. (1981) 'Popular Recreation and Social Conflict in Derby, 1800–1850', in E. and S. Yeo (eds), *Popular Culture and Class Conflict 1590–1914: Explorations in the History of Labour and Leisure* (Brighton: Harvester).

Dennis, M. and J. Grix (2012) *Sport under Communism: Behind the East German Miracle* (Basingstoke: Palgrave Macmillan).

Department of Culture Media and Sport (2000) *Annual Report* (London: DCMS).

Department of Culture, Media and Sport (2002) *A Safe Bet For Success* (London: DCMS).

Department of Culture, Media and Sport (2005) *Gambling Act 2005* (London: DCMS).

Department of Culture, Media and Sport (2010) *The Parry Report* (London: DCMS).

Department of Justice (1977) *Fraud and Corrupt Payments Act* (Washington DC: DOJ).

Department of State Division of State Athletic Commission (1985) Alvarado v State, 488 New York Appeal Court, NYS, 2. 177 (New York: DOSSAC).

Derevensky, J. and R. Gupta (2004) *Gambling Problems in Youth: Theoretical and Applied Perspectives* (New York: Plenum Press).

Dietl, H. M. and E. Franck (2007) 'Governance Failure and Financial Crisis in German Football', *Journal of Sports Economics*, vol. 8, no. 6, pp. 662–669.

Dimeo, P. (2007) *A History of Drug Use in Sport 1876–1976: Beyond Good and Evil* (New York: Routledge).

Dixon, D. J. (1991) *From Prohibition to Regulation: Bookmaking, Anti-gambling, and the Law* (Oxford: Clarendon Press).

Dittenhofer, M. A. (1995) 'The Behavioural Aspects of Fraud and Embezzlement', *Public Money and Management*, vol. 15, no. 1, pp. 9–14.

Dobel, J. P. (1978) 'The Corruption of a State', *The American Political Science Review*, vol. 72, no. 3, pp. 958–973.

Dobson, S. and J. Goddard (2001) *The Economics of Football* (Cambridge: Cambridge University Press).

Dohley, R. (2000) *Want to Make a Bet? Gambling and Crime in Australasia*, Critical Issues in Policing Paper no. 4 (Adelaide: Australasia Centre for Policing Research).

Doig, A. (2006) *Fraud* (Cullumpton: Willan Publishing).

Doig, A., S. Johnson and M. Levi (2001) 'New Public Management, Old Populism and the Policing of Fraud', *Public Policy and Administration*, vol. 16, Spring, pp. 91–111.

Doig, A. and M. Levi (2009) 'Inter-agency Work and the UK Public Sector Investigation of Fraud, 1996–2006: Joined-up Rhetoric and Disjointed Reality', *Policing and Society*, vol. 19, no. 3, pp. 199–215.

Doig, A. and M. Macaulay (2008) 'Decades, Directions and the Fraud Review: Addressing the Future of Public Sector Fraud', *Public Money & Management*, vol. 20, no. 3, pp. 185–192.

Domazlicky, B., R. and P. M. Kerr (1990) 'Baseball Attendance and the Designated Hitter', *American Economist*, vol. 34, no. 1, pp. 62–68.

Donaghy T. (2009) *Personal Foul: A First Person Account of the Scandal That Rocked the NBA* (Sarasota: Four Daughters LLC).

Donnelly, L. (2011) 'NHS "own goal over sport gifts" ', *The Sunday Telegraph*, 6 March, p. 14.

Dow, C. (1998) *Major Recessions: Britain and the World, 1920–1995* (Oxford: Oxford University Press).

Duggan, M. and S. Levitt (2002) 'Winning Isn't Everything: Corruption in Sumo Wrestling', *American Economic Review*, vol. 92, no. 5, pp. 1594–1605.

DuBoff, L. D. (1977) 'Auction Problems: Going Going Gone', *Cleveland State Law Review*, vol. 26, pp. 499–513.

Duke, V. and L. Crolley (2001) 'Fútbol, Politicians and the People: Populism and Politics in Argentina', *The International Journal of the History of Sport*, 18, no. 3, pp. 93–117.

Dunning, E. (1999) *Sport Matters: Sociological Studies of Sport, Violence and Civilization* (London: Routledge).

Dunning, E. and K. Sheard (1979) *Barbarians, Gentlemen and Players: A Sociological Study of the Development of Rugby Football* (New York: New York University).

Durney, J. A. (1992) 'Fair or Foul, The Commissioner and MLB Disciplinary Process', *Emory Law Journal*, vol. 21, no. 3, pp. 581–623.

Egan, M. (2010) 'The Role of the Regulated Sector in the UK Anti-money-laundering Framework: Pushing the Boundaries of the Private Police', *Journal of Contemporary European Research*, vol. 6, no. 2, pp. 272–288.

Ellen, L. (2008) 'Football Agents: A Critique of the Football Association's New Regulation', *Sport and the Law Journal*, vol. 15, no. 3, pp. 8–26.

Ericson, R. (1981) 'Rules *for* Police Deviance', in C. Shearing (ed.), *Organizational Police Deviance* (Toronto: Butterworths), pp. 83–110.

Ericson, R. (2007) 'Rules in Policing: Five Perspectives', *Theoretical Criminology*, vol. 11, no. 3, pp. 367–401.

European Rugby Cup (2009) *Decision Disciplinary Committee* (Ireland: European Rugby Cup).

Evans, R. (2004) 'Horse Trading Scandal Puts Sport of Kings Back in Dock', *The Daily Telegraph*, 27 January.

Everett, J., D. Neu and A. S. Rahaman (2007) 'Accounting and the Global Fight against Corruption', *Accounting, Organisations and Society*, vol. 32, no. 6, pp. 513–542.

Figone, A. (1989) 'Gambling and College Basketball: the Scandal of 1951', *Journal of Sport History*, vol. 16, no. 1, pp. 44–61.

Financial Action Task Force (2009) *Strategic Surveillance Survey* (Paris: FATF/OECD).

Financial Action Task Force (2009) *Money Laundering Through the Football Sector* (Paris: FATF/OECD).

Financial Action Task Force (2011) *Laundering the Proceeds of Corruption* (Paris: FATF/OECD).

Finneran, S. R. (1996) 'Knowing Silence of Nonentreprenurial Information Is Not Sporting', *Albany Law Review*, vol. 59, pp. 511–514.

Firth, D. (1978) *The Golden Age of Cricket* (Guildford: Lutterworth Press).
Firth, D. (2003) *Bodyline Autopsy* (London: Aurum Press).
Fletcher, C. and D. Herrmann (2012) *The Internationalisation of Corruption* (Farnham: Gower).
Flick, U. (2010) *Qualitative Research* (London: Sage).
Foreman, I. (1996) 'Boxing in the Legal Arena', *Sports Law Journal*, vol. 3, no. 1, pp. 75–101.
Foot, J. (2007) *Calcio: a History of Italian Football* (London: Harper Perennial).
Football Association Inquiry (1995) *Hansard*: 253, pp. 827–834.
Football.co.uk (2012) 'Man Jailed over Carling Cup Ticket Scam', at: www.football.co.uk/cardiff_city/man_jailed_over_carling_cup_ticket_scam_rss2136437.shtml (accessed 10 April 2012).
Forrest D. and R. Simmons (2010) 'Sport and Gambling', *Oxford Review of Economic Policy*, vol. 19, no. 4, pp. 598–601.
Forster, J. (2006) 'Global Sports Organizations and Their Governance', *Corporate Governance*, vol. 6, no. 1, 72–83.
Forster, J. and N. Pope (2004) *The Political Economy of Global Sporting Organisations* (London: Routledge).
Fraud Review Team (2006a) *Final Report: A Consultation Response by the Office of Fair Trading* (London: OFT).
Fraud Review Team (2006b) *Final Report, The Legal Secretariat to the Law Officers* (London: OFT).
Freeman, S. (2000) *Own Goal! How Egoism and Greed Are Destroying Football* (London: Orion).
Frick, B. (2003) 'Contest Theory and Sport', *Oxford Review of Economic Policy*, vol. 19, no. 4, pp. 512–529.
Furnell, S. (2002) *Cybercrime: Vandalising the Information Society* (London: Addison-Wesley).
Gambling Commission (2011) *Betting Integrity Issues Paper: Inside Information and Fair Open Betting*, Department of Culture, Media and Sport (London: HMSO).
Gannon, R. and A. Doig (2010) 'Ducking the Answer? Fraud Strategies and Police Resources', *Policing and Society: An International Journal of Research and Policy*, vol. 20, no. 1, pp. 39–60.
Gardham, D. (2007) 'Kieron Fallon Attacks Police after Trial Collapse', *Daily Telegraph*, 7 December, at: www.telegraph.co.uk/news/1571787/Kieren-Fallon-attacks-police-after-trial-collapse.html (accessed 5 June 2012).
Gee, J., G. Brooks and M. Button (2012) *Fraud in Football; Research into How Well Football Protects Itself against Fraud* (London: PKF).
Gee, J., M. Button and P. Bassett (2010) *Fraud Loss Measurement: A Short Guide to the Methodology and Approach* (London: PKF).
Gee, J., M. Button and G. Brooks (2009) *The Financial Cost of Fraud: What Data from around the World Shows* (Milton Keynes: MacIntyre Hudson).
Gee, J., M. Button and G. Brooks (2010) *The Financial Cost of UK Public Sector Fraud: A Less Painful Way to Reduce Public Expenditure* (Milton Keynes: MacIntyre Hudson).

Gee, J., M. Button and G. Brooks (2011) *The Financial Cost of Healthcare Fraud: What Data from around the World Shows* (London: PKF).
Gee, J., M. Button and G. Brooks (2012) *The Financial Cost of Fraud 2011: What Data from around the World Shows* (London: PKF).
Gems, G. (2006) *The Athletic Crusade: Sport and American Cultural Imperialism* (Nebraska: University of Nebraska Press).
Giacopassi, D. and B. Stitt (1993) 'Assessing the Impact of Casino Gambling in Crime in Mississippi', *American Journal of Criminal Justice*, vol. 18, no. 1, pp. 117–131.
Gibbons, K. M. and D. C. Rowat (1976) *Political Corruption in Canada* (Toronto: McClelland and Steward).
Gibbs, J. (2007) *Point Shaving in the NBA: An Economic Analysis of the National Basketball Association's Point Spread Market*, mimeo, Stanford University.
Gill, M. (2005) *Learning from Fraudsters* (London: Provtiviti Group).
Gill, M. and J. Hart (1997) 'Exploring Investigative Policing', *British Journal of Criminology*, vol. 37, no. 4, pp. 549–567.
Gill, M. and J. E. Goldstraw-White (2010) 'Theft and Fraud by Employees', in F. Brookman, M. Magurie, H. Pierpoint and T. H. Bennett (eds), *Handbook of Crime* (Cullumpton: Willan Publishing).
Gillespie, K. and G. Okruhlik (1991) 'The Political Dimensions of Corruption Cleanups: A Framework for Analysis', *Comparative Politics*, vol. 24, no. 1, pp. 77–95.
Ginsburg, D. E. (1995) *Gambling and Game Fixing Scandals* (Jefferson: McFarland & Company).
Giulianotti, R. (1999) *Football: A Sociology of the Global Game* (Cambridge: Polity Press).
Giulianotti, R. and R. Robertson (2009) *Globalisation and Football* (London: Sage).
Glazer, M. P. and P. Glazer (1989) *The Whistleblowers* (New York: Basic Books). New York.
Gleaves, J. (2012) 'Enhancing the Odds: Horse Racing, Gambling and the First Anti-doping Movement in Sport 1899–1911', *Sport in History*, vol. 32, no. 1, pp. 1–27.
Gilovich, T., R. Vallone, and A. Tversky (1985) 'The Hot Hand in Basketball: On the Misconception of Random Sequences', *Cognitive Psychology*, vol. 17, no. 3, pp. 295–314.
Glynn, P., S. J. Kobrin and M. Naim (1997) 'The Globalisation of Corruption', in *Corruption and the Global Economy* (Washington DC: Institute for International Economics), pp. 7–27.
Golbert, J. and M. Punch. (2000) 'Whistleblowers, the Public Interest, and the Public Interest Disclosure Act 1998', *The Modern Law Review*, vol., 63, no. 1, pp. 25–54.
Gobert, J. and M. Punch (2007) 'Because They Can: Motivations and Intent of White Collar Criminals', in H. Pontell and G. Geis (eds), *International Handbook of White Collar Crime* (New York: Springer).

Goldsmith, M. (1991) 'Judicial Immunity for White-collar Crime: The Ironic Demise of Civil Rico', *Harvard Journal on Legislation,* vol. 93, Winter (Harvard: Cambridge Press).

Goldspink, R. and J. Cole. (2002) *International Commercial Fraud* (London: Sweet and Maxwell).

Goode, E. and N. Ben-Yehuda (1994) *Moral Panics: The Social Construction of Deviance* (Oxford: Blackwell).

Gorse, S. and S. Chadwick (2010) 'Conceptualising Corruption in Sport: Implications for Sponsorship Programmes', *The European Business Review*, July/August, pp. 40–45.

Gorse, S. and S. Chadwick (2012) *The Prevalence of Corruption in International Sport, A Statistical Analysis* (Coventry University: Centre for International Business of Sport).

Grabosky, P. (2001) 'Virtual Criminality: Old Wine in New Bottles?', *Social and Legal Studies*, vol. 10, no. 2, pp. 243–249.

de Graaf, G. (2007) 'Causes of Corruption: Towards a Contextual Theory of Corruption', *Public Administration Quarterly*, Spring, pp. 39–48.

Greenfield, S. and G. Osborn (2001) *Regulating Football: Commodification, Consumption and the Law* (London: Pluto).

Greer, D. L. (1983) 'Spectator Booing and the Home Advantage: A Study of Social Influence in the Basketball Arena', *Social Psychology Quarterly*, vol. 46, no. 3, pp. 252–261.

Griffiths, M. (1995) *Adolescent Gambling* (London: Routledge).

Griffiths, M. (1999) 'Gambling Technologies: Prospects for Problem Gambling', *Journal of Gambling Studies*, vol. 15, no. 3, pp. 265–283.

Gropman, D. (1979) *Say It Ain't So, Joe! The Story of Shoeless Joe Jackson* (Boston: Little, Brown and Company).

Groschel, C. E. (2012) 'Down for the Count: The Muhammad Ali Boxing Reform Act and Its Shortcomings, *Nova Law Review*, vol. 26, pp. 927–931.

Guardia de Finanza (2010) *Annual Report 2010*, at: www.gdf.gov.it/repository/ContentManagement/information/N614484291/Rapporto_Annuale_2010_Dati.pdf?download=1 (accessed 5 May 2012).

Guha, R. (2003) *A Corner of a Foreign Field: The Indian History of a British Sport* (London: Picador).

Guriev, S. (2004) 'Red Tape and Corruption', *Journal of Development Economics*, vol. 73, no. 2, pp. 489–504.

Guthrie-Shimizu, S. (2009) 'Architects of a Masquerade Peace: The United States and the 1936 Berlin Olympic Games', *The Japanese Journal of American Studies*, vol. 20, pp. 67–87.

Guttmann, A. (2004) *From Ritual to Record: The Nature of Modern Sports* (New York: Columbia Press).

Hamil, S., S. Morrow, C. Idle, R. Giambattista and S. Faccendini (2010) 'The Governance and Regulation of Italian Football', *Soccer and Society*, vol. 11, no. 4, pp. 373–413.

Hamil, S. and G. Walters (2010) 'Financial Performance in English Professional Football: an Inconvenient Truth', *Soccer and Society*, vol. 11, no. 4, pp. 354–372.

Handy, C. (1993) *Understanding Organisations* (London: Penguin).

Harbison, G. (1995) 'A Win by Split Decision', *Time Magazine*, 27 November, p. 35.

Hannigan, N. S. (2006) 'Blowing the Whistle on Healthcare Fraud: Should I?', *Journal of the American Academy of Nurse Practitioners*, vol. 18, no. 11, pp. 512–517.

Hard, M. (2010) 'Caught in the Net: Athletes' Rights and the World Anti-doping Agency', *Southern California Interdisciplinary Law Journal*, vol. 19, no. 3, p. 533.

Hart, A. J. (2010) 'Barry Bonds and the Baseball Hall of Fame: Is it in the Best Interest of Baseball?, *Southwestern Law Review*, vol. 40, pp. 175–198.

Harte, C. and B. Whimpress (2008) *A History of Australian Cricket* (London: Carlton Books).

Harvey, J. (2005) 'An Evaluation of Money Laundering Policies', *Journal of Money Laundering Control*, vol. 8, no. 4, pp. 339–345.

Haugen, K. K. (2004) 'The Performance-Enhancing Drug Game', *Journal of Sports Economics*, vol. 59, no. 1, pp. 67–86.

Hauser, T. (2003) *The View from Ringside: Inside the Tumultuous World of Boxing* (Wilmington: Sport Media Publishing).

Helies, H. N. (2009) 'Baseball's Growth Problem: Can Congress Require Major League Baseball to Test Its Athletes for Human Growth Hormone', *Arkansas Law Review*, vol. 62, pp 315–361.

Henning, P. J. (2001) 'Public Corruption: A Comparative Analysis of International Corruption Conventions and United States Laws', *Arizona Journal of International and Comparative Law*, vol. 18, no. 3, pp. 794–865.

Henry, H. (1992) ' "Them Dodgers Is My Gallant Knights": Fiction as History in "The Natural" ', *Journal of Sport History*, vol. 19, no. 2, pp. 110–129.

Henry, I. P. and P. C. Lee (2004) 'Governance and Ethics in Sport', in J. Beech and S. Chadwick (eds), *The Business of Sport Management* (Harlow: Pearson Education).

Henry, I. P., M. Amara, J. Liang and K. Uchiumi (2005) 'The Governance of Professional Soccer: Five Case Studies: Algeria, China, England, France, and Japan', *European Journal of Sports Sciences*, vol. 5, no. 4, pp. 189–206.

Hesch, J. D. (2007) 'Understanding the Original Source Exception to the False Claims Act's Public Disclosure Bar in Light of the Supreme Court's Ruling in Rockwell v. United States', *DePaul Business & Commercial Law Journal*, vol. 7, no. 1, pp. 1–34.

Hill, D. (2008) *The Fix: Soccer and Organised Crime* (Toronto: McClelland and Stewart).

Hill, D. (2009) 'How Gambling Corruptors Fix Football Matches', *European Sport Management Quarterly*, vol. 9, no. 4, pp. 411–432.

Hill, D. (2010) 'Strategies of Corruption: How Corrupt Football Players and Referees Perform Fixed Matches', in Martin Kreutner (ed.), *Practice Meets*

Science: Contemporary Anti-Corruption Dialogue, papers presented at the International Anti-Corruption Summer School, Hernstein, Austria, 2009.

Hoberman, J. (2001) *Mortal Engines: The Science of Performance and the Dehumanization of Sport* (Caldwell: Blackburn Press).

Hobson, R. (2012) 'Players Urged to Come Clean in Campaign to Beat Cheats', *The Times*, 13 January, p. 92.

Hood, S. J. (1996) 'Political Change in Taiwan: The Rise of Kuomintang Factions', *Asian Survey*, vol. 36, no. 5, pp. 468–482.

Hodess, R. (2004) 'Introduction', in R. Hodees, T. Inowlocki, D. Rodriguez and T. Wolfe (eds), *Transparency International Global Corruption Report* (London: Pluto Press).

Holdaway, S. (1983) *Inside the British Police: A Force at Work* (Oxford: Blackwell).

Holdaway, S. (1994) 'Academic Whistleblowing on the Beat: The Policeman's Lot', in G. Vinten (ed.), *Whistleblowing, Subversion or Corporate Citizenship?* (London: Paul Chapman).

Hollinger R. and J. P. Clark (1983) *Thefts by Employees* (Lexington: Lexington Books).

Holt, R. (1989) *Sport and the British: A Modern History* (New York: Clarendon Press).

Home Office (2000) *Terrorism Act 2000* (London: HMSO).

Home Office (2006) *The Fraud Act 2006* (London: HMSO).

Home Office (2007) *Money Laundering Regulations* (London: HMSO).

Home Office (2006) *The Fraud Act 2006* (London: HMSO).

Home Office (2011) *The Bribery Act* (London: HMSO).

Hope, K. (2011) 'Suspects Named as Match-fixing Scandal Rocks Greek Football', *Financial Times*, 25 June, p. 2.

Horne, J., A. Tomlinson and G. Whannel (1999) *Understanding Sport: An Introduction to the Sociological and Cultural Analysis of Sport* (London: Routledge).

Horne, J., A. Tomlinson, G. Whannel and K. Woodward (2012) *Understanding Sport: A Social Cultural Analysis* (Abingdon: Routledge).

Horning, D. (1970) 'Blue Collar Theft: Conceptions of Property, Attitudes towards Pilfering; Work Group Norms in a Modern Industrial Plant', in E. D. Smigel and H. L Ross (eds), *Crimes against Bureaucracy* (New York: Van Nostrand Reinhold Company).

Hornle, J. and B. Zammit (2010) *Cross-border Online Gambling Law and Policy* (Cheltenham: Edward Elgar).

Howard, K. C. (1997) 'Regulating the Sport of Boxing – Congress Throws the First Punch with Professional Boxing Safety Act', *Seton Hall Journal of Sport Law*, vol. 7, pp. 103–127.

Hugel, P. and J. Kelly (2002) 'Internet Gambling, Credit Cards and Money Laundering', *Journal of Money Laundering Control*, vol. 6, no. 1, pp. 57–65.

Huggins, M. (2003) *Horseracing and the British 1991–1939* (Manchester: Manchester University Press).

Hughes, S. (2010) *And God Created Cricket* (London: Black Swan, Random House).

Humphreys, B. R. (2011) 'Online Sports Betting and International Relations', *SAIS Review*, Winter–Spring, pp. 103–115.

Hums, M. and J. MacLean (2004) *Governance and Policy in Sport Organizations* (Scottsdale: Holcomb Hathaway).

Hung, T. F. (1989) 'Grassroots Organizers', *Free China Review*, vol. 39, no. 12, pp. 24–29.

Huntingdon, S. P. (1968) *Modernisation and Corruption: Political Order in Changing Societies* (New Haven: Yale University Press).

Huntingdon, S. P. (1989) 'Modernisation and Corruption', in A. J. Heidenheimer, M. Johnston and V. T. Levien (eds), *Political Corruption: A Handbook* (New Brunswick: Transaction Publishers).

Hyo-Sik, L. (2011) 'Key Figures Indicted in Game-fixing Scam', *The Korea Times*, 10 June, p. 3.

ICC (2011) *ICC Anti-Corruption Code for Players and Player Support Personnel* (Dubai: International Cricket Council).

Improper Payments Elimination and Recovery Act (2012) *Background, Implementation, and Assessment* (Washington, DC: Congressional Research Service).

Improper Payments Information Act (2002) *A Brief Introduction* (Washington, DC: CRS Report for Congress).

International Cricket Council (2001) *Report on Corruption in International Cricket 2001* (London: International Cricket Council).

Ingles, G. (2007) *'The Foreign Legion' in Football Money League 2007* (Manchester: Deloitte).

Inglis, S. (1985) *Soccer in the Dock: A History of British Football Scandals 1900 to 1965* (London: Willow).

Issac, N. (1984) *All the Moves – a History of College Basketball* (New York: Harper).

Iyer, N. and M. Samociuk (2006) *Fraud and Corruption: Prevention and Detection* (Aldershot: Gower).

Jar, M. (2006) *Cybercrime and Society* (London: Sage).

Jenkins, R. (2010) 'Rugby Scandal Doctor Saves Her Career', *The Times*, 1 September, p. 3.

Jennings, A. (1996) *The New Lord of the Rings* (London: Pocket Books).

Jennings, A. (2007) *Foul! The Secret World of FIFA: Bribes, Vote Rigging and Ticket Scandals* (London: HarperCollins).

Jennings, A. and C. Sambrook (2000) *The Great Olympic Swindle* (London: Simon and Schuster).

Jeswald, W. S. (1999) 'Law and Power in Agency Relationships', in Robert H. Mnookin and Lawrence E. Susskind (eds), *Negotiating on Behalf of Others: Advice to Lawyers, Business Executives, Sports Agents, Diplomats, Politicians and Everybody Else* (Thousand Oaks: Sage Publications).

John, T. and M. McGuire (2003) *The National Intelligence Model: Key Lessons from Early Research* (London: Home Office).

Johnson, V. R. (2005) *Cybersecurity, Identity Theft, and the Limits of Tort Liability* (Berkeley: Bepress Legal Series, Berkeley Electronic Press).

Johnson, R. A. (2003) *Whistleblowing: When It Works – and Why* (Boulder: Lynne Rienner).

Jones, M. (2010) *On the Right Track: From Olympic Downfall to Finding Forgiveness and the Strength to Overcome and Succeed* (Washington: Howard Books).

Jones, T. (2007) *The Dark Heart of Italy* (London: Faber & Faber).

Junwei, Yu (2007) *Playing in Isolation: A History of Baseball in Taiwan* (Norman: University of Nebraska).

Jupp, V. (1989) *Methods of Criminological Research* (New York: Unwin Taylor).

Kapardis, A. and M. Krambia-Kapardis (2004) 'Enhancing Fraud Prevention and Detection by Profiling Fraud Offenders', *Journal of Criminal Behaviour and Mental Health*, vol. 14, no. 3, pp. 189–201.

Kau, M. Y. M. (1996) 'The Power Structure in Taiwan's Political Economy', *Asian Survey*, vol. 36, no. 3, pp. 287–305.

Khan, M. H. (2002) 'Corruption and Governance in Early Capitalism: World Bank Strategies and Their Limitations', in J. Pincus and J. Winters (eds), *Reinventing the World Bank* (Ithaca: Cornell University Press).

Kidd, P. and R. Broadbent (2012) 'BOA Defiant after Court Lifts Games Ban on Chambers', *The Times*, 1 May, p. 54.

King Commission (2000) *Commission of Inquiry into Cricket Match Fixing and Related Matters* (Cape Town: UCB).

Klitgaard, R. (1988) *Controlling Corruption* (Berkeley: University of California Press).

Kluka, D., G. Schilling and W. F. Stier (2004) *Sport Governance* (Oxford: Meyer & Meyer Sport).

Kochan, N. and R. Goodyear (2010) *Corruption: The New Corporate Challenge* (Basingstoke: Palgrave Macmillan).

Korean Herald (2010) 'Clemens Indicted', *Korean Herald*, 21–22 August, p. 16.

Korean Herald (2011) 'Prosecutors Indict Key Figures in Football Match Fixing Furore', *Korean Herald*, 10 June, p. 20.

Korean Times (2011a) 'NBA Labor Deal Proposes Off-season Drug Tests', *Korean Times*, 9 December, p. 24.

Korean Times (2011b) 'Probe Begins over German Football License Corruptions', *Korean Times*, 16 December, p. 23.

Knoop, T. (2004) *Recessions and Depressions: Understanding Business Cycles* (Westport: Praeger).

KPMG (2004) *KPMG Forensic Fraud Survey*, KPMG Australia.

KPMG (2008) *Anti-Bribery and Anti-Corruption Survey*, KPMG Australia.

KPMG (2009) *KPMG Forensic Fraud Barometer*, KPMG Australia.

Kuo, C. T. (2000) 'Taiwan's Distorted Democracy in Comparative Perspective', *African and Asia Studies*, vol. 35, no. 1, pp. 85–111.

La Motta, J. (1997) *Raging Bull* (Lewes, DE: De Capo Press).

Lavelle, L. (1995) 'From the Diamonds to the Courts: Major League Baseball v the Commissioner', *North Carolina Central Law Journal*, vol. 21, pp. 97–121.

Lazaroff, D. E. (1990) *Torts and Sports: Participant Liability to Co-participants for Injuries Sustained During Competition* (Coral Gables: Entertainment and Sports Society of the University of Miami School of Law).

Leahy, J. and K. Fontanella-Khan (2010) 'Indian Cricket Scandals Out Investors on Sticky Wicket', *Financial Times*, 27 November, p. 9.

Lee, H. S. (2011) 'Key Figures Indicted in Game-fixing Scam', *Korean Times*, 10 June, p. 3.

Leitzel, J. (2008) *Regulating Vice: Misguided Prohibitions and Realistic Controls* (Chicago: Cambridge University Press).

Leff, N. H. (1970) 'Economic Development through Bureaucratic Development', in A. J. Heidenheimer (ed.), *Political Corruption: Readings in Comparative Analysis* (New Brunswick: Transaction Publishers).

Lehman, D. R. and A. Reifman (1987) 'Spectator Influence on Basketball Officiating', *Journal of Social Psychology*, vol. 127, no. 6, pp. 673–675.

Lewis, M. (2004) *Moneyball: The Art of Winning an Unfair Game* (New York: W. W. Norton and Company).

Levi, M. (1987) *Regulating Fraud* (London: Tavistock Publications).

Levi, M. (1988) *Prevention of Fraud*, Crime Prevention Unit Paper 17 (London: HMSO).

Levi, M. (1999) *Fraud: Organisation, Motivation and Control*, Vols 1 and 11 (Aldershot: Dartmouth).

Levi, M. (2002) 'Money Laundering and Its Regulation', *American Academy of Political Science*, vol. 582, no. 1, pp. 181–194.

Levi, M. (2008) *The Phantom Capitalist: the Organisation and Control of Long-firm Fraud*, 2nd edition (Aldershot: Ashgate).

Levi, M., J. Burrows, H. Fleming and M. Hopkins (2007) *The Nature, Extent and Economic Impact of Fraud in the UK* (London: ACPO).

Long, M. (2003) 'Leadership and Performance Management', in T. Newburn (ed.), *Handbook of Policing* (Cullompton: Willan Publishing), pp. 628–644.

Lord, R. (2010) 'Indian Cricket Works Over Its Teams', *The Wall Street Journal*, 22–24 October, p. 10.

Loveday, B. (1999) 'The Impact of Performance Culture on Criminal Justice Agencies in England and Wales', *International Journal of Sociology of the Law*, vol. 27, no. 4, pp. 140–160.

Loveday, B. (2007) 'Re-engineering the Police Organisation: Implementing Workforce Modernisation in England and Wales, *Police Journal*, vol. 80, no. 1, pp. 3–27.

Macaloon, J. J. (2007) *Muscular Christianity and the Colonial and Post-Colonial World* (London: Routledge).

Maennig, W. (2005) 'Corruption in International Sports and Sport Management: Forms, Tendencies, Extent and Circumstances', *European Sport Management Quarterly*, vol. 5, no. 2, pp. 187–225.

Martindate, J. and C. Lehr (1997) 'Two Strikes: A History and Analysis of Major League Baseball, Its Anti-trust Exemption, and Reserve Clause', *Journal of Legal Aspects of Sport*, vol. 3, pp. 174–180.

Maesschalck, J. and Y. Vanden Auweele (2010) 'Integrity Management in Sport', *Journal of Community and Health Sciences*, vol. 5, no. 1, pp. 1–9.

Maguire, M., (2007) 'Crime Data and Statistics', in M. Maguire, R. Morgan and R. Reiner (eds), *The Oxford Handbook of Criminology* (Oxford: Oxford University Press), pp. 241–302.

Mahmood, M. (2011) 'How I Broke the Cricket Scandal', *The Sunday Times*, 6 November, p. 21.

Mahmood, M. (2012) 'Bollywood Honeytrap Seduces Cricket Stars into Match-fixing', *The Sunday Times*, 11 March, pp. 14–15.

Majumdar, B. (2006) *Lost Histories of Indian Cricket: Battles off the Pitch* (London: Andre Deutsch).

Majumdar, B. and N. Mehta (2010) *Sellotape Legacy: Delhi and the Commonwealth Games* (Delhi: HarperCollins).

Malcolm, D. (2012) *Globalizing Cricket: Codification, Colonization and Contemporary Identities* (London: Bloomsbury Academic).

Manfred, R. D. (2008) 'Federal Labour Laws to Achieving a Completely Independent Drug Program in Major League Baseball', *Marquette Sports Law Review*, vol. 19, no. 1.

Mars, G. (1982) *Cheats at Work: Anthropology of Workplace Crime* (London: Allen and Unwin).

Mars, G. (1984) *Cheats at Work: Anthropology of Workplace Crime*, second edition (London: Allen and Unwin)

Mars, G. (2001) *Occupational Crime* (Dartmouth: Ashgate).

Mason, A. (1980) *Association Football and English Society, 1863–1915* (Brighton: Harvester).

Mason, A. (1989) *Sport in Britain – A Social History* (Cambridge: Cambridge University Press).

Matza, D. (1964) *Delinquency and Drift* (New York: Wiley).

Mbatu, J. M. (1991) 'Military Expenditures and Bureaucratic Competition for Rents', *Public Choice*, vol. 71, no. 2, pp. 19–31.

Mbaku, J. (1996) 'Bureaucratic Corruption in Africa: The Futility of Cleanups', *Cato Journal*, vol. 16. no 1, pp. 99–118.

McCarthy, M. (2007) 'Point-shaving Remains a Concern in College Athletics', *USA Today*, 9 May (Sports Section) at: http://usatoday30.usatoday.com/printedition/sports/20070509/c1scov09.art.htm (accessed 7 June 2011).

McDonald, S. and K. Ahern (2002) 'Physical and Emotional Effects of Whistleblowing', *Journal of Psychosocial Nursing and Mental Health Services*, vol. 40, no. 1, pp. 14–27.

McGuire, J. (2012) *Reflection on Process Sociology and Sport* (Abingdon: Routledge).

McElroy, S. J. (1999) 'Current and Proposed Federal Regulation of Professional Boxing', *Seton Hall Journal of Sport Law*, vol. 9, pp. 463–519.

McMullan, M. (1961) 'A Theory of Corruption: Based on a Consideration of Corruption in the Public Services and Governments of British Colonies and Ex-colonies in West Africa', *Sociological Review*, vol. 9, no. 2, pp. 181–201.

McMullan, J. L. and D. Perrier (2007) 'The Security of Gambling and Gambling with Security: A Rejoinder', *International Gambling Studies*, vol. 7, no. 3, pp. 377–382.

Méndez, F. and F. Sepúlveda (2009) 'What Do We Talk About When We Talk About Corruption?, *Journal of Law, Economics and Organization,* vol. 26, no. 3, pp. 493–514.

Miah, A. (2004) *Genetically Modified Athletes: Biomedical Ethics, Gene Doping and Sport* (London: Routledge).

Michie, J. (2000) 'The Governance and Regulation of Professional Football', *The Political Quarterly,* vol. 71, no. 2, pp. 184–191.

Michie, J. and C. Oughton (2005) 'The Corporate Governance of Professional Football Clubs in England', *Corporate Governance. An International Review,* vol. 13, no. 4, 517–531.

Miers, D. (2004) *Regulating Commercial Gambling, Past, Present and Future* (Oxford: Oxford University Press).

Millar, R. S. (1986) 'American Singing: The Role of Custom and Usage in the Thoroughbred Horse Business', *Kentucky Law Journal,* vol. 74, pp. 781–788.

Millward, P. (2011) *The Global Football League: Transnational Networks, Social Movements and Sport in the New Media Age* (Basingstoke: Palgrave Macmillan).

Mitchell Report (2007) *Report to the Commissioner of Baseball of an Independent Investigation into the Illegal Use of Steroids and Other Performance Enhancing Substances by Players in Major League Baseball,* George J. Mitchell, Office of the Commissioner of Baseball, 13 December. Available at: http://files.mlb.com/mitchrpt.pdf (accessed 16 March 2013).

Mitsilegas, V. and B. Gilmore (2007) 'The EU Legislative Framework against Money Laundering and Terrorist Finance: A Critical Analysis in Light of Evolving Global Standards', *International and Comparative Law Quarterly,* vol. 56, no. 1, pp. 119–140.

Morgan, W. J. (2006) 'Fair Is Fair, Or Is It? A Moral Consideration of the Doping Wars in American Sport, *Sport in Society,* vol. 9, no. 2, pp. 177–198.

Morris, A. D. (2011) *Colonial Project: National Game: A History of Baseball in Taiwan* (Berkeley: University of California Press).

Mostrous, A. (2011) 'NHS Trust Gag Doctors to Conceal Safety Fears', *The Times,* 12 November, p. 11.

Munting, R. (1997) *An Economic and Social History of Gambling* (Manchester: Manchester University Press).

Nas, T. F., A. C. Price and C. T. Weber (1986) 'A Policy-oriented Theory of Corruption', *American Political Science Review,* vol. 80, no. 1, pp. 107–119.

Nathan, D. A. (2003) *Saying It's So: A Cultural History of the Black Sox Scandal* (Chicago: University of Illinois Press).

Nathanson, M. (2008) *Major League Baseball as Enron: The True Meaning of the Mitchell Report, Outside the Lines* (Arizona: SABR Business of Baseball Committee).

National Fraud Authority (2010) *Annual Fraud Indicator* (London: NFA).

National Gambling Impact Study Commission Report (1999) *National Gambling Impact Study Commission Report* (Washington DC: NGISC).

Near, J. and M. Miceli (1985) 'Organizational Dissidence: The Case of Whistle-Blowing', *Journal of Business Ethics,* vol. 4, no. 1, pp. 1–16.

Neff, E. (2006) 'Fight Doctors', *Las Vegas Review Journal,* 5 January, p. 7.

Neiman, M. (2008) 'Protecting Profesional Boxers: Federal Regulation with More Punch', *Sports Law Journal*, vol. 15, pp. 60–85.

Nelson, M. (2009) *The National Basketball League: A History, 1935–1949* (Jefferson: McFarland and Company).

Newfield, J. (2003) *The Life and Crimes of Don King: The Shame of Boxing in America* (New York: Harbour Press).

Newman, G. and R. Clarke (2003) *Superhighway Robbery: Preventing e-commerce Crime* (Cullompton: Willan Press).

Nisbet, J. (2011) 'Fenerbahce Furious over Champions League Ban', *The Independent*, 26 August, p. 70.

Norridge, J. (2008) *Can We Have Our Balls Back, Please? How the British Invented Sport* (London: Allen Lane).

Nye, J. S. (1967) 'Corruption and Political Development: A Cost–Benefit Analysis', *American Political Science Review*, vol. 56, no. 2, pp. 417–427.

Nye, J. S. (1970) 'Corruption and Political Development: Cost–Benefit Analysis', in A. J. Heidenheimer (ed.), *Political Corruption: Readings in Comparative Analysis* (New Brunswick: Transaction Publishers).

O'Connor, A. (2010) 'Fifa Executive Committee Pair Banned after Investigation into Corruption', *The Times*, 19 November, p. 14.

OECD (1997) *OECD Convention on Combating Bribery of Foreign Public Officials in International Business Transactions, Directorate for Financial and Enterprise Affairs* (Paris: OECD).

Ok, G. (2006) *The Transformation of Modern Korean Sport: Imperialism, Nationalism and Globalisation* (Korea: Hollym Corp Publishers).

Orford, J. (2001) *Excessive Appetites Psychological View of Addictions*, second edition (Chichester: John Wiley).

Orford, J. (2003) *Gambling and Problem Gambling in Great Britain* (Hove: Brunner-Routledge).

Orford, J., M. Griffiths, H. Wardle, K. Sproston and B. Erens (2009) 'Negative Public Attitudes toward Gambling: Findings from the 2007 British Gambling Prevalence Survey Using a New Attitude Scale', *International Gambling Studies*, vol. 9, no. 1, 9–54.

Ormerod, D. (2007) 'Criminalising Lying', *Criminal Law Review*, March, pp. 193–219.

Ormerod, D. and D. H. William (2005) 'Introduction', in A. Brown, L. Dobbs, A. Doig, G. Owen and G. Summers (eds), *Fraud: Law and Practice and Procedure* (London: LexisNexis).

Otusanya, O. J. (2011) 'Corruption as an Obstacle to Development in Developing Countries: A Review of the Literature', *Journal of Money Laundering Control*, vol. 14, no. 4, 387–422.

Parsons, C. A., J. Sulaeman, M. Yates and D. S. Hamermesh. (2007) *Strike Three: Umpires' Demand for Discrimination*, Research Paper Series: Discussion Paper No. 3899 (Bonn: Institute for the Study of Labor [IZA]).

Pawar, A. (2011) *Consolidated Financial Statements 31 December 2010: Independent Auditors report to the Members of the International Cricket Council by Ernst and Young*, available online at: http://static.icc-cricket.com/ugc/documents/DOC_1BB823FE870FF9DD74B088EDB22E3D49_1303051786243_116.pdf.

Pedowitz, L. (2008) *Report to the Board of Governors of the National Basketball Association* (New York: Wachtell, Lipton, Rosen and Katz).

Pfanner, E. (2011) 'Corruption Scars the Playing Fields of Europe', *International Herald Tribune*, 8–9 January, p. 16.

Philips, D. and A. Tomlinson (1992) 'Homeward Bound: Leisure, Popular Culture and Consumer Capitalism', in D. Strinati and S. Wagg (eds), *Come on Down? Popular Media Culture in Post War Britain* (London: Routledge).

PKF (2010) *Annual Survey of Football Clubs Finance Directors Report* (London: PKF).

PKF (2011) *The Annual Survey of Football Club Finance Directors 2010* (London: PKF).

Pomeranz, F. (1995) 'Fraud: the Root Causes', *Public Money and Management*, January–March, pp. 15–18.

Pound, D. (2004) *Inside the Olympics: A Behind the Scenes Look at the Politics, the Scandals, and the Glory of the Games* (Toronto: John Wiley and Sons).

Preston, I. and S. Szymanski. (2003) 'Cheating in Contests', *Oxford Review of Economic Policy*, vol. 19, no. 4, pp. 612–624.

Price, J., M. Remer and D. F. Stone (2012) 'Sub-Perfect Game: Profitable Biases of NBA Referees', *Journal of Economics and Management Strategy*, vol. 21, no. 1, pp. 210–300.

Price, J. and J. Wolfers (2007) *Racial Discrimination among NBA Referees*, Working Paper 13206 (Cambridge, MA: National Bureau of Economic Research).

Punch, M. (1985) *Conduct Unbecoming* (London: Tavistock Publications).

Punch, M. (2000) 'Police Corruption and Its Prevention', *European Journal of Criminal Policy and Research*, vol. 8, no. 3, pp. 301–324.

Qayyum Commission (2000) *Qayyum Report* (Lahore: Pakistan Cricket Board).

Radford, B. (2011) *Caught Out: Shocking Revelations of Corruption in International Cricket* (London: John Blake).

Reaves, J. A. (2002) *Taking in a Game: A History of Baseball in Asia* (Lincoln: University of Nebraska Press).

Reid, J. (1995) *A Licence to Print Money: A Journey through the Gambling and Bookmaking World* (Edinburgh: Mainstream).

Remote Gambling Association (2010) *Sports Betting: Legal, Commercial and Integrity Issues* (London: RGA).

Reith, G. (2002) *The Age of Chance: Gambling and Western Culture* (London: Routledge).

Riess, S. (1984) *The American Sporting Experience* (West Point: Leisure Press).

Riordan, J. and A. Kruger (1999) *The International Politics of Sport in the 20th Century* (Abingdon: Routledge).

Roberts, M. (2011) *The Same Old Game, Volume 2: Codification. The True Story of the Origins of the World's Football Games* (Createspace.com).

Roberts, R. and J. S. Olson (1991) *Winning Is the Only Thing: Sports in America Since 1945* (Baltimore: Johns Hopkins University Press).

Rodenberg, R. M. and H. L Choong (2009) 'Payback Calls: A Starting Point for Measuring Basketball Referee Bias and Impact on Team Performance', *European Sport Management Quarterly*, vol. 9, no. 4, pp. 375–387.

Roots, C. (2012) 'Corruption Scandal: Trainer Gets 10-year Ban', *Sydney Morning Herald*, 1 February.

Rose-Ackerman, S. (1978) *Corruption: A Study in Political Economy* (London: Academic Press).

Rose-Ackerman, S. (1999) *Corruption and Government: Causes, Consequences and Reforms* (Cambridge: Cambridge University Press).

Rosen, D. (2008) *A History of Performance Enhancement in Sports from the Nineteenth Century to Today* (Westport: Praeger).

Russell, N. (1998) *Dealing with Fraud: A Survey of UK Companies* (London: Neville Russell).

Sack, A. L. (1991) 'The Underground Economy of College Football', *Sociology of Sport Journal*, vol. 8, no. 1, pp. 1–15.

Sakuri, Y. and R. Smith (2003) *Gambling as a Motivation for the Commission of Financial Crime. Trends and Issues in Crime and Criminal Justice No 25* (Canberra: AIC).

Sammons, J. T. (1990) *Beyond the Ring: The Role of Boxing in American Society* (Chicago: University of Illinois Press).

Sandholtz, W. and M. M. Gray (2003) 'International Integration and National Corruption', *International Organization*, vol. 57, no. 4, pp. 761–800.

Schwartz, D. (2005) *Cutting the Wire: Gaming Prohibition and the Internet* (Reno: University of Nevada Press).

Schmotzer, B. P., D. Kilgo and J. Switchenko (2009) 'The Natural? The Effect of Steroids on Offensive Performance in Baseball'. *Chance*, vol. 22, no. 2, pp. 21–32.

Scott, J. C. (1972) *Comparative Political Corruption* (Englewood Cliffs: Prentice-Hall).

Seligson, M. A (2006) 'The Measurement and Impact of Corruption Victimisation: Survey Evidence from Latin America', *World Development*, vol. 34, no. 2, pp. 381–404.

Serious Fraud Office (2010) *Annual Report 2009/10* (London: SFO).

Serious Fraud Office (2011) *Annual Report 2010/11* (London: SFO).

Seshagiri, S. (2012) 'IPL 5 Spot-fixing Scandal: BCCI Bans Five Players Found Guilty; Former Cricketers Embrace Decision', *International Business Times*, 1 July, at: www.ibtimes.co.in/articles/358245/20120701/bcci-ban-five-cricket-players-ipl-spot.htm (accessed 29 June 2012).

Sheptycki, J. (2002) 'Accountability across the Policing Field: Towards a General Cartography of Accountability for Post-Modern Policing', *Policing and Society*, vol. 12, no. 4, pp. 323–338.

Shivaji, B. (2011) 'Corruption, Human Rights and Development', *Asia Pacific Journal of Research Management*, vol. 2, no. 5, pp. 265–273.

Shleifer, A. and R. Vishny (1993) 'Corruption', *Quarterly Journal of Economics*, vol. 108, no. 3, pp. 599–617.

Shropshire, K. L. (1992) *Agents of Opportunity: Sport Agents and Corruption in Collegiate Sports* (Philadelphia: University of Pennsylvania Press).

Siegel, B. (2010) 'Playing Host Is Hard to Do: The Allure of the World Stage and Shiny New Stadiums', *World Policy Journal*, vol. 27, no. 4, pp. 59–66.

Simmons, R. (1997) 'Implications of the Bosman Ruling for Football Transfer Markets', *Economic Affairs*, vol. 17, no. 3, pp. 13–18.

Simson, V. and A. Jennings (1992) *The Lords of the Rings: Power, Money, and Drugs in the Modern Olympics* (London: Simon and Schuster).

Smith, G., M. Button, L. Johnston and K. Frimpong (2010) *Studying Fraud as White Collar Crime* (Basingstoke: Palgrave Macmillan).

Slapper, G. and S. Tombs (1999) *Corporate Crime* (London: Longman).

Soebbing, B. P. and D. S. Mason (2009) 'Managing Legitimacy and Uncertainty in Professional Team Sport: The NBA's Draft Lottery', *Team Performance Management*, vol. 15, no. 3, pp. 141–157.

Soule, B. and L. Lestrelin (2011) 'The Puerto Affair: Revealing the Difficulties of the Fight against Doping', *Journal of Sport and Social Issues*, vol. 35, no. 2, pp. 186–208.

Spaaij, R. (2012) *The Social Impact of Sport* (Abingdon: Routledge).

Sproat, P. (2007) 'The New Policing Assets and New Assets of Policing: A Tentative Financial Cost–Benefit Analysis of the UK's Anti-money-laundering and Asset Recovery Regime', *Journal of Money Laundering Control*, vol. 10, no. 3, pp. 277–299.

Sproat J. (2009) 'To What Extent Is the UK's Anti-money-laundering and Asset Recovery Regime Used against Organised Crime?', *Journal of Money Laundering Control*, vol. 12, no. 2, pp. 134–150.

Staudohar, P. D. (2002) 'Baseball Negotiations: A New Agreement', *Monthly Labour Review* (December), pp. 15–22.

Stevens, L. (2006) *Major Inquiry into Alleged Irregularities within the Sporting Industry, The Quest Inquiry* (London: Quest).

Sudgen, J. (1996) *Boxing and Society – An International Analysis* (Manchester: Manchester University Press).

Summers, B. (2008) 'The Fraud Act: Has It Had Any Impact?', *Amicus Curiae*, Issue 75, Autumn.

Sutherland, E. H. (1949) *White Collar Crime* (New York: Holt, Rinehart & Winston).

Svensson, J. (2003) 'Who Must Pay Bribes and How Much? Evidence from a Cross Section of Firms', *Quarterly Journal of Economics*, vol. 118, no. 1, pp. 207–230.

Sykes, G. M. and D. Matza (1957) 'Techniques of Neutralization: A Theory of Delinquency', *American Sociology Review*, vol. 22, no. 6, pp. 664–670.

Szczepanik, M. (2007) 'Sirens Sound as Inquiries Follow Hot on Heels of Stevens' Report', *The Times*, 17 July.

Szeftel, M. (2000) 'Clientelism, Corruption and Catastrophe', *Review of African Political Economy*, vol. 27, no. 85, pp. 427–441.

Taylor, B. and J. Trogdon (2002) 'Losing to Win: Tournament Incentives in the National Basketball Association', *Journal of Labor Economics*, vol. 20, no. 1, pp. 23–41.

Taylor, I. (1971) '"Football Mad": A Speculative Sociology of Football Hooliganism', in E. Dunning (ed.), *The Sociology of Sport* (London: Frank Cass).

Taylor, I. (1999) *Crime in Context: A Critical Criminology of Market Societies* (Oxford: Polity Press).

Taylor, M. (2008) *The Association Game: A History of British Football* (London: Pearson-Longman).

Taylor, R. (1992) *Football and Its Fans: Supporters and Their Relations with the Game, 1885–1985* (Leicester: Leicester University Press).

Tendler, S., O. Kay and R. Syal (2007) 'Police Will Investigate Corruption in Football', *The Times*, 16 June.

Thelin, J. R. (1994) *Games Colleges Play: Scandal and Reform in Intercollegiate Athletics* (Baltimore: John Hopkins University Press).

Thomas, K. (2010) 'Once under Oath, Now under Indictment', *International Herald Tribune*, 21–22 August, p. 12.

Thoroughbred Owners and Breeders Association (TOBA) (2004) *Sales Integrity Program*, at: www.toba.org/programs/sales-integrity-program.aspx (accessed 14 April 2012).

Thu, K. M., K. Hattman, V. Hutchinson, S. Lueken, N. Davis and E. Linboom (2002) 'Keeping the Game Close: "Fair Play" among Men's College Basketball Referees', *Human Organisation*, vol. 16, no. 1, pp. 1–8.

Tischler, S. (1981) *Footballers and Businessmen – The Origins of Professional Soccer in England* (New York: Holmes and Meier).

Transparency International (2009) *Global Corruption Barometer* (London: Transparency International).

Transparency International (2010) *Corruption in the UK: Overview and Policy Recommendations* (London: Transparency International).

Transparency International (2011) *Corruption in the UK: Part Two: Assessment of Key Sectors* (London: Transparency International).

Tranter, N. (1998) *Sport, Economy and Society in Britain 1750–1914* (Cambridge: Cambridge Univerity Press).

Trevino, K. T. and G. R. Weaver (2003) *Managing Ethics in Business Organizations* (Stanford: Stanford University Press).

Tucker, J. (1989) 'Employee Theft as Social Control', *Deviant Behaviour*, vol. 10, no. 4, pp. 319–334.

UEFA (2010) *The European Club Footballing Landscape Report* (Nyon: UEFA).

Ungerleider, S. (2001) *Faust's Gold: Inside the East German Doping Machine* (New York: St Martin's Press).

United Nations (2004) *The United Nations Convention against Corruption* (New York: UN Office on Drugs and Crime)

United States Congress, Senate Committee on Governmental Affairs (1994) *Corruption in Professional Boxing*, No. 3 103–408 (Washington DC: GPO).

Urra, F. (2007) *Assessing Corruption, Analytical Review of Corruption Measurement and its Problems: Perception, Error and Unity* (Washington DC: Georgetown University).

Vamplew, W. (1976) *The Turf: A Social and Economic History of Horse Racing* (London: Viking).
Vamplew, W. (2004) *Pay Up and Play the Game: Professional Sport in Britain, 1875–1914* (Cambridge: Cambridge University Press).
Ventresca, M. (2011) 'There's Something about Barry: Media Representations of a Home Run King', *A Journal of Baseball History and Culture*, vol. 20, no. 1, pp. 56–80.
Verschoor, C. (2005) 'To Blow the Whistle or Not Is a Tough Decision!', *Strategic Finance*, vol. 87, no. 4, pp. 21–22.
Vincent, F. (1991) *Baseball's Drug Policy and Prevention Program: Major League Baseball Drug Policy and Prevention Program* (New York: Major League Baseball).
Wagg, S. (1984) *The Football World: A Contemporary Social History* (Brighton: Harvester Press).
Walker, J. S. (2011) *ACC Basketball: The Story of the Rivalries, Traditions, and Scandals of the First Two Decades of the Atlantic Coast Conference* (Durham: University of North Carolina Press).
Walsh, D. (2006) *From Lance to Landis: Inside the American Doping Controversy at the Tour de France* (New York: Ballantine Books).
Walsh, D. (2011) 'A Cycle of Deceit', *The Sunday Times*, 22 May, pp. 11 and 18.
Walsh, D. (2012) 'Off Yer Bike', *The Sunday Times*, 26 August, p. 18.
Walsh, K. M. (1994) 'Boxing: Regulating a Health Hazard', *Journal of Contemporary Health. Law and Policy*, vol. 11, no. 1, pp. 63–78.
Wang, F. (1994) 'The Political Economy of Authoritarian Clientelism in Taiwan', in L. Roniger and A. Gunes-Ayata (eds), *Democracy, Clientelism, and Civil Society* (Boulder: Lynne Rienner).
Wardle, H., K. Sproston, J. Orford, B. Erens, M. Griffiths, R. Constantine and S. Pigott (2007) *British Gambling Prevalence Survey 2007* (London: National Centre for Social Research).
Waxman, D. (2008) 'Auctioning Off Integrity: The Legitimacy of Seller-Rebate Agreements in the Thoroughbred Auction Context', *Kentucky Law Journal*, vol. 96, pp. 139–161.
Weinstock, J., J. P. Whelan, A. W. Meyers and J. M. Watson (2007) 'Gambling Behavior of Student-Athletes and a Student Cohort: What Are the Odds?', *Journal of Gambling Studies*, vol. 23, pp. 13–24.
Weir, M. J. (2008) 'The Ugly Side to the Beautiful Game: Bungs and the Corruption of Players' Agents in European Football', *Southwestern Journal of Law and Trade*, vol. 14, no. 1, pp. 145–170.
Weisburd, D., E. Warning and E. F. Chayet (2001) *White Collar Criminal Careers* (New Haven: Yale University Press).
Wells, J. T. (1997) *Occupational Fraud and Abuse* (Dexter: Obsidian).
Westin, A. F. (1981) *Whistle-blowing: Loyalty and Dissent in the Corporation* (New York: McGraw-Hill).
Wetzel, D. and D. Yaeger (2000) *Sole Influence: Basketball, Corporate Greed, and the Corruption of America's Youth* (New York: Warner Books).
Wheatcroft, G. (2003) *Le Tour: A History of the Tour De France* (London: Simon and Schuster).

Wilde, S. (2011) 'How Many More Have Overstepped the Mark?', *The Sunday Times*, 11 November, p. 4.

Williams, J. (2003) *Cricket and England: A Cultural and Social History of the Inter-war Years* (London: Frank Cass).

Williams, R., J. Royston and B. Hagen (2005) 'Gambling and Problem Gambling within Forensic Populations: A Review of the Literature', *Criminal Justice and Behaviour*, vol. 32, no. 6, pp. 665–689.

Willisch, M. J. (1993) 'Protecting the Owners of Baseball: A Governance Structure to Maintain the Integrity of the Game and Guard the Principals' Money Investment', *Northwestern University Law Review*, vol. 88 (1993–1994), pp. 1619–1650.

Wilson, E. M. (2009) *Government of the Shadows: Parapolitics and Criminal Sovereignty* (London: Pluto Press).

Winfield, M. (1994) 'Whistleblowers as Corporate Safety Net', in G. Vinten (ed.), *Whistleblowing, Subversion or Corporate Citizenship?* (London: Paul Chapman).

Winfree, J. J. McCluskey, R. Mittelhammer and R. Fort (2004) 'Location and Attendance in Major League Baseball', *Applied Economics*, vol. 36, no. 19, pp. 2117–2124.

Wolfers, J. (2006) 'Point Shaving: Corruption in College Basketball', *American Economic Review*, vol. 96, no. 2, pp. 279–284.

Wu, C. L. (2001) 'Taiwan's Local Factions and American Political Machines in Comparative Perspective', *China Report*, vol. 3, no. 7, pp. 51–71.

Wu, C. L. (2003) Local Factions and the Kuomintang in Taiwan's Electoral Politics'. *International Relations of the Asia Pacific*, vol. 3, no. 7, pp. 89–111.

Yilmaz, M., S. Chatterjee and M. Habibullah (2001) 'Improvement by Spreading Wealth: The Case of Home Runs in Major League Baseball', *Journal of Sports Economics*, vol. 2, no. 2, pp. 181–193.

Zeitlin, L. R. (2001) 'A Little Larceny Can Do a Lot for Employee Morale', *Psychology Today*, vol. 5, no. 1, pp. 22–24.

Zimbalist, A. (1999) *Unpaid Professionals: Commercialism and Conflict in Big-time College Sports* (Princeton: Princeton University Press).

Zitzewitz, E. (2006) 'Nationalism in Winter Sports Judging and Its Lessons for Organizational Decision Making', *Journal of Economics and Management Strategy*, vol. 15, no. 1, pp. 67–99.

Index

Printed and bound in the United States of America